Reconciliati
The Continuing Agenda

Reconciliation:
The Continuing Agenda

Robert J. Kennedy, editor

THE LITURGICAL PRESS
Collegeville, Minnesota

Cover design by Janice St. Marie

Library of Congress Cataloging-in-Publication Data

Reconciliation : the continuing agenda / Robert J. Kennedy, editor.
    p.   cm.
    Papers from the 1986 conference of the Notre Dame Center for Pastoral Liturgy.
    ISBN 0-8146-1568-6 (pbk.) : $8.95
    1. Penance—Congresses. 2. Reconciliation—Religious aspects—
Catholic Church—Congresses. 3. Pastoral theology—Catholic
Church—Congresses. 4. Catholic Church—Liturgy—Congresses.
5. Catholic Church—Doctrines—Congresses. I. Kennedy, Robert J.,
1947-   .   II. Notre Dame Center for Pastoral Liturgy. Conference
(1986).
BX2260.R343 1987
265'.6—dc19   87-25965
                                                                  CIP

ISBN 0-8146-1568-6

To the prophets of justice and peace

    whose voices are a two-edged sword
    whose hearts call us to be reconciled in Christ

    and

in gratitude

    for all who have inspired the readers of this book
    to be ambassadors of reconciliation

Contents

Contents

Contents

Contributors

MOTHER TESSA BIELECKI is Abbess of the Spiritual Life Institute, a community of men and women following the spirit of the primitive Carmelite rule for apostolic hermits, with centers in Crestone, Colorado and Kemptville, Nova Scotia.

WILLIAM M. CIESLAK, O.F.M. CAP., is professor of liturgy at the Franciscan School of Theology, Graduate Theological Union in Berkeley, California, and an adviser to the Bishops' Committee on the Liturgy.

JAMES DALLEN, priest of the diocese of Salina, Kansas, is associate professor of religious studies at Gonzaga University, Spokane, Washington.

DORIS DONNELLY, author of *Learning to Forgive* and *Putting Forgiveness into Practice,* is co-director of the Center for Spirituality at Saint Mary's College, Notre Dame, Indiana.

CATHERINE DOOLEY, O.P., is assistant professor in the Department of Religion and Religious Education, The Catholic University of America, Washington, D.C.

EDWARD FOLEY, Capuchin, is assistant professor of liturgy at the Catholic Theological Union, Chicago, Illinois.

LINDA L. GAUPIN, C.D.P., is director of liturgy for the diocese of Wilmington, Delaware.

RICHARD M. GULA, S.S., author of *To Walk Together Again: The Sacrament of Reconciliation,* is associate professor of moral theology at Saint Patrick's Seminary, Menlo Park, California.

CHARLES W. GUSMER is professor of liturgy and sacramental theology at Immaculate Conception Seminary at Seton Hall University, Darlington, New Jersey.

JOSEPH A. HART is associate professor of systematic theology at Saint Bernard's Institute, Rochester, New York.

KATHLEEN HUGHES, R.S.C.J., is associate professor of word and worship at the Catholic Theological Union, Chicago, Illinois, and an adviser to the

International Committee on English in the Liturgy and the Bishops' Committee on the Liturgy.

BROTHER JOHN and BROTHER JEAN-MARIE are both American-born members of the Ecumenical Community of Taizé and have been active in the international meetings of young adults and the worldwide pilgrimage of reconciliation sponsored by Taizé.

ROBERT J. KENNEDY, priest of the diocese of Rochester, New York, is a doctoral candidate in liturgy at the University of Notre Dame.

JAMES LOPRESTI, S.J., is associate professor of liturgy at the Seminary of the Immaculate Conception, Huntington, New York, and is coordinator for workshops on reconciliation for the North American Forum on the Catechumenate.

JOHN ALLYN MELLOH, S.M., directs the John S. Marten Program in Homiletics and Liturgics in the department of theology, University of Notre Dame, and was formerly director of the Notre Dame Center for Pastoral Liturgy.

JON NILSON is associate professor and chairperson of the department of theology at Loyola University of Chicago, Illinois.

ELLEN O'HARA, C.S.J., is a canon lawyer and director of the marriage tribunal for the diocese of Boise, Idaho.

Contributors

Foreword

In June, 1986, the Notre Dame Center for Pastoral Liturgy hosted the conference "Reconciliation: The Continuing Agenda." Participants came from parishes and dioceses, schools and universities, hospitals, retreat centers, and seminaries in the United States and Canada, and from as far away as Australia.

As this diverse group filed into Washington Hall that balmy Monday evening for the opening of the conference, a familiar image awaited them: an artist's dramatic representation of the reconciling cross of Jesus Christ. Against the burgundy velvet stage curtains, the walnut processional cross, studded with blue and green and gold jewel-like chips of glass, stood as a powerful sign and sacrament of the unity all shared through the victorious death of Jesus Christ.

In a real sense it was that unity which brought the participants together. It was to serve that unity that the conference on reconciliation came to be, and it is to extend that vision of unity beyond the four-day conference that we publish these proceedings.

"That they may be one . . . :" the prayer of Jesus the reconciler echoes down through the generations, disturbing our complacent acceptance of a war-torn world, an alienated society, fragmented individuals. That prayer continues to call us to attend to the ministry of reconciliation both within and beyond the Church.

To see reconciliation as the heart of the Christian mystery and to explore its meaning theologically, liturgically, and pastorally was the challenge we set before our speakers. The topic is considerably broader than preparing communal penance services or catechizing young children. It is a process inseparable from the life and mission of the Church, and therefore inseparable from the life and mission of every Christian.

Yet it is no secret that despite the reform of the Rite of Penance promulgated on the first Sunday of Advent in 1973, reconciliation remains a problematic sacrament in this post-Vatican II era. There are still questions not satisfactorily answered, issues not adequately explored, relationships not clarified. How does the Church today reverence the authentic gospel tradition and faithfully hand it on to a society yearning for healing, unity and peace? How do

Christians *live* a reconciling way of life? How do we as a sacramental people *celebrate* that reconciliation in the renewed rituals of the Church?

The 1986 conference was an effort to broaden and deepen the discussion, to contribute responsibly to the ongoing dialogue, to reflect upon the topic in the broader context of Christian life, so that the sacrament of reconciliation could be for the Church what all sacraments are meant to be—a ritual expression of a deep underlying reality, a saving encounter with the redeeming Christ.

Reconciliation: the continuing agenda. The conference and the publication of these proceedings is a modest beginning. But if these papers assist in bringing about a renewed vision and commitment to make the continuing agenda a continuing challenge in our personal and communal lives, then the effort will have been fruitful. It is in that hope that we publish these proceedings.

The Center for Pastoral Liturgy expresses gratitude to those whose papers are contained within this volume and to Robert Kennedy who served as its editor.

Eleanor Bernstein, c.s.j.
Director
Notre Dame Center for
Pastoral Liturgy

Preface

This is above all a pastoral book: born of a commitment to the Church's mission of continuing Christ's work of reconciliation, born of a compassionate care for the weak and sinful members of the Church, born of a concern that liturgy always express and nourish the faith of the whole people who move toward the fullness of God's reign.

Apart from the celebration of the eucharist, perhaps no other segment of the liturgical life of the Church has been scrutinized more thoroughly than the sacrament of penance. For well over twenty-five years, theologians, pastors, canon lawyers, catechists and indeed the faithful have raised serious discussions about the form of the sacrament, its history and theology, its use (or nonuse) by parishioners, and the thorny problems related to it that have challenged pastoral practice before and after the promulgation of the revised Rite of Penance in 1973. We are all familiar with these questions and problems whether we came early or late to the discussion.

So why another book on penance?

It is precisely because the agenda continues, even after twenty-five years of pastoral theological reflection: the agenda for the recovery of the meaning of reconciliation in the life of the Church and the renewal of the liturgies which celebrate it. We are still debating the usefulness and expressiveness of the revised rites, the rediscovery of a sense of sin and reconciliation in the baptized, the appropriateness of penance for young children and the more vexing problem of "second confession," the legal and pastoral uses of the communal forms of penance, and the relationship of penance to the social justice mission of the Church and to the spiritual strength of each believer.

This collection of essays does not answer all the questions or solve all the problems. In fact it offers quite distinct, if not contradictory, assessments and suggestions about the uses of the rites and about the larger contexts and meanings of reconciliation in which they are celebrated. Even the words "penance" and "reconciliation" are used here without a clear agreement on their meaning. Is one the name of the sacrament and the other the mystery celebrated? Is one a virtue and the other a liturgy? Or are they just two ways of saying the same thing—one just a little more old-fashioned than the other? When even the basic vocabulary finds no consistent meaning, it is clear that answers and solutions for the pastoral practice of reconciliation in the Church and world still elude us. Nevertheless the presentations here advance the conversation by reviewing historical data with new eyes, by making bold proposals for addressing complex issues, by providing fresh insights into familiar material.

In addition, two elements do stand in clear relief throughout all these essays. First, if the need for Christian reconciliation is to be recognized and met, it is necessary to accept our solidarity with all persons, solidarity in two senses. On the one hand, we are "the fellowship of the weak" (to use Henri Nouwen's phrase), bonded in the Spirit of the reconciling Christ with the marginalized, weak, alienated, powerless, oppressed, confused, and weary among us, all of us equally dependent on the power of God alone. On the other hand, we are among the band of sinners, conspiring with the evil ones to commit the works of individual and social injustice, all of us equally in need of conversion to the outlook of the gospel of Christ. So whether our authors speak of the role of the Church in reconciliation or the recovery of a sense of sin or the way the ritual formulas express (or fail to express) repentance of social sin, they recognize that solidarity with weak and sinful alike is foundational for cooperating with the dynamics of reconciliation. That is gospel revolution.

The second consistent element is the ecclesial dimension of penance and reconciliation. Karl Rahner's retrieval of this "forgotten truth" about the sacrament has at last taken deep root in the imaginations of historian, theologian, canon lawyer, and pastor alike. This understanding brings into sharp focus the fact that penance is considered neither a private affair of the individual nor an isolated moment in the confessional (or reconciliation room); rather, it is a process which occurs in the midst of the believing community, taking time and having transforming impact on the wide network of relationships in the Church and beyond. Thus individual confession is a celebration of the Church; Lent is the time of conversion for the whole community as well as the individual believer; all the activities of a parish participate in and are aimed at reconciliation with Christ; and even fasting and other ascetical practices make sense only in the social context of believing brothers and sisters.

On these two pillars rests the arch of continuing dialogue on reconciliation. The essays have been divided into three main sections. The *theological agenda* considers the foundations of reconciliation in the faith tradition and its communal context against the background of "the Church as sinful reconciler." The connections of the three sacraments of reconciliation are explored, as well as the possible shape of a lifestyle of reconciliation. A provocative examination of sin rounds out this section. The *historical agenda* on the distant past of the early Church and the nearer past of the last fifteen years of magisterial teaching on penance offers critical insights on where we might be headed in the future. The *pastoral agenda* is the largest section of this book and begins with apologizing to dozens of people on the streets of New York. Discussion on the rites of reconciliation risks yet another review of the three forms of the 1973 Rite of Penance, proposes a renewed Order of Penitents and an approach to Lent as a penitential season, and prophetically calls for the use of rites which seek forgiveness and reconcile for social sin. Reconciliation in parish life embraces the relationship of penance and anointing of the sick, penance and children, canon law, preaching repentance and fasting, all in the context of the parish as reconciling community.

All in all, it is a hearty agenda to get the meeting started!

From the beginning all the authors have been eager participants in continuing the discussion on reconciliation. Their enthusiasm, as well as their good work, made the editorial task a joy. In addition, I thank John Brooks-Leonard, Janet Schlichting and David Stosur for editing the editor, Beverly Robinson and Lorraine Strope for their expert typing skills and endless patience, and Eleanor Bernstein, csj, for her ill-advised but steady faith in me.

Robert J. Kennedy
Feast of Cyril and
Methodius
14 February 1987

Abbreviations

CLD   *Canon Law Digest*

DS   H. Denzinger, A. Schönmetzer, eds., *Enchiridion Symbolorum* (33rd ed., Freiburg i. B., 1965)

GCD   *General Catechetical Directory (Directorium Catechisticum Generale,* Congregation of the Clergy) English translation Washington, D.C.: United States Catholic Conference, 1971

ICEL   International Commission for English in the Liturgy

IDB   G. A. Buttrick, ed., *Interpreters' Dictionary of the Bible,* 4 vols. (Nashville, 1963)

NCCB   National Conference of Catholic Bishops

PG   J. P. Migne, ed., *Patrologia Graeca,* 161 vols. (Paris, 1857–66)

PL   J. P. Migne, ed., *Patrologia Latina,* 221 vols. (Paris, 1844–64)

RCIA   Rite of Christian Initiation of Adults

RP   Rite of Penance, 1973

SLF   *Sharing the Light of Faith,* National Catechetical Directory for Catholics of the United States (Washington, D.C.: United States Catholic Conference, 1979)

USCC   United States Catholic Conference

James Lopresti, s.j.

The Church as Sinful Reconciler

> In the evening of that same day, the first day of the week, the
> doors were closed in the room where the disciples were for fear of
> the Jews. Jesus came and stood among them. He said to them:
> "Peace be with you," and showed them his hands and his side.
> The disciples were filled with joy when they saw the Lord, and he
> said to them again: "Peace be with you. As the Father has sent me,
> so I am sending you." After saying this he breathed on them and
> said: "Receive the Holy Spirit. For those whose sins you forgive,
> they are forgiven; for those whose sins you retain, they are re-
> tained" (John 20:19–23).

When Jesus breathed his spirit into the apostolic community on
that night of the first day of the week, as told in this passage
from John's Gospel, he gave a charge to the assembled embryonic
Church. These followers were to be sent as Jesus was sent,
namely to effect the reconciliation of estranged humanity. Attentive to that same breathed-in spirit, Paul tells the Corinthians that
we, the Church, are to be ambassadors of reconciliation (2 Cor
5:20). That task defines who we are and what we are about in this
world. Reconciliation of all who are alienated is to be the mark of
our way of life as followers of Jesus.

I want to make a few claims—some theoretical and some
pastoral—about what being ambassadors of reconciliation means
for the Church today. All of these claims will follow from a first
principle, namely, that remembering is at the heart of being ambassadors of reconciliation. We will attend to two nuances of
meaning contained in the word "remembering." Remembering
means both "not forgetting" and "being made a member once
again." With all puns intended I claim that reconciliation has to
do both with not forgetting who we are and with becoming who
we are once again. I think the converse is true as well. Alienation
is forgetting who we are and refusing or being unable to become
who we are once again. Furthermore, I claim that the Church is
meant preeminently to be the gathering around the table of those
who do not forget and continually make members once again.

By now the reader may be gasping for air, suffocated by all these aphorisms mercilessly heaped on top of one another at the very beginning of this paper. Let me lift some of their weight and dispel some of their density with some images of alienating forgetfulness and reconciling remembrance.

My first image comes from the upper west side of New York City where there is an increasing number of homeless people walking the streets. While a construction worker deftly maneuvers a huge crane to lift tons of brick to build more apartments for the expanding class of wealthy young professionals, a bag lady clumsily roots and picks through the refuse of the playfully chic new *gelato modo* next door. The two don't even notice each other. One day I approached one of these women, offering her one of the peaches I had just purchased from the neighborhood green grocer. Snarling and curled in mindless terror, she turned away from me and screamed in indecipherable gibberish. Her dignity had so long been forgotten by all of us, including herself, that we could not communicate at all, let alone satisfy a part of her hunger for food (or mine for being a good samaritan). She and I were aliens to each other. She had been forgotten into irretrievable isolation. I felt helpless and shut out. I walked away.

Alienation is forgetting who we are and refusing or being unable to be re-membered.

My second image comes from Luke's account of Jesus' temptation in the wilderness (Luke 4:1–13). A hungry man could wish for nothing more satisfying than to have the power to change stones into food (first temptation). A solitary and powerless man could wish for nothing more satisfying than to control the common life of countless subjects in his very own kingdom (second temptation). A man suffering the befuddlement that only painfully gives birth to hope and faith could wish for nothing more satisfying than unassailable proof that he will never suffer loss or hurt (third temptation). Each of these possibilities (the last being the cleverest ruse of all) was voiced by the tempter who feared not so much Jesus' divinity as his unwillingness to attempt to escape his limited creatureliness, his humanity. The tempter's tricks had worked before in the garden when the first man gave in to the master of deceit and forgot his humanity. He seized the forbidden fruit of godlike awareness. Primal alienation was generated in that

James Lopresti

2

elemental forgetfulness. Perhaps the first sin was not so much to seek after the life of God as to refuse to re-member who we are in trying to seize that life. We are alienated from our true center in that forgetfulness.

The Nazarean, on the contrary, treasured his humanity in the desert. He suffered stones to be stones; he accepted the struggles to form human community in bonded servant-love rather than sovereign rule; and he embraced hard-won faith rather than the easy certitudes and divine guarantees as the path of life. The sinlessness of Jesus is this: he never forgot his humanity and he re-membered himself with humankind over and over, ever more deeply until he died (not so much for us as) into us, fully one with us. In that passing of his life-breath from Calvary into the room of the johannine Pentecost, he became the model and source of reconciliation.

Jesus then, as the one who remembered his humanity, is our starting point for reflecting on the meaning of reconciliation. A woman lost in forgetfulness is our starting point for reflecting on the meaning of alienation. Jesus connected with the rest of humankind in his poverty; the woman was isolated from human community by her hostile destitution.

There is more to be said about what it means to forget one's humanity and more to be said about what it means to remember it. But I think we are, for the most part, ill-equipped to deal with issues of forgetfulness and remembrance. Forgetfulness is a deeper matter than the mere loss of memory about facts, and remembrance is fuller than their recall. I say we are ill-equipped because we live in the aura of forgetfulness and only achieve momentary glimpses of remembrance. Our imagination is narrowed by a kind of presupposition that the individual precedes the community. This shows up in our zero-sum commodity culture: for me to win, you must lose. In national and international political language we call it "protecting our vital interests abroad." We build arsenals of weapons to defend ourselves and to keep competing others away. Occasionally the isolation of it all wells up in lonely dissatisfaction. We sense that something is wrong. Accordingly we struggle to connect with one another. Yet our deepest experiences of being in love and the passionate attempt to cross over the boundaries to enter one another's hearts can seem to be futile attempts to break out of isolation. All the while we have left unquestioned the

Church as Reconciler

3

presupposition that we are disconnected subjective cells trying to bridge the insufferable gap between us. We seldom stop to ask ourselves whether we might have presupposed things to be opposite of what they really are. It may well be that our fundamental imagination is at fault. Perhaps we have forgotten something so basic that our whole starting point is backwards. Let me explain.

I daresay that the story of Jesus' fidelity in the wilderness is so powerful because it is an account of one who rescues us from this primary forgetfulness. He remembered the deeper truth that sharing humanity precedes being an isolated individual. Jesus remembered forgotten human community and felt the primal human bondedness. That is to say, he is without original sin. He is the coalescence of the human community, and he knew the full horror of forgetful abandonment by those to whom he was so fully attentive. The good news is that he has overcome the power of forgetfulness. He lives and generates remembrance anew.

I realize that this is all rather dense theology to parse out. What I am trying to say is that true reconciliation is a breakthrough to (or, if you will, a breaking-in-upon) this primary, mostly unconscious, corporate memory. We the Church are meant to be the ambassadors of that profoundly human *memoria*. We are stewards of memory about the primary blessing of human community and we are rescued by our baptism from the original forgetfulness which alienated us in the beginning.

Perhaps another set of images will make all this abstract language a little less troublesome and tedious. This set comes from the eucharistic assembly itself. Everything about our liturgy bespeaks the mystery of the human community which equals more than the sum of its parts.

We who assemble for eucharist gather with no distinction according to class, rank, privilege, age, ideology, color, economic status or even temperament. The only distinctions have to do with facilitating the service of the assembled body. We sing our prayer as much as possible, the music uniting our voices into one continuous sound, the same note in 5000 vocal chords. We hear one word proclaimed. We exchange the sign of peace uniting us one to another once again without distinction. We process to one table to eat of one bread and drink of one wine. These are all corporate acts; they are acts done by a community, not by a collection of juxtaposed individuals.

James Lopresti

Our eucharistic assembly is one very special time in our lives when we are uniquely free to loosen our grip on everything which intensifies our differences and to acknowledge our primal common humanity. In the ideal, we give shape, sound, flesh and blood to a deep *memoria:* that we humankind are one before we divide up into individuals. We momentarily see and show ourselves as Jesus sees and shows us, as part of himself and part of one another, a corporate whole. Through the lens of that mystical awareness, poetically manifest in eucharistic assembly, we see the rest of our lives, insofar as they are marked by division and hostilities, as so much forgetfulness, so much alienation from our true and (were it not for the eucharist) invisible center in common life. In the liturgy we don't so much make human community happen as we chance to discover or re-member the primary human community already given to us in our original blessedness.

That is why, from one perspective at least, the eucharist is called the sacrament of reconciliation. The Greeks called it *anamnesis*, or "not-forgetting." Here we re-member who we are. We are blessed humankind, a mosaic of many contrasting pieces, the image of the Holy One. The eucharist, then, is the life strategy of remembrance. That's the point.

STRATEGIES OF FORGETFULNESS

Like remembrance, forgetting begets, and then is nurtured in, life strategies of its own. As already stated, forgetfulness is not merely an innocent matter of the loss of recall of facts. Forgetfulness, of the kind we are considering here, has an agenda, often an unconscious and thereby more dangerous one. The life strategies of forgetfulness have to do with protective hiding. They protect the lie they generate by psychologically destroying the evidence. That is to say, we forget what some part of ourselves does not want to re-member and, simultaneously, we wrap or hide that forgetfulness in a garment of truth-avoiding escapes. Why? In the end, the only reason to hide, i.e., to forget, is fear, and in particular the fear of our mortality, our creatureliness, the unshakable suspicion mocking all our life plans that we will wither away and nothing will be left. Everything dies sooner or later. We have no clear evidence, save what faith and hope afford us in their fragile ways, that such is not the case. There is no way to escape that, but there seems to be no way to accept it either. We can only *risk* the

Church as Reconciler

belief and the hope against the evidence to the contrary. We cannot supplant the risk with security. Clearly to re-member our common humanity is to re-member our death-destiny. Along with taxes, so we are told, that's about all we can count on. Forgetfulness grows, then, as an attractive alternative.

It seems that forgetfulness of this kind generates, and then feeds on, four strategies for truth avoidance, four ways to generate the self-protective lie. They are the opposites of eucharist, and they have their own liturgies: rituals of status and the sacraments of privilege. They are each hostile and they are each futile, yet they remain so attractive, given the deep risk of remembrance. They are the tempter's way to get us to pretend that stones are bread, to pretend that power is the means of assuaging loneliness, and to pretend that certitude can replace the dark faith. Paradoxically, as we shall see, they reinforce the death they seek to avoid and escape. Two are aggressive measures of forgetfulness: they are breaking out and getting ahead. Two are passive measures: they are opting out and opting ahead. Let's look at the aggressive forms first.

Surely one way to escape re-membrance of our death-destined common humanity is to use force to escape. Jerzy Kosinski tells a story which painfully illustrates this strategy.

> During the war an adolescent boy is the butt of a peasant family—the farmer horsewhips him and spits in his face for amusement. One day a peasant's child dies of poisoning, and the ill-treated boy, measuring from the father's grief how much peasants love their children, thinks up a revenge for his humiliations—he will make the children swallow balls of bread concealing a hook. The first victim is a little girl. "I turned away so as not to see her face and forced myself to think only of the lash from her father's whip. And from that moment I could look my persecutors fearlessly in the face, even provoking their blows and ill treatment. I felt no pain at all. For every stroke I received they're going to pay with a pain a hundred times worse than mine. Now I was no longer their victim; I was their judge and their torturer . . . ." In spite of the peasants' magic spells death persistently took its toll and the children continued to die.[1]

Is that too obvious and crude an evil? Then perhaps staying within the system offers an alternative: getting ahead, an option chosen by many. Like breaking out, getting ahead is rooted in vio-

James Lopresti

6

lence, but it is a violence sanctioned within the system, even institutionalized. There are many genteel and legal ways to climb over others to get to the secure place of having more barns to store more grain, reaped in the bigger harvest of the larger bank account. We know what happened to the man in the parable who chose that route.

So we turn to the more passive types of forgetfulness: opting out and opting ahead. For some, the grand opera provides the anesthesia; for others it is the release of sex; still others waft it on crack and cocaine. Opting out is the symptomatic relief. It is the choice of Anacin or Pepto-Bismol or Preparation H, advertised during the evening news when we've had just about enough of the world's pains and horrors. It also shows up in the way we specialize our social life. No need for me to see the pain of another. We have hired people to take care of that for us. Specialized out of all responsibility, I can sit back on my assets and let the scapegoating go on. There is a thinly veiled promise in all this exposure to specialization and anesthesia that one can opt out of the pain all the time. Yet we all know that anesthesia wears off, that problems come home to roost, and that addiction adds the problem of never having enough. There is one more option left.

The last option is the most insidious of all. It is the tempter's best shot at the religious types. It is opting ahead. It is claiming a superior plane. It is, in what appears to be the more benign form, thanking God for making me not like the rest. It shows in the tragedy of religious who appropriate their theology in such a way as to believe that the monotheism they profess is the spirituality they live. Celibate and poor men and women who obey their superiors surely are guaranteed some vague promise of acceptability and prestige which others have foregone by choosing to live in the corporate world of compromise and consumerism. With only a few twists and turns opting ahead mutates into its more malignant form. To be a member of the Aryan race is to be of superior blood and not subject to the indignity of being identified with common humanity. The holocaust is the monstrous offspring of evil nurtured in the pseudo-religious temptation to opt ahead.

As Jesus is the archetype of remembrance, so our bag lady from upper Broadway is an archetypal victim of forgetfulness. Perhaps she is victim on many levels. She is (1) preyed upon by those who are seeking to break out of their poverty and frustration, (2) ignored by those who are scurrying past her en route to their new important position one step ahead of the competition, (3) anesthetized by her own addictions to the point of brain damage, and (4) the object of condescension from religious types like me who need to be the good samaritan every now and then. She embodies what happens to us when we forget and cannot be re-membered any more.

FORGETFULNESS AND REMEMBRANCE IN THE CHURCH
Still we the Church, like the master who has breathed his spirit into us, are to be ambassadors of reconciliation. That is to say, the four strategies of forgetfulness are not permitted us. Only the strategy of remembrance is ours, the deep memory of the common blessedness of all humankind as the image of God.

All this leads to some pastoral reflections on the Church today, some observations on the Church as sinful reconciler, that is, as both a forgetting and a remembering community.

While examples of the strategy of breaking out would be hard to find in the Church, except perhaps in the many holy wars we have fought over the years against Turks, heretics, infidels, Protestants and "C-rated" movies, still there are many examples of getting ahead strategies. It is dealing in cliché to highlight the faults of a community's life wherein positions of authority and prestige are sought not for the common good but for personal aggrandizement. Stories of forgetfulness undermining the common good as churchmen clutch for power and position are as old and celebrated as the institution itself.

The passive forms of forgetfulness are another matter. It took the courageous witness of physicians of the soul like Daniel Berrigan, Dorothy Day, Thomas Merton and Raymond Hunthausen to call to mind a certain selective forgetfulness exercised by a whole people, including the Church. Two decades ago our corporate selective moral consciousness, fully awake to the perils of inappropriate behavior in the bedroom, overlooked the incestuous and obscene military huddlings in Pentagon boardrooms. As a faith community, we had opted out of involvement in the painful lives of the poor who were, and still are, constantly and systematically dispossessed of even the most meager sustenance. Rather we sought to join in this nation's effort to build stronger defense of an unquestioned way of life. Many of us had become unaware

James Lopresti

8

that the American Dream had already become the tortured night-mare of the world's poor here and abroad. Having opted out of the fray, we let the cancerous cells of militarism, nuclear madness and their underlying interdependencies metastasize. Things are different now. To mix the metaphor a bit, we now see how seam-less the life-protection garment is. We are opting back in; remem-brance has a chance. Two pastoral letters are a very important start-up of new *memoria* on behalf of our common humanity.

It is forgetfulness' strategy of opting ahead, however, that re-mains for us the most nasty and seductive trick of the demon, be-cause it hides in what seems to be our virtues. This fourth tempter, like Becket's in T. S. Eliot's *Murder in the Cathedral*, coun-sels the highest treason: to do the right thing for the wrong rea-son. I cannot help but think of recent slick advertising campaigns taken on by a few dioceses eager to fill the heretofore emptying Sunday pews. "Come Home for Christmas," some of them say. The unspoken message within the very laudable gesture of hospi-tality can be a very condescending one. It calls on the image resi-dent in basic human memory of mamma and pappa who welcome errant sons and daughters back. As virtuous as the image may seem, even as resonant with scriptural images of reconciliation, it easily forgets that the socially real analogues of mamma and pappa are part of the reason son or daughter has been absent. Here ascends the strategy of opting ahead of the sinner. The root image insufficiently identifies with the sinner.

Returning to the Church is not really returning home. It is get-ting back on the corporate road en route to the kingdom-home. Furthermore, no one dares welcome the errant ones back unless the welcomers themselves are ready to be changed by what the returning members bring with them. Such a return is not that much different, in part, from what is the expected outcome of ecumenism. So-called errant churches do not return to Rome for Christmas. That is condescending forgetfulness, opting ahead of our sinfuless. Rome, Constantinople, Canterbury and Geneva need to fashion new roads to the kingdom together. The returning so-called sinner brings reminders to us of our corporate journey of conversion. Unless we are ready to re-member that fact as we re-member them, then we had best not send out such teasing messages.

Church as Reconciler

Given the fragile and faulted condition of the human community and aware of the tragedies of forgetting who we are, how do we the Church go about the task of remembrance, true to our eucharistic identity? More precisely, how do we ambassadors of reconciliation show forth the victory of Christ over primal forgetfulness and go about the pastoral task of membering once again?

Let me approach this final set of questions by offering another image within a story. A special way of victorious re-membering appears in the account I heard from a Maryknoll missioner about a certain weaver she knows in the Philippines. Whenever the old woman fashioned a garment or tapestry on her loom, she treated mistakes in her pattern in a very unusual way. Instead of returning to the place of her fault to excise the errant threads, she simply incorporated the mistake into her original design. Ironically, some of her most beautiful works emerged out of what people of lesser wisdom would have considered a flawed effort. She did not forget her mistakes; she recollected them and regathered them into the fabric of her life's work. In her remembering she offered a little bit more of herself to her appreciating customers. Curiously, by re-membering the fault the woman overcame it. In fact it would be better to say that she rescued the fault and transformed it into victory.

Each one who is entrapped in forgetfulness—those who in "helpless hostility"[2] have tried to break out, or get ahead, or opt out, or opt ahead of fragile human community—is a fault in the warp and woof of the human fabric. We the Church, eschewing the violence of both the aggressive and the passive forms, overcome the fault, or share in the victory over forgetfulness, by allowing or suffering the fault into the pattern. It is a radical non-violence we must practice, a profound pacifism. We remember the sinner with us the sinners.

How might that look in practice, especially given the crisis of our means of reconciling the sinner, our crisis of the form of penance? While it is true that our present penitential discipline is in trouble, and that trouble may well have roots in our forgetfulness at a fundamental level, still it is not true that Christ's reconciling victory over our elemental forgetfulness is in doubt. Our seeming lack of appropriate means to mediate that victory does not cancel it. We will know how to member once again as we discover the

James Lopresti

10

ways the victory of Christ over forgetfulness is seeping through the cracks of our cultural and ecclesial defense against it. Then we can tap the reservoir of victory in channels of its natural flow.

Let us consider briefly what people do these days to effectively relieve their troubles when they find themselves victims of active or passive forgetfulness. We may find in this inchoate redemptive search some hints at the way the victory may be making its appearance in spite of our institutional myopia. First, people in trouble connect with others who suffer the same deprivation, malaise, or captivity. Self-help groups, base communities, affiliations, therapy groups and numerous other organizations show that one way out of the trouble is to cross over a bridge of isolation into a corporate life of some kind. We might call this the "community principle." Second, people in trouble seek out others who have navigated these same treacherous waters at least slightly ahead of them. Alcoholics Anonymous sponsors, cancer patients who have suffered through to some new physical and/or spiritual integrity, and old hands in the resistance underground all act as mentors, guides, and witnesses to the novice sufferer. We might call this the "sponsorship principle." Third, people in trouble seek out people of wisdom and specific expertise who will meet their needs. The helping professions are among the fastest growing professions in the job market in our society. Health care professionals constantly increase both in number and in diversity of approaches. We might call this the "leadership principle." Fourth, people in trouble learn that relief usually comes only slowly and with effort and often, as well, in marked stages. AA members celebrate steps of sobriety. Process-aware self-help publications are constantly on the New York Times best seller lists. We might call this the "process principle."

In some way, each of these components where people find relief from trouble could be a realization of the God-touched human spirit yearning for, and reaching out towards, the integrity and wholeness we are meant to have. The simple point of all this is that these experiences are inchoate efforts to re-member the forgotten human core of blessedness, to re-member common humanity preceding our being individuals.

Yet the Church itself has the mission to be the preeminent sign in the world of the core of human blessedness. To be true to the needs of our time, then, that mission will be enfleshed in ways

Church as Reconciler

that (1) reverence the function of bonded ties of "sinners" to one another, (2) encourage the development of sponsor relationships, (3) make use of the fully reconciling expertise of the community, beyond merely what the priest can now do, and (4) take time for process. These features must show up more than they have so far in our pastoral practice of penance. But there is more. The Church must do all these things while committed to the strategy of remembrance and have nothing to do with the strategies of forgetfulness. It is not that the Church is the place where there is never any forgetful alienation, but that the Church is the place where people nevertheless choose to member once again. This is a kind of behavior which enfleshes a commitment to recall our humanity, our peace and harmony, and to seek it out in witness to the world. That is to say, the Church behaves in such a way that others who see what these communities of believers are all about may themselves begin to trust their yearnings for deeper human bondedness and fuller completion than their forgetfulness has allowed them. The Church is a reconciling agent in the world inasmuch as it is a living witness to belief in the opposite of forgetful alienation within and without its own borders. Insofar as it is not that witness, it is part of the problem of forgetfulness.

The Church re-members itself and enfleshes the victory of Christ over forgetfulness by becoming a true community on the journey to the kingdom of the fulfillment of God's promise. The Church's mission of reconciliation comes to life, then, as it embraces the alienated and nurtures those so embraced as they turn toward a new wholeness.

Giving voice to our deep bondedness with all, even those who have chosen the strategies of forgetfulness, we immediately fracture the defense of the lie and call memory out of its hiding place. In other words, the bag lady's isolated destitution is transformed into shared poverty. And there the victory resides, precisely and finally. The victory undercuts opting ahead in order to become the guarantor of moral rectitude. The victory opts into human struggles on all levels. The victory gets underneath those who get ahead and gathers in those who break out. That is to say, the victory suffers death for life. That means living without defense even of our virtues. It means rejoicing in our being limited human creatures as God did in Jesus who would not escape that fragility. It means favoring rather than fearing the stranger or the social and

James Lopresti

12

moral outcast, for no one is alien. It means replacing the old bromide "forgive and forget" with "forgive by re-membering."

There is some pain in remembering that who we are includes our death-destined fragility. As one silly popular poster puts it: "The truth will make you free, but first it will make you miserable." But there is more pain in forgetting. There is tragedy and alienation. We the Church, the sinful reconciler, the "embassy of reconciliation,"[3] do no better than be the place to discover the blessedness of being human in a world where even God couldn't resist trying it out.

NOTES

1. Christian Duquoc, "Sacramental Reconciliation and Real Reconciliation," in *Sacramental Reconciliation*, Concilium 61, ed. E. Schillebeeckx (New York: Herder and Herder, 1971) 32.

2. This phrase is used as an alternative for sin and is richly developed by Nathan Mitchell, *The Rite of Penance: Commentaries, Background and Directions*, vol. 3 (Washington: The Liturgical Conference, 1978) 12.

3. Robert J. Kennedy, "The Church: Embassy of Reconciliation," *Assembly* 12:5 (June 1986) 332–333.

Church as Reconciler

James Dallen

Theological Foundations of Reconciliation

The theology and practice of the sacrament of penance has under-gone more significant developments in the twentieth century than it had for centuries before. The changing ways in which we name it suggest those developments. For a millenium we called it "con-fession" and approached it individually to obtain forgiveness of sins. Earlier in this century we recognized that the sacrament had a broader thrust than ritual forgiveness, that it was oriented to-ward conversion, and we restored the ancient name of "pen-ance." Now we are seeing that our individualistic preoccupations have prevented us from realizing the full scope of conversion as a dimension of Church mission and we are trying to call the sacra-ment "reconciliation."

But have our understanding and experience undergone the revo-lution that the change in terminology implies? When we say "reconciliation," do we still mean "forgiveness of sins"? What are the foundations and implications of this approach? In particular, what does it say about the Christian way of life?

In suggesting some aspects of the answers to these questions I will, first of all, indicate how several twentieth-century develop-ments have reoriented our understanding of the sacrament and have been incorporated into the reformed Rite of Penance. Then I will attempt to situate the sacrament within an overview of recon-ciliation as the human experience of God's presence in our world. My hope is that we will then be in a better position to see the ministry and sacrament of conversion and reconciliation as part of the Church's mission in the world.

TWENTIETH-CENTURY DEVELOPMENTS

The major developments to which I wish to call attention may be summarized in the form of three statements: (1) the sacrament is social and ecclesial in its nature as well as its effects; (2) the sacra-ment is an act of ecclesial worship; (3) the deepest meaning of the sacrament is conversion and this conversion goes beyond ritual to the whole of the Christian life as mission. Each indicates a radical departure from the prior understanding of the sacrament, but tensions between the two understandings still remain.[1]

1. *The sacrament is social and ecclesial in its nature as well as its effects.* The twentieth-century emphasis on the social and ecclesial character of the sacrament was slow to develop in theology and even slower in pastoral practice. Once the trend took shape, however, it stood in sharp contrast with the privacy, individualism, and clericalism that characterized the sacrament during the era of the Counter-Reformation. A majority of theologians came to see reconciliation with the Church as an effect of the sacrament. Many theologians went further, concluding that the means whereby God's reconciling love entered into penitents' experience was not through an individual experience of interior repentance, but through the experience of reconciliation with the Church; that is, they judged that reconciliation with the Church, not interior repentance, is the *res et sacramentum* of penance and the means to reconciliation with God. Communal celebrations that prepare for or celebrate the sacrament gave practical, pastoral expression to this social and ecclesial character.

2. *The sacrament is an act of ecclesial worship.* Several historical factors diminished the sense of the sacrament as an act of worship: individualism, clericalism, a mechanistic understanding of *ex opere operato,* and a corresponding fixation on the essentials emphasized in doctrinal polemics and needed for canonical validity. Liturgical minimalism streamlined the rite until little more than confession and absolution remained. The symbolic encounter with God in the confessional was a means of grace for individuals but hardly an act of community worship. But by the time this development had peaked in the mid-twentieth century, theologians had begun to view sacraments in a liturgical rather than canonical and ascetic context, and to see them in relation to the mystery of Christ and Church. Communal celebrations began to restore the sense of community worship and individual celebrations began to be based on a shared-prayer model.

3. *The deepest meaning of the sacrament is conversion and this conversion goes beyond ritual to the whole of the Christian life as mission.* Over the centuries the individual's symbolic encounter with God in confession came to be a ritual means of therapeutic purification (forgiveness of sins) and of sanctification (grace), generally in

Theological Foundations

preparation for communion. As communion became more frequent, so did confession, until the experience of full eucharistic participation (though it was still minimally communal) led to reevaluation. A renewed appreciation of baptism as the foundation of Christian living made growth in likeness to Christ—rather than avoidance of sin—the goal of disciples. Conversion came to be seen as broader than ritual, and reconciliation as broader than forgiveness. Sacramental liturgy was integrated into the everyday life and mission of Christians and the experience of reconciliation with God and neighbor there.

VATICAN COUNCIL II AND THE CONCILIAR REFORMS
The overall pastoral intent of Vatican II and its effort to revitalize the Church's mission in the modern world meant that these twentieth-century developments were incorporated as part of the Church's contemporary understanding and practice of the sacrament.

The Teaching of Vatican II

What the Council says about penance in its documents expresses the perspectives of these developments.

1. *The sacrament is social and ecclesial in its nature as well as its effects.* At the time of the Council theologians were by no means unanimous in their views regarding the social and ecclesial character of the sacrament. This lack of theological unanimity makes the Council's position on the matter even more striking. The Constitution on the Liturgy called for a reform to express the sacrament's nature and effect more clearly.[2] A declaration accompanying the final text presented to the Council[3] and an official interpretation by Archbishop Hallinan[4] indicated that the word "nature" had been added alongside "effects" to stress the sacrament's social and ecclesial character. The Constitution on the Church was more explicit: "Those who approach the sacrament of penance obtain pardon from God's mercy for the offense committed against him, and are, at the same time, reconciled with the Church which they have wounded by their sins and which by charity, by example and by prayer labors for their conversion."[5] Thus, in relating the sacraments to the priestly community of the Church, *Lumen gentium* set reconciliation with God and reconciliation with the Church side by side—as did the Decree on the Ministry and Life

James Dallen

16

of Priests[6]—though without trying to state the precise relationship between the two ("at the same time").[7] The same text affirmed two closely related realities: the social and ecclesial character of sin ("which they have wounded by their sins") and the social and ecclesial character of conversion ("which by charity, by example, and by prayer labors for their conversion"), both of which had earlier been stated in the Constitution on the Liturgy in connection with lenten penance.[8]

2. *The sacrament is an act of ecclesial worship.* The Constitution on the Liturgy likewise made clear the communal nature and effects of the liturgy and the Council's preference for communal celebrations rather than individual and quasi-private celebrations.[9] The Council thus gave primacy to communal celebrations of the liturgy; affirmed the social and ecclesial nature and effect of sin, conversion, and the sacrament of penance; and called for reform to express these realities more clearly. Among the guidelines it gave for liturgical reform, the Council specifically affirmed the place of Scripture[10] and the need for adaptation to pastoral needs in different cultures.[11]

3. *The deepest meaning of the sacrament is conversion and this conversion goes beyond ritual to the whole of the Christian life as mission.* The Council also stated explicitly that the sacraments are acts of worship whose effects extend into people's lives and it related the sacraments to the Church's overall mission and community life.[12] By relating the sacraments to Christian spirituality and growth in faith[13] because of their relationship to the Easter mystery[14] and their character as priestly acts of Christ,[15] the Council made the completion of the likeness to Christ which begins in baptism the goal of the Christian life.[16] Continual repentance, renewed in the sacrament of penance whereby people are reconciled to God and Church, is thus the constant dynamic of Christian holiness achieved by living in the community of the Church and sharing in the Church's mission.

The 1973 Rite of Penance

Besides incorporating these developments, the 1973 Rite of Penance introduced a change of terminology to reorient our awareness. "Penance," synonymous with conversion, is the title of the ritual and is often used in the Introduction to the Rite, yet "recon-

Theological Foundations

ciliation" is both the preferred term for the sacrament and the broader reality. The Rite of Penance generally prefers "reconciliation" when it speaks of the sacrament and uses "penance" for the conversion process which culminates in reconciliation. This preference for the term "reconciliation" emphasizes both the divine initiative and the human response and sees Church community as the context for both; "penance" and "confession" suggest a more individualistic encounter. ("Confession," once used by metonymy for the sacrament, is not used by the Rite in that sense, except possibly in numbers 7b and 10b.) Reconciliation is the broader reality because it includes both God's initiative and human beings' response, while penance generally seems to accent the human effort needed to receive God's gift. Reconciliation is also broader because it puts greater emphasis on the social and ecclesial character of the sacrament as well as on the reciprocal encounter that takes place between God and people and among people.

The Introduction to the Rite of Penance was the first in the new rituals to outline the doctrinal and theological understanding on which the ritual is based. It begins by showing that the mystery of reconciliation is the key to perceiving God's work in our world and to understanding redemption in Christ and sacramental conversion in the Church (nos. 1–2). That mystery is, consequently, also the key to understanding the Church, its life and worship, and its pastoral and sacramental ministry to repentant sinners (nos. 3–7). Because of this focus on reconciliation, there is a communal and ecclesial character to the sacrament, to the ministers who have responsibility for it, and to the penitents who, led by the Church's minister, celebrate its liturgy (nos. 8–11). The same outlook, for the most part, colors remarks on the manner and forms of celebrating the sacrament (nos. 12–35) and related liturgies (nos. 36–37) and on adapting and developing the ritual (nos. 38–40).

The orientations of conciliar teaching on the sacrament were thus incorporated into the reformed Rite of Penance of 1973.

1. *The sacrament is social and ecclesial in its nature as well as its effects.* The 1973 Rite of Penance clearly expresses the social and ecclesial character of sin and penance. It does so in particular by speaking of reconciliation rather than forgiveness of sins or confession in the decree of promulgation,[17] the section titles of the in-

James Dallen

troduction, and the chapter titles of the ritual. Salvation history (no. 1), the sacraments (no. 2), and the life of the Church (nos. 3–5) manifest the mystery of reconciliation. The Church, as a reconciling community (nos. 1–5, 18), is where God and humanity are reconciled (nos. 4, 8) and baptism, eucharist, and penance are sacraments of reconciliation (nos. 2, 4, 5). Reconciliation with God and Church is the purpose of penance (no. 5 and throughout the document); absolution expresses it (no. 6d) and the formulas of absolution recall and proclaim salvation history as the mystery of reconciliation (nos. 46, 62).

The Rite of Penance emphasizes the ecclesial role of the penitent in speaking of the acts of the penitent (no. 6) and the penitent as co-celebrant of the sacrament (no. 11). The penitent is called faithful (nos. 2, 4), a member of the Church (no. 3), and a disciple of Christ (no. 6), as well as sinner (nos. 3, 5, and throughout) and penitent (no. 6 and throughout). The laity not only participate in the celebration of the sacrament but also in the planning and preparation of celebrations (no. 40b). Their wider role as agents of reconciliation is also mentioned (nos. 5, 8).

The Rite clearly regards reconciliation with the Church as an effect of the sacrament (e.g., nos. 4, 5, 31) and expresses this in its rituals (e.g., nos. 203–204) as (part of) the nature of the sacrament. Although it takes no position on the debated issue of reconciliation with the Church as the *res et sacramentum* of penance, it does seem to prefer this over the more individualistic interior repentance. Reconciliation with the Church, symbolized by the imposition of hands, restores the penitent sinner to the community in which the Spirit of Jesus is active (e.g., nos. 5, 6d, 9a, 19, 24) and by this renewal of grace the sinner is reconciled with God (no. 2, in the Latin). The penitent is once more part of the Easter mystery by being restored to the Church (nos. 1, 2, 7, 19) and the broken covenant is remade as the penitent is restored to the covenant-community (nos. 5, 6d).

The Christian goal is likeness to Christ (nos. 6a, 15), not conformity to law. For this reason, the Rite of Penance understands sin relationally (no. 5). Like Trent, it sees sin primarily in terms of its effects and consequences; unlike Trent, it emphasizes social sin and the social dimensions of all sin (e.g., nos. 4, 5, 7, 18, 25c). It states the distinction of sins in terms of grave and venial (rather than mortal and venial) and is more inclined to identify sin with

Theological Foundations

the "fundamental direction of life" (Appendix III, 3, iii, 1, in the Latin) than with particular acts.

The 1973 Rite encourages communal celebrations because they more clearly manifest the ecclesial nature of penance (no. 22) and show the Church's involvement in sinners' conversion (no. 4). The whole Church acts in the ministry of reconciliation (no. 8) and it is through the Church that God grants remission of sins (no. 6). The Church exercises the ministry of reconciliation through bishops and priests (no. 9), ministers of God (nos. 6, 10d) and of the Church (no. 6) acting in the person of Christ (nos. 6, 9). Though the Rite of Penance puts greater emphasis on the power of the priest than does much of contemporary theology (nos. 1–2, 8), the priest's role is clearly an ecclesial one (cf. nos. 9a, 9b) and goes beyond the exercise of judgment to include leadership in prayer, discernment of spirits, pastoral dedication, and human warmth (cf. no. 10).

2. *The sacrament is an act of ecclesial worship.* The priest's ministry is thus related to liturgical presidency. In the Rite of Penance the celebration of the sacrament is clearly an act of worship and its atmosphere is obviously one of prayer (nos. 4, 7, 11, 15, 16, 19, 20, 22, 23, 27, 29, 36, 37). The focus is on the present action of a merciful God rather than on the penitent's past sins (no. 6); praise of God (nos. 20, 29) and joy (no. 6d) are central. The use of Scripture, emphasized by the Council, is the foundation for this liturgical character. The Word of God reveals sinfulness, calls people to conversion, encourages them to trust God's mercy, and reveals the true nature of conversion and penance (nos. 17, 22, 24, 36–37). For this reason Scripture has a place in every form of celebration in the Rite, although it is—strangely—optional in the rite for reconciling individuals (nos. 17, 43).

Providing communal celebrations of the sacrament and penitential celebrations is the most obvious indication that the sacrament is regarded as ecclesial worship. Still, even the individual rite is presented as worship (no. 11) by its emphasis on the dialogue (nos. 6d, 16, 18), on the ecclesial dimensions of the sacrament, on prayer in the rite, and on the Word; there is also greater flexibility regarding the place of celebration (nos. 12, 38). The formulas of absolution summarize the biblical, ecclesial, and Trinitarian orientations of the Rite's understanding of penance.

James Dallen

3. *The deepest meaning of the sacrament is conversion and this conversion goes beyond ritual to the whole of the Christian life as mission.*
Both the introduction (nos. 1, 2, 7, 19) and the celebrations (nos. 44, 54, 57; Appendix II, 8–19) present baptism as the paradigmatic experience of reconciliation through Christ's Easter mystery; the sacrament of penance and reconciliation is thus clearly related to initiation, the sacramental base of the Christian life. The purpose of penance is deeper love and friendship, reconciliation with God and Church (no. 5 and throughout). The season of Lent is a special time for a community experience of conversion; reconciliation with God is its goal (no. 13) and it is marked by communal celebrations (no. 40b). But the specific discussion of conversion (no. 6) and repeated references (nos. 4, 6a, 7, 20) see it as a continual reality characterizing the Christian life. The presentation of the acts of the penitent brings this out more fully.[18]

This penitential dimension of the Christian life links Christian life and liturgy but not in an individualistic fashion. The Rite of Penance sees sacrament as an aid in attaining full freedom and likeness to Christ, thus completing the direction given at baptism (nos. 2, 4, 6a, 7b). But the Rite explicitly states that penitent sinners "should help each other in doing penance so that freed from sin by the grace of Christ they may work with all of good will for justice and peace in the world" (no. 5). (This is the first correlation of the sacrament and work for social justice in an official document.) The strongest correlation between the sacrament, everyday penance, and social action is in number 7: "In order that this sacrament of healing may truly achieve its purpose among Christ's faithful, it must take root in their whole lives and move them to a more fervent service of God and neighbor."

As a consequence, though the Rite of Penance speaks of the value of frequent celebration, it requires that this be done carefully and emphasizes (in contrast with Pius XII's statement in *Mystici corporis*) that it is not a "mere ritualistic repetition or psychological exercise, but a serious striving to perfect the grace of baptism" (no. 7b). It affirms means other than the sacramental ritual for expressing repentance and achieving reconciliation (nos. 4, 7, 37) and, overall, gives primacy to living the gospel message of repentance as a dimension of the Christian mission to bring salvation to the world by proclaiming the gospel and working with all people of goodwill for justice and peace. A residual preoccupation with

Theological Foundations

the Tridentine requirements prevents the eschatological character of the Church's mission of reconciliation from being developed.

GOD'S WORK AND THE CHURCH

Following the lead of the 1973 Rite of Penance, I regard "reconciliation" as the prime category for understanding God's work in our world and for understanding the Church's mission to participate in that work. "Conversion" and "penance"— synonymous terms—are for the sake of reconciliation. "Forgiveness of sins" is an inadequate and misleading term if it is given primacy, since it is only a secondary part of the personal (individual) experience of reconciliation. This will become clearer as we attempt to situate the sacrament of penance and reconciliation within an overview of the Church's mission in relation to God's work in the world.

A basic Christian intuition about God is that God reconciles, brings together in loving union, those who continue to be marked by differences. To realize how deeply God is committed to reconciliation requires attention to the Trinitarian character of our faith.[19] Daring to enter within the Holy of Holies, the inner life of the triune God, Christian thinkers have gone so far as to claim that God is reconciler by nature. Thus classical theology maintains that in God there are three subjects with a single consciousness;[20] or, in Rahner's phrasing, there is in God one self-presence in three distinct manners of subsisting.[21] Trinitarian theology may sound like cerebral speculation, dry and remote, but the divine reality has all the passion of a love affair: "There are these three," Augustine said, "the one who loves, the one who is loved, and the love itself."[22] In dynamic tri-unity divine love is self-expressed in the Word and bonded in the Spirit. God, one and three, is reconciler, the loving union of those who remain distinct. By rejecting both a "monarchical" subordinationism and a "democratic" tritheism, Christians have affirmed their faith that God is reconciling community.

When the Holy Spirit is seen as the common gift, the bond, of Father and Son, the Spirit is the community of Father and Son. This Spirit is also Gift of God in human experience and the eternal sending of the Spirit (spiration) takes historical form in cosmic and human community. The Preface of the Holy Trinity proclaims our faith in doxological terms: "three Persons equal in majesty,

James Dallen

22

undivided in splendor, yet one Lord, one God, ever to be adored in . . . everlasting glory." But since God's glory is the ground for God's being called divine and "God cannot be glorious without being glorified,"[23] the God who is tri-unity freely expresses self in creation through the Word; and the Spirit who bonds Father and the Son is God's power moving in creation that the many be one. In the beginning, the Spirit of God hovering over the waters (Gen 1:2) is creation's breath of life, enlivening all those things that God freely makes to be different, maintains in their difference, and yet brings together. "The Spirit of the Lord, indeed, fills the whole world" and "holds all things together" (Wis 1:7).

Yet this reconciling power of God which brings all things together—which "gathers to a greatness," as Hopkins puts it in "God's Grandeur"—not only does so freely but also with respect for the reality of the creatures who participate in that freedom. Creatures are free to withdraw themselves from what is being brought together and from this love which brings all things together—are free to sin. Our experience of creation is not simply an experience of unity but of a unity threatened by the absurdity, the nothingness, of chaotic fragmentation. The threat is too often of our own making. (I remember being struck, years ago, when I read Maritain's reflections on how God says to creatures, "without me, you can do nothing." That is to say, creatures can negate God's creative purpose, and introduce a vacuum into being, can make that "thing" which is nothing.)[24]

But the God who is reconciler, in inmost being, cannot witness such an outcome dispassionately. God seeks to complete creation by bringing all things together and, in the case of sin, by bringing back together. Thus we know God not only as creator but also as redeemer. For us, reconciliation is not simply a matter of union but of reunion, with the connotation of oneness after estrangement. At-one-ment involves an atonement which is liberation or conversion, our being freed from what is divisive or our being changed so as to fit together once more.

Scriptural usage aids clarification. The New Testament Greek katallagē ("reconciliation") is a legal term used of husband and wife, as in 1 Corinthians 7:11, and thus deals with personal relations—the end of hostility and the restoration of friendship. In the four Pauline applications of reconciliation to salvation, it is always God who takes the initiative to restore what was meant to be. In 2 Corinthians 5:18–20 God reconciles us to God's own self in and through Christ by not holding our sins against us. In Romans 5:10–11 Christ's death is the means whereby God destroys the hostility. In Colossians 1:20–22 Christ's death is the means whereby peace is made, although there are two ambiguities: whether it is God or Christ who acts and whether the peace is between God and creatures, among creatures, or (probably) both. Ephesians 2:11–16 is clear—Christ, by his death, restores friendship with God by breaking down the walls of separation among people, with the Jew-Gentile distinction, so radically divisive for the early Church, the archetype of how change takes place and what we are freed from.

There are thus two very different applications of "reconciliation" to salvation. In the first, "reconciliation" has a metaphorical character since the hostility is one-sided—human beings have chosen to separate themselves from God. In the other, the term is used literally—differences among people have indeed become divisive and separated them from what God is creating; their reunion reunites them with God. What both usages have in common is a focus on God's eternal purpose realized in time. Although our history is, in fact, not simply creation but new creation, this new creation is nevertheless no afterthought or repair job: it is a restatement of God's original creative intention. (This is explicit in Ephesians 1:10 where *anakephalaíōsis* has the sense of "recapitulation," a summary restatement of the main point.)

Whether in creation or in salvation, what God is by nature God does by choice. Thus Teilhard de Chardin, like Richard of St. Victor before him, is able to see in creation itself a reflection of the life of the Trinity, especially as creation moves toward its eschatological goal. (As I mentioned, the eschatological character of the sacrament—service to the kingdom—is present in the Rite of Penance but not explicitly developed.) God's creative action, centered in Christ, moves toward a mysterious synthesis, creative union, the complete fulfillment of the universe in God.[25] In the one movement of creation, incarnation, and redemption, whereby God expresses who God is, the God who is triune reconciler—reconciling community—continually reconciles until finally "God will be all in all" (1 Cor 15:28). The whole work of God in creation and salvation is reconciliation, a bringing together in loving union,

James Dallen

even if our factual experience is of redemption, a union re-established after estrangement.

The second Eucharistic Prayer for Masses of Reconciliation expresses this Trinitarian reconciliation beautifully: "In the midst of conflict and division, we know it is you who turn our minds to thoughts of peace." This power of God present and working in creation is the Spirit: "Your Spirit changes our hearts . . . Your Spirit is at work when understanding puts an end to strife, when hatred is quenched by mercy, and vengeance gives way to forgiveness." But Church worship, as Geoffrey Wainwright has noted,[26] gives a strong christological cast to pneumatology, and so this prayer praises God through Jesus, the Incarnate Word: "He is the Word that brings salvation, He is the hand you stretch out to sinners, He is the way that leads to your peace."

For us, then, Jesus makes apparent in his life, death, and resurrection that God is unalterably and unreservedly committed to reconciling all things—"through him and for him, everything in heaven and everything on earth" (Col 1:20–22). The infancy narratives describe him, at his birth, drawing to himself the poor and despised of Israel (Luke) and the gentile Magi (Matthew). Jesus used the political image of the "reign of God" for this reconciling work, a work which produced him and which was enacted in his ministry. He drew people's attention to it through his parables, surrendered himself to it in his prayer, let its presence have its effect through his miracles, celebrated it in his meals.

Jesus' death and resurrection made clear the irrevocable character of God's commitment to make peace, to redeem, by reconciling all things: since sinners wished it that way, it was done by the blood of his cross. By manifesting God's love for people, his dying and rising enable us to discover that we are thereby gifted with the capacity to love (see Rom 5:5). The love whereby God identifies self with us creates within us the human analogue to creative divine love: a radical openness by which we identify ourselves with God and with other human beings instead of just ourselves. Thus the power of love by which God reconciles us to others and to God in Christ is the same power whereby we are able to love both God and neighbor. God's gift of reconciling love, most evident in the Easter mystery, makes us one: one with others, one within ourselves, one with creation, and thereby one with God. Conversion or liberation is thus an aspect of reconciliation: in reconciling us to others, self, creation, and God, God changes us so that we can be united or frees us from the barriers, divisions, and distinctions—the sin—that prevent union.

God's eternal sending of the Word (generation) becomes human in the person of Jesus and God's eternal sending of the Spirit (spiration) takes further historical form in Christ's Body, the Church, as his *anamnesis* or memorial, part of what happened to Jesus in the resurrection. God's work and message is now entrusted to us, Paul told the Corinthians (2 Cor 5:18-20). Thus the work and message of the Church is reconciliation.

However, when this work and message are seen in the context of creation, incarnation, redemption, and salvation—all understood as reconciliation—some basic ecclesiological shifts become necessary. The first shift needed is to realize that the Church does not exist for the sake of its members, so that they can save their souls, but in order to serve humanity, the kingdom, and God. It serves its members and is reconciled not only by reconciling its sinful members but by working for reconciliation throughout the world. A second shift leads to the same conclusion: as God does what God is, so the Church is what it does—a reconciling community. It is reconciled only by reconciling.

The ecclesiology of Vatican II situates the image of the Church as Body of Christ within the context of the broader image of the Church as People of God and abandons the institutional model of Church. Cardinal Ratzinger may not be in complete sympathy with this,[27] but the broader image of the Church as People of God puts the Church in its place as part of God's overall plan and work, avoiding any idolization of the Church through a spirit of exclusivism or elitism. It does so by complementing the christological character of the Church with the (historically prior) pneumatological character. The movement of God's Spirit in all of creation takes shape in human history as the People of God. So far as this People of God is memorial of Jesus, it is Body of Christ. But in any case, the movement or mission extends beyond the Church. God's work of reconciliation is primary and is not confined to the Church, which is the "universal sacrament of salvation" but not salvation exclusively: as sacrament it is sign and instrument of union with God and the unity of humankind, but it is not the only way in which those are realized.[28] But neither can it be such a sacrament if it is not fulfilling its mission. It is as a reconciling

James Dallen

26

community that the Church is People of God. It is by maintaining and manifesting Christ's Easter mystery in every time and place through its own commitment until he comes again that the Church is memorial of Jesus and Body of Christ; and since that mystery is reconciliation, the Church is Body of Christ only as a reconciling community.

It is possible that one reason for the current crisis of sin and penance—if there is one—is that people do not experience the Church as a reconciling community. At the least, that this be a reality in people's experience requires the abandonment of the institutional model of Church. Otherwise, the community that is called to be prophet in order to proclaim God's saving work sounds like it's nagging and the community that is called to be Good Samaritan to humanity's needs looks more like a robber. Only a converting community that recognizes and struggles to overcome its own sin knows how to welcome and work with penitent sinners. A disincarnate, transcendent and perfect institution, standing apart from its members, may be able to channel an abstract forgiveness and grace, but it is unable to be a community that supports conversion and promotes reconciliation. Nor is it possible for the Church to be a converting community without being a reconciling community—conversion or transformation involves beginning to do what we exist for.

The nature of the Church is thus evident only from its mission as a participation in the work of God in creation, incarnation, redemption, and salvation—a work of reconciliation. It is not divine but created. It is sinful but converting. It is a reconciling community.

Ecclesiological shifts require that we reimage Christian life. Who we are as Christians follows from the mission which determines the nature of the Church, the mission of God to reconcile all things. As we are initiated into the Christian community, we recognize God's commitment and choose to be aligned with it. We set ourselves to conversion, being transformed so as to contribute to the work of a reconciling community, and we are converted as we reconcile. As we are aligned with God's commitment, we are God's action in Christ in the Spirit, marked out as one, holy, catholic, and apostolic. To be Christian is to commit ourselves to being public property.

Theological Foundations

One aspect of this, catholicity, is particularly relevant today. As unity does not require uniformity, so the acceptance of pluralism is a consequence of the Church's recognition of its call to be catholic.[29] As the Spirit unites Father and Son without the Father ceasing to be Father or the Son ceasing to be Son, as God unites humanity to God while maintaining the distinction between Creator and creation, so the Church unites without erasing differences. There is necessarily a pluralism of persons, rites, races, opinions, lifestyles, and all the rest in the Church. The reconciling Spirit of Jesus brings together in loving union while respecting differences.[30]

THE PASTORAL MINISTRY AND SACRAMENT OF PENANCE AND RECONCILIATION

Within this perspective we are better able to appreciate both the pastoral ministry and sacrament of penance and reconciliation. Neither exists to keep individuals in line or to enable them to have their sins forgiven (i.e., experience wholeness through liberation from sin). Both exist so that the Church may exercise its mission of being a reconciling community by keeping together those who have committed themselves to that mission. This is, I think, a sufficient rationale both for real collegiality and for the priority of communal celebrations of the sacrament over individual confession.

Here we see the importance of the vision of Church in the Rite of Christian Initiation of Adults. It will be difficult for people to see the sacrament of penance and reconciliation as a reordination to conversion for the sake of reconciling all things in Christ if they have never made that vision their own or committed themselves to making it a reality. The sacrament of penance and reconciliation exists for the sake of the Church's mission both in worship and in life. Its worship, the response of praise and thanks to God for what God is doing, and its action, aligning it with what God is doing, must necessarily be correlated.

We need to recognize that the sacrament unites these dimensions of worship and (social) action. To keep them united the sacrament must clearly be an ecclesial activity oriented toward the Church's mission. This has not always been the case in the historical development of the sacrament. During the first centuries the pastoral ministry and sacrament of penance and reconciliation

James Dallen

28

were primarily oriented toward maintaining the Church in apostolic holiness so that it might fulfill its mission of being a sacrament of salvation for pagan society. In time the orientation shifted. Already in the era of canonical penance the ministry and sacrament were focusing more on the need for the Church to maintain certain standards of behavior and on the needs of individuals. By the late Middle Ages this shift was complete and the focus was primarily on individual holiness. By this time, the original orientation (toward ecclesial holiness for the sake of its mission) had practically been forgotten. Beginning in the twelfth and thirteenth centuries a new ecclesial focus began to develop: maintaining apostolic unity in the face of threats from Albigensianism and other heresies. In the era of the Counter-Reformation this focus on individual holiness was maintained and strengthened. The ecclesial focus on apostolic unity was also extended and solidified in opposition to the Protestant reformers.

In our own time global Christianity has become a real possibility and for the first time in its history the Church is able to become fully catholic. The pastoral ministry and sacrament of penance and reconciliation, in order to enable the Church to fulfill its mission to serve humanity, the kingdom, and God in this new situation and in order to serve the Church's members so that they may take their part in this mission, should therefore focus on maintaining the Church in apostolic catholicity, consciously seeking to respect differences that are not opposed to the accomplishment of its mission. Thus, if there is a hierarchy of truths in Christian doctrine,[31] there is also a hierarchy of virtues in Christian living and a corresponding distinction of sins. Keeping this in mind, the Church's pastoral ministry and sacrament of penance and reconciliation must have as its primary goal keeping the Church faithful to its mission of reconciliation. It does so by supporting conversion, the movement toward full union with the Father, through Christ, in the power of the Holy Spirit active in the Church, *for the sake of its mission of reconciliation.* It does not do so if, as has been the case, the Church ignores its own sinfulness, restricts sin to certain areas in individuals' lives (especially sex), and prevents people from assuming responsibilities in line with the gospel's demands.[32]

Conversion is both ecclesial and personal. Moreover, individual or personal experience of the sacrament is in the context of the ecclesial experience. Personal conversion (considered in Scholastic

Theological Foundations

theology in terms of the acts of the penitent) is the way in which the individual Christian lives as a member of the Church, itself created, sinful, redeemed, and converting. But conversion is only part of reconciliation. The community that seeks reconciliation is a reconciling community and thus reconciled; the same is true of its members. Authentic conversion does not take place except as a part of the effort to realize reconciliation.

We see this in the ancient understanding of penitential practices, the external expression of conversion. The early Church considered it important to link together prayer, fasting, and almsgiving (works of charity): individuals should deny something to themselves while, at the same time, reaching out to God in prayer and to others in sharing what they had denied to themselves. In this way, whether in the order of penitents or in everyday penance, Christians learned to live as agents of reconciliation. (Paul VI's *Paenitemini* sought to revitalize this in the contemporary Church.)

The same recognition of conversion as part of reconciliation is needed in the sacramental celebration. It too must link personal conversion and the integration of converting sinners into the Church with the Church's mission. It must not simply focus on the forgiveness of the individual's sins or leave the impression that sin is something only between individuals and God, as though it were something invisible and interior which God could forgive without the whole human situation being changed. God, in fact, does not forgive sins, if that is taken to mean that God's attitude towards people changes or that the human situation is left unchanged.[33] Rather, our conversion allows God's love to become operative within us so that we can love with the same love (see Rom 5:5), proclaiming the good news of reconciliation and working so that others can experience it. It is a cooperation with God's love and sets us free from whatever hinders us from being a part of what God is doing. Forgiveness is thus only one part of conversion, the experience of liberation. And conversion itself has an essentially social function in a community moving through history toward the kingdom of God. The absolution proclaimed in the sacramental celebration makes that explicit. It consecrates the whole conversion process—intrinsically, not extrinsically—by showing that its term and goal is not simply forgiveness of sins but reconciliation with the Church so as to take part in its mission.

James Dallen

The sacrament of conversion and reconciliation is thus the source and summit of a life of conversion lived in a reconciling community. By establishing reconciliation as the primary category for understanding God's work and the Church's mission, the 1973 Rite of Penance laid out new theological foundations for the pastoral ministry and sacrament of penance and reconciliation. Those foundations include the triune God as reconciling community, the work of God in creation and salvation as reconciliation, Jesus' redemptive work as reconciliatory, and the Church's mission as reconciliation. Building on those foundations we recognize that the pastoral ministry and sacrament of penance and reconciliation are oriented toward the conversion of the Church and its members into agents of reconciliation. The celebration of the sacrament is part of the Church's mission and shows that mission to be social, the formation of a reconciling community as the memorial of Jesus until he comes. "And when everything is subjected to him, then the Son himself will be subject in his turn to the One who subjected all things to him, so that God may be all in all" (1 Cor 15:28).

NOTES

1. See my "Recent Documents on Penance and Reconciliation" in this volume.

2. *Sacrosanctum concilium*, no. 72.

3. *Acta Synodalia Sacrosancti Concilii Oecumenici Vaticani II* 2, pars 2 (Rome: Typis Polyglottis Vaticanis, 1962) 558–559.

4. Ibid., 567.

5. *Lumen gentium*, no. 11, in *Vatican Council II: The Conciliar and Post-Conciliar Documents*, ed. Austin Flannery, O.P. (Collegeville: The Liturgical Press, 1975) 362.

6. *Presbyterorum ordinis*, no. 5.

7. However, almost all theologians who regarded reconciliation with the Church as an effect of penance had come to see it as the *res et sacramentum* of penance and thus reconciliation with God as its consequence. See Rahner, "Penance as an Additional Act of Reconciliation with the Church," in *Theological Investigations, Volume X: Writings of 1965-67: 2*, trans. David Bourke (New York: Herder and Herder, 1973)

Theological Foundations

130; and especially Clarence McAuliffe (who does not agree that it is the *res et sacramentum*), "Penance and Reconciliation with the Church," *Theological Studies* 26 (1965) 1–39.

8. *Sacrosanctum concilium*, nos. 109–110.

9. Ibid., nos. 26–27.

10. Ibid., nos. 24, 35.

11. Ibid., nos. 27–40, 62.

12. Ibid., nos. 9, 59.

13. In addition to *Sacrosanctum concilium*, no. 59, see *Presbyterorum ordinis*, nos. 13, 18, and *Christus Dominus*, no. 30.

14. *Sacrosanctum concilium*, no. 61.

15. E.g., *Sacrosanctum concilium*, nos. 6–7; *Presbyterorum ordinis*, no. 5.

16. *Lumen gentium*, nos. 7, 11, 32–36, 40, 42.

17. "Reconciliationem inter Deum et homines," 2 December 1973, *Acta Apostolicae Sedis* 66 (1974) 172–173.

18. For a detailed discussion, see my *The Reconciling Community: The Rite of Penance* (New York: Pueblo Publishing Company, 1986) 269–286.

19. An influence from Trinitarian theology is evident in nos. 5, 6d, 9a, 10c, 19.

20. See Bernard Lonergan, *De Deo Trino*, 3rd ed. rev. (Rome: Gregorian University, 1964) 2: 186–193.

21. Karl Rahner, *The Trinity* (New York: Herder and Herder, 1970) 109ff.

22. *De trinitate 9, 2, 2, Corpus Christianorum, Series Latina* (Turnhout: Brepols, 1953–) 50:294.

23. Robert C. Neville, "Creation and the Trinity," *Theological Studies* 30 (1969) 26.

24. See Jacques Maritain, *Existence and the Existent: An Essay on Christian Existentialism* (Garden City: Doubleday Image, 1948) 98–99.

25. See Christopher F. Mooney, *Teilhard de Chardin and the Mystery of Christ* (New York: Harper and Row, 1966) 168–188.

26. Geoffrey Wainwright, *Doxology: The Praise of God in Worship, Doctrine and Life* (New York: Oxford University Press, 1980) 103.

27. He regards "People of God," at least as used in postconciliar ecclesiologies, as a conception of the Church which returns us to the "Old Testament." See *The Ratzinger Report: An Exclusive Interview on the State of the Church* (San Francisco: Ignatius Press 1985) 46–47.

28. For the Church as universal sacrament of salvation, see *Lumen gentium*, no. 48. This is cited in *Gaudium et spes*, no. 45, and *Ad gentes*,

James Dallen

no. 1. For the meaning of sacrament here (sign and instrument of union and unity), see especially *Lumen gentium,* no. 1.

29. Cf. *Lumen gentium,* no. 13.

30. Implications for Church organization and government of Trinitarian (not monadic) unity in the Trinity are noted by Jürgen Moltmann, *The Trinity and the Kingdom* (San Francisco: Harper and Row, 1981) 191ff.

31. See *Unitatis redintegratio,* no. 11. Pius XI's 1928 encyclical *Mortalium animos* condemned the concept of such a distinction; see DS 3683.

32. This was well stated by Archbishop Paul Grégoire in the 1971 Synod. See "The Use of Penance and the Sense of Sin," *Doctrine and Life* 22 (1972) 32–34. His claim is that it is not so much the concept of sin which is today in question as a concept without root in the gospels. He saw the Church's problem structurally rooted in its institutions and intensified by a practice of the sacrament inadequate to Christians' social responsibility.

33. Whatever change there is, is on the human side. God loves all that is, simply because it is. Reconciliation, insofar as it is a return of sinners to loving union, transforms what is unlovable by removing barriers to union (i.e., the sin that negates God's creative purpose). Cf. Thomas Aquinas, *Summa Theologiae* III, q. 49, a. 4.

Theological Foundations

Doris Donnelly

Reconciliation and Community

There is a natural connection between reconciliation and community. Words like hurt, sin, offense, pardon, forgiveness, and reconciliation do not make sense outside the context of relationships; they presuppose community. And it is probably fair to say that the only sure way to avoid being hurt or hurting another and to spare oneself the effort and joy of union after disunion is to live without spouse, children, parents, co-workers, friends, God—even to live outside a relationship with oneself because forgiving oneself and integrating (or reconciling) a divided personality is a very real and an often profound experience.

Yet the fundamental connection between the terms "reconciliation" and "community" must not be as self-evident as we think if so many of us admit uncertainty about how their interdependence works or does not work. The plan of the first part of this paper, then, is to deal with difficulties that explain the disconnection between reconciliation and community. The second part of the paper will consider situations where community and reconciliation are able to flourish.

DIFFICULTIES CONNECTING RECONCILIATION AND
COMMUNITY

There are six difficulties which would seem to explain the disconnection between reconciliation and community.

(1) The theme of community and our interconnectedness as people (our coresponsibility in sin and our cooperation in repentance) is difficult to link with the experience of the collapse of family and social structures surrounding us. On one hand, we want to talk about Church as community; on the other hand, fewer and fewer persons are living in units that bear the nurturing, caring, challenging, generative, committed, enduring qualities of "community."

(2) Even when community *is* present, reconciliation is an infrequently exercised option by which to resolve conflict, divisiveness, hostility and violence. In fact, forgiveness and reconciliation are

34

often viewed as spineless and weak responses to injury, with aggressive behavior patterns (vengeance, separation, counterviolence) the preferred responses. In the popular imagination, Rambo, the Liquidator, and the Exterminator have the right idea when it comes to dealing with the opposition.[1]

Recently, a friend of mine who was about to make a career change investigated how conflicts were resolved at his prospective new firm. (Not incidentally, ground rules concerning conflict resolution are wisely decided early in any relationship where investment of self and commitment are part of the picture). My friend learned that when disagreements arose, the person who questioned the *status quo* was labeled a "troublemaker" and was usually fired, occasionally transferred. Or the "troublemaker" was ostracized from the social life of the organization, and in his or her alienation, was encouraged to resign.

This pattern of axing or chilling the opposition is common enough in families, neighborhoods, and institutions. There is no room for dialogue in this approach—no settlement, no compromise, no negotiation. The message that gets through loud and clear is that forgiveness is equivalent to being pushed around, to being the doormat, the sucker, the weakling, and that the world respects more assertive tactics. This is the experience people live with from day to day.

(3) For reconciliation and forgiveness to be attractive and realistic options in daily life situations—in families, in communities, neighborhoods, on the job, among friends, and so forth—they need to be modeled effectively in the Church community. We all want to see how a parish team composed of mortals who disagree, annoy, and argue with each other learn to forgive and move on in service to the community. We want to learn how a Christian family deals with an unmarried pregnant teenage daughter in a way that is confrontative *and* forgiving. We want to witness leaders in the Church admitting mistakes while trusting in the support of a forgiving community. And we yearn to see over and over again *in practice*, not merely in theory, how victims of injustice forgive as the community of blacks did in Montgomery, Alabama, during the civil rights confrontation in that city, again proving that love is the most powerful force in the world.

This is another way of saying that symbols both on and off the altar need to be "in sync."

Reconciliation and Community

I believe many of our religious symbols and, in particular, many of our liturgical symbols (in baptism, the eucharist, penance, for example) are powerful signs of repentance, healing, and reconciliation. But I am not sure they are strong enough to withstand the countersigns which visually and viscerally assault the imaginations of the faithful.

That visual drama is disquieting. A community preaches economic justice but pays its own employees substandard salaries; and another community talks of a *koinonia* reaching out to all but declines to wash the feet of women at a Holy Thursday footwashing. Certainly, there are many reconciling gestures within the Church communities, and we lap these up like hungry little puppies; the Pope visits Ali Agca in a prison cell and speaks to him "like a brother to a brother;" a mother forgives the drunk driver who killed her child and then founds Mothers Against Drunk Driving (M.A.D.D.) to see that no one else suffers the same tragedy; a bishop asks forgiveness of the alienated in his diocese for sins of omission and commission that may have driven some from their spiritual roots. But these gestures are all too rare and are often offset by disturbing divisive symbols. The community is getting mixed signals. You and I are sending mixed signals. And the bottom line is that the Church is simply not as transparent as it could be in practicing what it preaches about reconciliation.

The tragic result of this opaqueness is that we have lost some of our credibility as preachers and teachers of repentance and heralds of the good news of the forgiveness of sins in Jesus Christ. The gospel is right on target when it suggests that we leave our gifts at the altar while we straighten our commitments as a repentant, forgiving, and reconciling people in the pews. It might just as accurately call us to leave our symbols at the altar if these are not paralleled elsewhere. We are light to the nations when both sets of symbols are working together, and we are darkness and confusion when the signals are scrambled.

(4) An individualistic (God and me) piety further threatens the tenuous hold we may have on breathing the words "reconciliation" and "community" in the same breath, for it seems to some that we can sin, we can be forgiven, and we can be reconciled without touching another human being along the way. For those who prefer a privatized spirituality, the notion of community involvement in reconciliation is regarded as intrusive, unnecessary,

Doris Donnelly

36

embarrassing, and for some, terrifying. We need to be pastorally sensitive to these fears.

At the same time, we need to correct the faulty theology that undergirds this solipsistic spirituality by asserting two fundamental truths.

The first has to do with sin. However much it may appear to the contrary, there is no such thing as a private sin or a sin that affects only the person who commits it. Even those sins committed in secret without witnesses have repercussions on everyone else because the divided and disordered person who lives among us is less fully a person and less free than he or she might otherwise be. In some cases (poverty, sexism, racism, violence), sin has even a collective origin. The essence of sin certainly is that it is an offense against God, but it also has an often neglected or forgotten social and ecclesial dimension.[2]

If we have any doubts about whether sin injures the members of the community, or how repentance redresses the wrong we do (or the good we don't do), or how reconciliation heals the division resulting from sin, I propose that we ask the experts.

Let's ask the Catholic bishops in Northern Ireland and their Protestant counterparts; let's ask the Nicaraguans who gather on the Honduran border as U.S. aircraft maneuver ominously over their heads; let's ask the grandparent who has not seen a grandchild for six years because of a bitter divorce judgment. Let's ask these people whether selfishness, revenge, injustice, and violence can be neatly contained so that no one is affected but the perpetrator of the deed. These people will tell us what we may fear knowing: that there are some places where the evil is so deep that if one were to drop a penny into one of these holes, it would take days before it would touch bottom. Untold numbers are affected by sin.

We need good preaching and catechesis on sin.

And lest we think this will drive the people from the pews and lessen the Sunday collection, remember that two mainline religious trade books that made it to the bestseller list in recent years have been Karl Menninger's *Whatever Became of Sin?* and M. Scott Peck's *People of the Lie.* The churches may not be talking about sin (and I can't remember the last sermon I heard on the subject), but people obviously want to hear about it and are paying good money to read about it.

Reconciliation and Community

We are lessened as a community if we refuse (or do not know how!) to acknowledge our culpability, and we are diminished as the redeemed Body of Christ by not celebrating that redemption. Jesus Christ offered his lifeblood for the "forgiveness of sins" and died to point us to victory over sin. If the Christian community denies its involvement with sin what do these fundamental credal tenets mean? Suffice it to say that the Christian community is not served responsibly without teaching about sin and its forgiveness in Christ.

The second truth which does not sit well with a privatized spirituality has to do with the forthright declaration of Jesus that once forgiveness is received, it needs to be passed on. In fact, the gospel would have us believe that the only way we have of determining whether a person has received the forgiveness of God is by that person's offer of unconditional forgiveness to another.

The parable of the unforgiving debtor (Matt 18:23–35) makes this point crystal clear. The unsettling ending of the story says that I cannot receive forgiveness and hoard it. If I do, it simply means that I may have been granted forgiveness (as the debtor was) but that I did not accept it through repentance (as the debtor did not). Jesus draws a scathing lesson: "You wicked servant! I forgave you all that debt because you besought me; and should you not have had mercy on your fellow servant, as I had mercy on you? And in anger his lord delivered him to the jailers, till he should pay all his debt. So also my heavenly Father will do to every one of you, if you do not forgive your brother from your heart."

(5) Still another difficulty has to do with our fear that justice is not served if the community forgives. The line of argumentation runs like this: Do we not owe it to the offender to teach her a lesson? Is it not our responsibility to give him a dose of his own medicine so that he mends his ways?

The truth of the matter is that forgiveness from Jesus is always raised in connection with justice, a new justice wherein Jesus removed the link between the offense and the debt, and takes upon himself payment of that debt.[3] The "eye for an eye" teaching of the old law is replaced in the New Testament by a teaching that asks we forgive our enemies and by a theology that Jesus has settled the debt due to the sins of all (Matt 5:38–42). Accepting that truth is what repentance is about, bringing in its tracks the awe-

Doris Donnelly

38

some recognition that through no merit of my own, no work of my own, no wish of my own, my sins have been forgiven.

This approach is hard to reckon with institutions—the Church of Jesus Christ among them—that sometimes function on a punitive rather than a forgiving model. Suppose we reflected on the way we run our schools, our religious communities, our parishes, our organizations. How often is it apparent in *our* dealing with offenders that Jesus Christ removed the link between the offense and the deed?

(6) There are always three terms involved in the process of reconciliation. *The first is the hurt itself,* and it frequently matters little whether the hurt was big or small, accidental or deliberate. To be hurt is to experience pain, to be wounded. It is often difficult to admit, to accept, to forgive.

The third and last step is reconciliation. To reconcile means to bring together that which belongs together but which is apart. It is the goal, the end term of the process we are describing, but it is frequently encouraged hastily and it is often pushed ahead before the time is right. Frequently, this rushing is equivalent to putting a Band-Aid on a wound before it is inspected and cleansed out. This is not a healthy procedure to follow for any kind of wound— emotional, physical or spiritual.

Forgiveness is the second step, often bypassed in the pell-mell race to reconciliation. Forgiveness provides the occasion to take stock of the hurt done to us, to acknowledge the pain and to determine with all our wits about us that we will choose, freely, to love. Sometimes that takes some doing.

This process, so common in ordinary life, can be easily transposed to the theological world. There, the first step is sin, and there are some of us old enough to be familiar with a pastoral practice that encouraged immediate reconciliation whenever sin was "discovered" or "fallen into." The first step was (is?) dealt with by rushing towards reconciliation (step three) through sacramental confession—and the sooner the better. Step number two, the experience of the forgiveness of God, was often missed entirely.

I believe that many of our pastoral, liturgical, and catechetical problems with regard to the sacrament of reconciliation might be resolved by reaffirming step two and allowing each other the

Reconciliation and Community

graced privilege of experiencing the forgiveness of God. Once we know that experience with the certainty of faith, once we experience the total, magnanimous forgiveness of God, then celebrating forgiveness is the logical, expected, hoped-for next step. However, if we do not experience God's forgiveness, reconciliation becomes a *pro forma,* innocuous, ineffectual and meaningless gesture.

SHAPING A RECONCILING COMMUNITY

Once the difficulties are acknowledged, the question that remains is this: what does a community look like when it mirrors the forgiving and reconciling Spirit of Jesus Christ? Such a community bears the following marks.

(1) It is a community that initiates forgiveness. It goes first. It reaches out to the offender and forgives. It does not wait for the offender to grovel, to beg pardon; in the spirit of Jesus, it extends forgiveness even before it is requested.

What this means in the concrete is that the Christian community not only goes first, but does so without arrogance (after all, the offender is being incorporated or reincorporated into a community of forgiven sinners). Then after the fact, the forgiving community does not lord it over the offender that has been magnanimously forgiven. Nor does it remind the offender of the offense by forgiving provisionally or conditionally, and/or by putting the offender on probation. Rather, in the spirit of the prodigal parent, the forgiving community does not let the offense stand in the way of the future relationship. Nothing breaks down the walls of resistance more effectively, than this: going first and asking forgiveness, or going first and accepting forgiveness.

(2) It is a community where the truth can be spoken, where insecurity and human frailty can be acknowledged, and where men and women are not forced to behave as hypocrites declaring themselves free from sin. It is a community where the power of sin is taken seriously, where sin is recognized as destroying not only the sinner but altering reality as well. And it is a community where there is support from other forgiven sinners once the truth is spoken.

For the Protestant pastor and martyr Dietrich Bonhoeffer, this inner honesty that allows one to stand naked before another

Doris Donnelly

breaks the hypocritical substructure that renders community impossible. In *Life Together,* Bonhoeffer puts it this way:

> The final breakthrough to fellowship [read "community"] does not occur because, though they have fellowship with one another as believers and as devout people, they do not have fellowship as the undevout, as sinners. The pious fellowship permits no one to be a sinner. So everybody must conceal his [her] sin from himself [herself] and from the fellowship. We dare not be sinners. Many Christians are unthinkably horrified when a real sinner is suddenly discovered among the righteous. So we remain alone with our sin, living in lies and hypocrisy . . . .[4]

The first letter of John had it the other way around: there is always hope with the truth because "if we acknowledge our sins, then God who is faithful and just will forgive our sins" (1 John 1:9).

(3) It is a community where reconciliation is a way of life, where hurts are acknowledged to the one who did the hurting, where hurts are "tested" so that misunderstandings are not permitted to fester, and where hurts are submitted to forgiveness and healing before reconciliations occur. There is sensitivity in this community to the truth that forgiveness is one of those use-it-or-lose-it facts of life, so forgiveness is practiced in all relationships—in marriage, friendship, parenting, ministry. It is a community marked by mercy in treating injury, opting as a matter of course for non-punitive ways of dealing with pain and hurt.

(4) It is a community rich in symbolic gestures—anointings, blessings, laying on of hands—with reverent instruction about the reconciling, peacemaking and healing rites in the full range of the Church's liturgy, especially the eucharist. But it is also a community which understands that everyone, ordained and non-ordained, is a minister of reconciliation, a peacemaker.

There is no stereotype of peacemaker.[5] They are as often men as women. They are tall, fat, short, thin—nurses, fathers, salespersons, executives, actors, athletes, bishops, busdrivers, students, senators. But whatever shape each peacemaker takes, all are personal "sacraments" expressing the reality of reconciliation rites. The call is for everyone to be a transparent sign of peace because the good news of forgiveness of sin and reconciliation of the world community to Jesus Christ depends on flesh-and-blood signs for its credibility.

Reconciliation and Community

I began this paper by writing that a natural connection exists between community and reconciliation. It is now time to tell you that its not exactly true. It is not a natural connection but a supernatural one that bonds these terms together. The Jewish philosopher Hannah Arendt was right when she said that a spiral of violence doomed humankind until forgiveness and eventual reconciliation was offered by Jesus of Nazareth as a way out of self-destruction.[6] It was Jesus of Nazareth who led the way, the way to peace, the way to reconciling the human race to himself. It was a costly business. It cost Jesus his life. And if we decide to follow in his footsteps, one way or another it will cost us ours too.

The paradox of the process is that in this death there is a new life. In the long run, we extend new life to the one who offended us, new life to ourselves (who could have been swallowed up and destroyed by hate), and new life to the relationship between us. It is only then that a community worth having comes into being.

NOTES

1. Melanie Klein, "Some Theoretical Conclusions Regarding the Emotional Life of the Infant," in *Envy and Gratitude and Other Works 1946-1963* (New York: Free Press, 1975) See especially, pp. 61-71 where Dr. Klein holds that at the most primitive level, retaliation, not forgiveness, functions as the persistent desire.

2. Karl Rahner, S.J., "Forgotten Truths Concerning the Sacrament of Penance," *Theological Investigations* II (Baltimore: Helicon Press, 1963) 135-174.

3. Christian Duquoc, "The Forgiveness of God," in *Forgiveness*, Concilium 184, ed. Cassiano Floristan and Christian Duquoc (Edinburgh: T. & T. Clark Ltd., 1986) 40.

4. Dietrich Bonhoeffer, *Life Together* (London: SCM Press, 1958) 86.

5. Doris Donnelly, *Putting Forgiveness into Practice*, (Allen, Texas: Argus Press, 1982) 32-33.

6. Hannah Arendt, *The Human Condition*, (Chicago: University of Chicago Press, 1958). See especially pp. 236-243.

Doris Donnelly

Robert J. Kennedy

Baptism, Eucharist, Penance: Theological and Liturgical Connections

This paper is about the story of humanity's reconciliation with God in Christ, and about how that story gets told in the Church so that each person's own story may intersect with it. This story could be told in terms of Ruby Turpin, the central character of Flannery O'Connor's short story "Revelation," who, thinking herself a generous and respectable Christian, sees in a momentary vision of the heavens opening, white and black trash, freaks and lunatics, entering heaven ahead of virtuous folks like herself. Or it could be told in terms of Grizabella the Glamour Cat, the ragged, spent and rejected figure of Andrew Lloyd Webber's musical *Cats*, who, instead of snarling and scratching when the other cats touch her, is transported to "the heavyside layer." Or it could be told in terms of Raleigh Whittier Hayes, the proper insurance agent of Michael Malone's novel *Handling Sin*, who comes to peace with himself, his father, and his whole family by hauling to New Orleans Grandma Tiny's trunk, the family Bible, PeeWee Jimson's plaster bust from the public library, his father's trumpet, and a gun. (Imagine what the sacrament would look like with those items!)

The story of humanity's reconciliation with God could be told in these terms; but I am only a struggling liturgical theologian and not a novelist, musician or librettist. I will attempt to tell the story in terms of theology and liturgy.

THE MYSTERY OF RECONCILIATION

When one searches the Scriptures for "the very pivot of salvation, the heart of the Christian confession of faith,"[1] one finds it summarized powerfully in Paul's words to the Corinthians:

> For anyone who is in Christ there is a new creation: the old is gone, and now a new one is here. It is all God's work. It was God who reconciled us to himself through Christ and gave us the work of handing on this reconciliation. In other words, God in Christ was reconciling the world to himself, not holding men's faults against

them, and he has entrusted to us the news that we are reconciled. So we are ambassadors for Christ; it is as though God were appealing through us, and the appeal that we make in Christ's name is: be reconciled to God. For our sake God made the sinless one into sin, so that we might become the goodness of God (2 Cor 5:17–21).

This passage, along with Romans 5:10–11, Ephesians 2:13–16 and Colossians 1:19–22, provides us with the core New Testament teaching on reconciliation. There are six aspects of the mystery of reconciliation as this teaching presents it.

First, these texts clearly and consistently attribute the act of reconciliation to God alone. There is never any suggestion of bargaining or striking a deal; reconciliation is not earned. It is a gift; and God, who has loved us first, is the agent of reconciliation.

Second, Christ is the means, the instrument of God's reconciling action. His whole ministry—the healing, teaching, caring outreach, miracles, table fellowship—is the medium for that reconciliation; but his death and resurrection are the central reconciling act. It is what Edward Schillebeeckx calls "the mystery of saving worship,"[2] that is, humanity-in-Christ opens out to God in longing, hope, and dependence, and God-in-Christ runs to meet and embrace humanity with grace and love.

Third, God reconciles us and the world (2 Cor 5:17–21), "everything in heaven, everything on earth" (Col 1:20). This occurred while we were still enemies (Rom 5:10)—hostile, alienated, separated (a fact which reinforces how much of a gift God's reconciliation is, unearned by us and undeserved). But what is the nature of our separation? Is it the separation we call "original sin"? Paul writes of "Adam's sin" (Rom 5:12ff.), but we cannot insert into the pauline teaching a later development of doctrine.[3] Is it the separation that naturally exists between creator and creature? This is the simplest and most basic form of separation that might apply. By way of limping analogy, if I write a poem, it is an extension or reflection or image of myself, but it takes on a life of its own independent of me. I can try to call it back from the preying analysis of literary critics, English teachers, and students so that it maintains its (my) integrity, but it is a struggle. Which is precisely the point here. The human creations in God's image have taken on a life independent of their Creator. Thus Paul understands humanity apart from Christ as lost, hostile and impotent, that is, unable to achieve what it is desirable to achieve. But the cross of

Robert J. Kennedy

44

Christ sets us free, liberates us and the world, so that we can surrender ourselves to the heart of God. No longer is the heart subject to paralyzing hostility, but it is free to romp in the fullness of God's love.[4]

Fourth, God reconciles us and the whole world to Godself, to God's order of things, to the logic (or illogic perhaps) of God's kingdom. This is capsulized in other words by Ephesians 2:14: "Christ is the peace between us." There are two dimensions of God's order of peace: the vertical in which humanity and the world are reconciled to God, and the horizontal in which Jew and Gentile (that is, culture and culture, human being and human being) are reconciled to one another. These clearly echo the two dimensions of "the greatest commandment" which requires love of God and love of neighbor. But be warned! In God's order of peace, God pulls down princes from their thrones and raises up the poor, he fills the hungry with good food and sends the rich away empty (cf. Luke 2:46–55).

> [God's] kingdom, Jesus suggested, defies all human expectations about how God works in the world. To the powerful, God's reign will appear shabby, incompetent and absurd: to the powerless, it will appear awesome, royal and overwhelming. To *all*, God's reign will be puzzling, controversial and even annoying.[5]

In God's kingdom-logic, Ruby Turpin finds white and black trash, "clean for the first time," going into heaven before her; Raleigh Hayes finds his upstanding self in the company of Hell's Angels, Sisters of Mercy, drug dealers, unwed mothers, jazz musicians, hardened criminals, ballet dancers and the Ku Klux Klan. But lest we get either too romantic or other worldly, in God's order of peace, God sees the world in such a way that Corazon Aquino and Imelda Marcos, Lee Iacocca and Mother Teresa, the homeless of the streets of Washington and Ronald Reagan, AIDS patients and Cardinal Krol are all brothers and sisters of one another. God wants us to see the world that way too, and so we have been "reconciled to himself."

Fifth, Christ's reconciling death and resurrection are definitive, "once and for all," but the reconciliation gained is not yet final (Rom 5:10–11). The reconciling act of God in Christ is not yet full and final salvation, but only opens the way for and is the means of our salvation; there is a final, eschatological reconciliation awaiting us and the world. Now that our separation from God has been bridged in Christ, "we wait in joyful hope for the coming of our savior Jesus Christ" by surrendering to the power of Christ's reconciling act (cf. 2 Cor 5:21). This leads into the final dimension of the mystery of reconciliation.

Sixth, those reconciled by God in Christ are "ambassadors for Christ," entrusted with the ministry of reconciliation until it is fulfilled in God's kingdom. Our appeal, "be reconciled to God," is the message we take into every situation of our lives. It is the underlying goal and dynamic of all ecclesial ministries: teaching, preaching, spiritual direction and pastoral counseling, human development, and social justice. It is also the underlying goal and dynamic in family life, neighborhood and workplace, in all the dimensions of human life. "What you have received as a gift, give as a gift" (Matt 10:8).

THE MINISTRY OF RECONCILIATION OF CHRIST AND THE CHURCH

It was Saint Leo the Great's insight that "what was visible in Christ has now passed over into the sacraments of the Church."[6] The Introduction to the Rite of Penance (no. 1) describes the reconciling work of Christ in three ways. First is Christ's preaching a prophetic word which lays bare human hearts before God. "The time has come, and the kingdom of God is close at hand. Repent, and believe the good news" (Mark 1:15). The prophetic call to conversion would blister and destroy human hope, however, if it were not accompanied in the second place by compassionate hospitality for the sinner (see for example, Matt 9:9–13). Such welcome makes conversion possible, even in the face of the gulf between human sinfulness and the holiness of God. In the third place, the reconciling ministry of Christ is underlined by the signs and wonders which accompany it: cure of illnesses, casting out of demons, meals with tax collectors and sinners. But most powerfully, there is the sign and wonder of his death and resurrection, the culmination of his whole reconciling life and ministry.

The Church's ministry is meant to extend the reconciling work of Christ, by the power of the Holy Spirit, in time and culture, until God is "all in all" (1 Cor 15:28). Thus the ecclesial work of reconciliation parallels Christ's in its preaching and teaching the prophetic word, its hospitality for the sinner, the alienated and the outcast (and everyone else!), and its sacramental processes and

Robert J. Kennedy

46

celebrations. It is this third dimension of the Church's ministry which is the concern of this paper.

THE CHURCH'S SACRAMENTS OF RECONCILIATION

It is common these days to describe penance as "the sacrament of reconciliation," but this terminology is inadequate and confusing. The mystery of reconciliation is expressed in multiple forms in the life and sacraments of the Church, so one cannot speak of one celebration of that mystery as though it were the only, or even principal, one. This problem of terminology was present in the committee charged with the postconciliar revision of the sacrament of penance: the title is "Rite of Penance," but the three forms of the Rite are labelled "rites for reconciliation."

Francis Mannion has recently attempted to give some stability to the terms "reconciliation" and "penance".[7] He begins with baptism: it is "the first and original sacrament of reconciliation and the forgiveness of sins, not only in the temporal sense, but in a primordial and paradigmatic one."[8] That is, it is the first such ritual in the Church's history and in each believer's life, *and* the foundation and model of all other forms and concepts of reconciliation. Mannion thus differentiates between baptismal and postbaptismal reconciliation. He further differentiates between reconciliation and penance within the postbaptismal context. Reconciliation is the process of return of serious sinners to communion of the Church; penance is the system of "those actions and processes that facilitate the sanctification, moral transformation, and ongoing conversion of the Church and its members at every level of corporate and individual Christian life."[9]

I concur with Mannion in his desire to find a way out of the confusion of terms, but I think he has given too narrow a definition of reconciliation in the postbaptismal context. Reconciliation is both broader and narrower than penance. It is broader (a) because it is the larger action of God and the Church within which penance is a crucial process; (b) because it is manifest in at least two postbaptismal sacraments (eucharist and penance) if not the whole sacramental economy; and (c) because it is manifest in the wider reconciling mission of the Church in the world. But reconciliation is also narrower than penance for it is "only" the goal and final step in the process of penance (conversion/contrition, confession of sins, acts of penance, absolution/reconciliation). Mannion's defi-

Connections

47

nition of penance affirms this process, of which reconciliation is the goal; but penance is not just the "interior aspect of reconciliation," as he suggests, but the interior *and* external "actions and processes that facilitate sanctification. . . ."[10]

However this terminological debate may eventually be resolved, it remains that the Church celebrates the mystery of reconciliation primarily in three sacraments: baptism, eucharist and penance.

Baptism. In considering baptism as a sacrament of reconciliation, it needs to be noted that this is only one dimension of meaning for this sacrament. There are other "lenses" for viewing baptism: initiation into the life and mission of Christ and the Church, original sin and the action of grace, vocation to participate in the worship and mission of the Church. The beauty and power of the Church's sacramental system is that these levels of meaning are not mutually exclusive, but intersect and enrich one another at newer and deeper levels of grace.

What connects baptism with reconciliation? The basic link is a faith which recognizes and acknowledges God active and present in the world, the constant love and offer of life God gives to all creatures. In that recognition and acknowledgement is the ever more progressive surrender to God's presence and power (= conversion) and the promise to live by the light of that presence and power. To put it in more christic terms, we enter through faith into Christ's reconciling death and resurrection, and Christ's victory over sin and death becomes our victory. We are released from slavery by dying with him, and are free to live a new life by rising with him. We cross over into God's vision of reality, into the new system of gospel values and into an entirely new hope. We are born into reconciled life, and commit ourselves to a lifestyle of solidarity with God and all our brothers and sisters; we commit ourselves to continuing Christ's reconciling ministry in the world. All this is accomplished of course by the Holy Spirit dwelling in us and the world, drawing us gently yet insistently into the circle of God's love and life. Even the first glimmer of recognition of God's presence is the loving work of the Spirit of the risen Christ.

From the earliest times of the Church, baptism has been associated primarily with conversion, forgiveness of sins and reconciliation. Peter at Pentecost repeats the instruction of Jesus:

Robert J. Kennedy

"Repent, believe the good news, and be baptized" (Acts 2:38; see Mark 1:15). In the Nicene creed, "we acknowledge one baptism for the forgiveness of sins." As the liturgies of baptism evolved they included rituals of conversion (exorcisms, scrutinies, liturgies of the word, renunciation of sin and the profession of faith, blessings) and rituals of incorporation and new life (anointings with oil, greetings of peace, new clothes, lighted candles, eucharistic meal). The central symbol of the water-bath communicates the conversion from death to life, the cleansing from the old life and the birth into the new creation.

Thus the conspiracy of individual and ecclesial faith, of rituals and creed, and of the prior love of God makes baptism the primordial sacrament of reconciliation.

Eucharist. Again, reconciliation is only one dimension of meaning in the eucharist; others include the nourishment, strength, health and healing of common meals, the ongoing formation in and celebration of faith (eucharist as mystagogy), commissioning for mission, the renewal of the paschal mystery. If the eucharist is model and summation of all other sacramental encounters with the living God, however, then reconciliation is a key theme.

Eucharist as reconciliation centers on the action of the sacramental memorial, "a cultic act by which a past salvific event is recalled—but in order to relive *hic et nunc* the grace of that event in praise and blessing, which revives hope in the ultimate accomplishment of that salvation at the very moment when God is reminded of his promise and asked to realize it."[11] The "past salvific event" is of course the paschal mystery, the cross of death and victory, *the* reconciling act. It is remembered in, and therefore, joined with, "the cultic act," that is, the human act of eating and drinking which itself speaks of encounter and unity, but which, when done in memory of Christ's death and resurrection, becomes the ecclesial magnification of reconciliation. As such it touches back to Jesus' table fellowship of mercy, his meals (including the Last Supper) with sinners. It also has an eschatological reference because it anticipates the full and final reconciliation of the heavenly banquet, and thus becomes "a model of the redemptive reconstruction of our society and world, . . . a turning to God in gratitude to acknowledge the gifts of creation and redemption and the price that Jesus paid to restore those gifts to us, and a turning to one another to share those gifts of creation and

Connections

49

redemption symbolically in the ritual in token of our commitment to do so extensively and fully in our lives."[12] In other words, the eucharist continually renews our visas as reconciling ambassadors for Christ.

The rituals of the eucharist support and express this theological understanding. The very act of gathering as the Church manifests the vision of reconciliation we have in Christ. The penitential rite, hearing the scriptures (see Neh 8:1–12; Luke 4:16–30), collecting gifts for the poor, the elements of bread and wine (many into one), the cup words of institution, the petitions of the eucharistic prayers, the Lord's Prayer, the greeting of peace, the breaking of bread (one to the many makes the many one), and the act of communion itself (the dual meaning of "the body of Christ")—all combine in a rich repertoire of symbols of reconciliation, a "cultic act" which makes present the past salvific act of Christ reconciling us and the world in hopeful anticipation of its fulfillment when he comes again.

Penance. Historically, penance as a separate sacrament has done two things: first, it has reconciled those who have seriously damaged the communion of the Church and who have repented of their sin; and second, it has encouraged the ongoing conversion of believers who are forever stumbling over their weaknesses and failings in Christian commitment. Theologically, penance extends to the sinner in both cases the reconciliation of baptism and moves reconciliation toward completion in the eucharist. Penance is the act of the Church which proclaims "the central paradox of Christian faith: the fact that the words 'God,' 'love' and 'sinner' must be put together in the same sentence."[13] The reconciled sinner then continues a conversion of life and expresses it "by a life renewed according to the Gospel and more and more steeped in the love of God,"[14] that is, a lifestyle of handing on the reconciliation one has been given. The symbol of imposition of hands both welcomes the sinner's return with love and forgiveness and recommissions the one now reconciled for the ministry of reconciliation.

SOME PASTORAL CONCLUSIONS

Theological and liturgical connections are valuable only if they ground a pastoral practice which touches the truth of Christ. Such truth is not primarily conceptual but lived. Knowing that there is

Robert J. Kennedy

no magical formula for finding and living of the truth of reconciliation in Christ, what pastoral strategies might at least send us in the right direction? I want to propose four simple and complementary ones.

(1) Every parish must continue the work of making the processes of initiation the foundation of ecclesial life. Not only do the initiatory processes form believers in the mystery of reconciliation, the baptismal life becomes the touchstone for recognizing sin and realizing the promise of mercy and forgiveness. Further, the vision of community embodied in the Rite of Christian Initiation of Adults is that of a community of hospitality and reconciliation. The more parishes practice the processes of initiation the more they will become the vision those processes describe.

(2) The season of Lent needs to be restored as the time of baptismal and postbaptismal reconciliation. It is the Church's time for learning again the ways of peace, for recognizing those who are brothers and sisters with us, and for committing ourselves to the mission of God's kingdom and not our own. It is time to put away our committee agendas, our own personal agendas, and most importantly our agenda of sin, and to agree with one another on God's agenda of life and peace.

(3) The lectionary should be preached with a year-long view to hospitality and reconciliation but it probably should be done, more often than not, without using these five- and six-syllable words. The gospel of reconciliation in Christ can be most powerfully conveyed through the stories of life's tragedies and delights. It would be important to remember that preaching hospitality and reconciliation will often be prophetic, as Jesus' own preaching was, and therefore the preacher may be a pain in the neck for the Ruby Turpins and Raleigh Hayeses of the parish.

(4) The sacrament of penance needs to be understood as a *process* of conversion and reconciliation, as *one of many rituals* which express the processes of conversion and reconciliation in the Church, and as *the intensification of all the personal and social processes of reconciliation*. This understanding will create an equation which will include confessing one's sins and eliminating the threat of nuclear war and communicating with your teenage daughter and making a good act of contrition and paying parish employees just wages and embracing our brother or sister with AIDS and

Connections

going in peace to love and serve the Lord. This is the sum of the Christian mystery of reconciliation.

NOTES

1. Jean-Marie Tillard, "The Bread and the Cup of Reconciliation," *Sacramental Reconciliation*, Concilium 61 (New York: Herder and Herder, 1971) 38.

2. Edward Schillebeeckx, *Christ the Sacrament of the Encounter with God* (New York: Sheed and Ward, 1963) 37.

3. Present theological discussion on original sin is a tangled one. See Brian O. Dermott, "Theology of Original Sin: Recent Developments," *Theological Studies* 38:3 (1977) 478–512, and James Gaffney, *Sin Reconsidered* (New York: Paulist Press, 1983), especially chapters 6 and 7.

4. See Nathan Mitchell, "Conversion and Reconciliation in the New Testament: The Parable of the Cross," *The Rite of Penance: Commentaries, Volume III: Background and Directions* (Washington: The Liturgical Conference, 1978) 11–15.

5. Ibid. 17.

6. *Sermon* 74:2, PL 54:398.

7. M. Francis Mannion, "Penance and Reconciliation: A Systemic Analysis," *Worship* 60:2 (1986) 98–118.

8. Ibid. 104.

9. Ibid. 108. Mannion suggests that the various forms of the 1973 Rite of Penance have the reconciliation of serious sinners as their primary purpose, although they are used for the two quite distinct purposes of penance and reconciliation. Solutions to this dilemma might either be the exclusive identification of sacramental confession with reconciling serious sin, thereby promoting other practices for ongoing penitential renewal, or creating an added rite of confession more adapted to penitential usage.

10. Ibid. 107, 108.

11. Tillard, *Bread and Cup* 40.

12. Monika Hellwig, "The Spirit of Jesus and the Task of Reconciliation," *New Catholic World* 227:1357 (1984) 5.

13. Mitchell, *Conversion and Reconciliation* 17.

14. Rite of Penance, no. 20.

Robert J. Kennedy

Brother John and Brother Jean-Marie
of the Taizé Community

The Christian Ethic as a Reconciliation Ethic

Reconciliation—the passage with Christ from a state of hostility to
a relationship of communion—lies at the very heart of the message
of the New Testament. Reconciliation between humanity and God,
and, as an immediate consequence, reconciliation of human beings
among themselves, sums up the gospel message. As St. Paul
writes: "God was reconciling the world to himself in Christ, not
counting people's sins against them, and he has entrusted to us
the message of reconciliation" (2 Cor 5:19). This reconciliation involves a breaking down of all the barriers between human beings;
differences are no longer divisive but complementary. Paul continues: "You are all children of God through faith in Christ Jesus,
for all of you who were baptized into Christ have clothed your-
selves with Christ. There is neither Jew nor Greek, slave nor free,
male nor female, for you are all one in Christ Jesus" (Gal 3:27-28;
see Col 3:11).

The Letter to the Ephesians presents these two dimensions of
reconciliation—reconciliation with God and among human
beings—as one single reality. It speaks of the mystery of God's
will "to bring all things in heaven and on earth together under
one head, even Christ" (Eph 1:10); and further on, using the Jew-
Gentile duality as a specific example, almost as a "type" of all divisions, the letter describes Christ's purpose "to create in himself
one new being out of the two, thus making peace, and in this one
body to reconcile both of them to God through the cross, by
which he put to death their hostility" (Eph 2:15-16). And the Letter to the Colossians, in an analogous passage, states that "God
was pleased . . . through him to reconcile to himself all things,
whether things on earth or things in heaven, by making peace
through his blood, shed on the cross" (Col 1:19-20).

Although the word "reconciliation" seems to be almost the exclusive property of the pauline writings (but cf. Matt 5:24), the reality is found everywhere in the New Testament. In John's gospel

Jesus states: "When I am lifted from the earth, I will draw all people to myself" (John 12:32). Here too, the link is very strong between Jesus' self-giving on the cross and the birth of a reconciled humanity. Elsewhere, John expresses the same thing in simpler terms, in terms of love: God's love manifested in the life of his only Son leads to the creation of a community centered on the "new commandment" of mutual love (e.g., John 15:9ff.; 17:20ff.). And in Mark's Gospel Jesus begins by announcing forgiveness to a paralyzed man and immediately afterwards makes this forgiveness concrete by sharing table fellowship with the outcasts of the Jewish society of his day (Mark 2:1–17). Finally, the Acts of the Apostles shows this reconciliation active in the lives of the first Christian community who "were one in heart and mind [and] . . . shared everything they had" (Acts 4:32).

RECONCILIATION AS GIFT AND CHALLENGE

We are all aware that the gospel is not first and foremost a blueprint for human activity but "good news": the God of love enters human history as a force for integral liberation. The gospel is not essentially something for us to accomplish, but rather something God accomplishes in us. Our primary task is thus to open our hearts, to welcome by an attitude of trust and faith God's entry into our lives through Jesus Christ (see John 6:29). In other words, reconciliation is first of all the free gift of God already become a reality through the life, death and resurrection of his only Son.

The consequences of this are far-reaching. It means that as believers our starting point is the reality of God's work of reconciliation in our world, the space of communion already opened up around the cross of Christ (see John 12:32; Luke 23:34). For Christians this reconciliation is not a utopia, a beautiful dream incapable of realization; our hope is absolutely sure, because it is rooted in Christ's coming and his gift of the Spirit of love and forgiveness (see Rom 5:5).

Yet how many Christians take as a fundamental reference point the individualistic outlook of secular society instead of the reality of reconciliation? They tend to consider the life of the isolated individual as the basic "given"; links with others are viewed as something secondary, and, as often as not, precarious. Small wonder, then, that we find it so difficult to build lasting relationships—our mind-set makes it practically impossible.

Brother John / Brother Jean-Marie

54

Scripture, however, offers us a very different understanding of reality; belief in the doctrine of creation means acceptance of our very existence as founded in a relationship with the Creator God in which we are related to the rest of God's creation. Relationship thus precedes individual existence and makes it possible, even on the level of creation. And this is even truer on the level of the "new creation," the work of redemption: we can forgive and live lives of reconciliation only because in Christ the barriers have already been broken through, hostility has been put to death (Eph 2:16). Seeing reconciliation as God's gift to us in Christ enables us to persevere in living lives of reconciliation and peacemaking, even in the face of apparent setbacks and difficulties.

Now if reconciliation is a free gift, it is at the same time a call to be lived out, a challenge to be undertaken. This is the paradox of the gospel: God's work does not replace or compete with human activity, but renders it possible and fruitful. The priority accorded to the divine initiative in no way leads to human passivity. In Paul's letters, the account of God's saving activity flows inevitably into an exhortation to the faithful to become what they are in their depths: "As God's fellow workers we urge you not to receive God's gift in vain . . . . As a prisoner for the Lord, then, I urge you to lead a life worthy of the calling you have received" (2 Cor 6:1; Eph 4:1). Faith leads necessarily to a way of life, an ethic; and if the essence of salvation lies in the reconciling passage from isolation to communion, then the corresponding ethic can only be an ethic of reconciliation. Reconciled by God, we are called to be reconcilers in all the dimensions of our lives.

The New Testament shows very clearly the link between the indicative of God's saving activity and the imperative of human behavior in terms of love and forgiveness. "Forgive as the Lord forgave you" (Col 3:13; see Matt 18:21-35), or as the Lord's Prayer inverts it in the form of a petition: "Forgive us our debts, as we also have forgiven our debtors" (Matt 6:12). John in his turn says, "Since God so loved us, we also ought to love one another. No one has ever seen God; but if we love each other, God lives in us and his love is made complete in us . . . . Anyone who does not love his brother, whom he has seen, cannot love God, whom he has not seen . . . . Whoever loves God must also love his brother" (1 John 4:11-12, 20-21). Here the two great commandments, love of God and love of neighbor, are shown to be two sides of the same coin. The love and forgiveness we offer to those around us testifies to the authenticity of the reconciling work of Christ in us and of our relationship to the Father. "As I have loved you, so you must love one another. All will know that you are my disciples if you love one another" (John 13:34–35).

LIVING AS PEOPLE WHO ARE RECONCILED

Having looked at the scriptural roots of the Christian ethic of reconciliation, we can examine some specific ways in which this ethic can take root in our existence. What does it mean to be "ambassadors of reconciliation" (see 2 Cor 5:20)? This can be answered by considering three aspects of reconciliation: in personal life, in the Church, and in human society at large.

First there is the personal dimension of reconciliation. It is this aspect which most clearly merits the name of forgiveness. How can we forgive those who have wounded us deeply, often in very intimate relationships? How can we seek forgiveness from those we have wounded, perhaps unintentionally? Brother Roger, the founder and prior of the Taizé Community, has called broken relationships "the worst trauma of our time."[1] Is it possible to live as reconciled people in a world marked by loneliness and abandonment, at a time when long-term commitments seem so very precarious if not impossible?

No easy answer to these questions exists. Close interpersonal relationships, particularly those of families and couples, are among the most delicate and complex of human realities. Healing the wounds of the parent-child relationship, for example, is often the work of an entire lifetime, even when there is an abundance of good will on all sides. It is as we grow and mature that God's forgiveness penetrates and transforms all the dimensions of our being. And often it can express itself only in tiny, seemingly insufficient gestures. Yet the willingness to keep on working towards this reconciliation, even with those who have already left this world, and the belief that in Christ it is already given, is of the utmost importance in leading us to the fullness of life offered by the gospel (see John 10:10).

One pitfall in this respect is that people often have the impression that they need to "forgive themselves" in order to advance, or at least convince themselves of ("feel") God's forgiveness. Were this the case, we would have no need of faith in Christ.

Brother John / Brother Jean-Marie

56

Such "subjective" forgiveness can easily become a form of that self-justification against which St. Paul cautions us constantly in his letters, and which in the end isolates us and makes authentic communion impossible. As an alternative to the futile search for self-justification Paul offers trust in Christ, through which the gift of reconciliation becomes a reality in our life. Rather than attempting to forgive or justify ourselves, or reduce the experience of God's forgiveness to a subjective feeling, we are called to believe in the reality of God's reconciling work in Christ, even when, subjectively speaking, we are not convinced of it: "[We can] set our hearts at rest in his presence whenever our hearts condemn us. For God is greater than our hearts, and he knows everything" (1 John 3:19–20). Such "objective" faith is the only way out of the vicious circle of self-justification and the path to a "transfigured subjectivity": sooner or later, God's forgiveness will transform our way of seeing ourselves, others and the world.

In this context, the sacrament of penance has an irreplaceable role to play. It provides, through the ministry of the Church and through another human being, that "objective" dimension of which we have been speaking. Hearing a fellow human being proclaim God's forgiveness in the name of the Church can be a truly liberating experience. It frees us from having to judge ourselves or aim at an impossible perfection. God's reconciling work becomes concrete and specific without running the risk of being viewed as a mere projection of our own subconscious.

As a complement to sacramental reconciliation, having a fellow Christian accompany us by listening can be a priceless step to inner healing. If Christians each had a friend in Christ (priest, religious or lay, male or female) to whom they could go in order to be listened to, their inner knots could be exposed to the light in a frank and compassionate dialogue, and the work of inner reconciliation, of growth in the Spirit, would be fostered immeasurably in our churches.

A practical suggestion presents itself here. Today as people live longer, there are many elderly persons in the Church, including many religious sisters, who often find themselves without an active ministry. Could they not be commissioned as "listeners" of others younger than themselves, to free them by their acceptance and understanding? What a ministry of liberation that would be!

Reconciliation Ethic

It may seem surprising to some, given the history of our community, that in Taizé today one rarely hears the word "ecumenism." It is not that we have abandoned the search for visible unity among Christians: it is more than ever our burning desire. But for many people ecumenism, which originally underlined the universal call and mission of the Church, has become just one concern among many, generally reserved to those experts engaged in the official dialogues. Certainly the work of theologians and other experts in the ecumenical movement has been, and still is, invaluable to bringing to light the great common inheritance of Christians, in pointing out where mutual reflection still needs to be undertaken and in indicating possible ways forward. Yet if in Taizé we prefer to speak, not of ecumenism, but of reconciliation among Christians, that is in order to emphasize that it is a matter of deep urgency for *all* believers if the Church is to be consistent with the message it proclaims.

We have seen that the reconciliation of human beings with God in Christ and the consequent reconciliation of human beings among themselves is at the heart of the good news of salvation. It follows that the community founded by Christ to continue his work in the world is called above all to offer a concrete image of this twofold reconciliation in the common life its members lead. "All will know that you are my disciples if you love one another" (John 13:35). But if this community is fragmented into competitive or mutually indifferent groups, what can it reflect of Christ? As Paul wrote long ago to the Christians of Corinth:

> I appeal to you, brothers, in the name of our Lord Jesus Christ, that all of you agree with one another so that there may be no divisions among you and that you may be perfectly united in mind and thought . . . . What I mean is this: One of you says, "I follow Paul," another, "I follow Apollos," another, "I follow Cephas," still another, "I follow Christ." Is Christ divided? Was Paul crucified for you? Were you baptized into the name of Paul? . . . When one says, "I follow Paul" and another "I follow Apollos," are you not acting in a merely human way (1 Cor 1:10, 12-13; 3:4)?

Divisions both old and new undermine the Church's claim to offer a radically new form of existence rooted in the living God which alone can liberate a fragmented humanity.

How can we forget the uncompromising words of Christ from

Brother John / Brother Jean-Marie

the Sermon on the Mount: "If you are offering your gift at the altar and there remember that your brother has something against you, leave your gift there in front of the altar. First go and be reconciled with your brother; then come and offer your gift" (Matt 5:23–24)?

Despite our individual responsibilities, how can all of us be ambassadors of reconciliation among Christians? In Taizé we put great faith in simple, grass-roots measures to build up trust. A text written by Brother Roger some years ago during a visit to Chile puts it this way: "When divisions and rivalries bring things to a standstill, nothing is more important than setting out to visit and listen to one another, and to celebrate the paschal mystery together."[2] Such visits and prayer together can do a great deal to create the sense of common belonging among Christians. For the past four or five years Taizé had been undertaking a "worldwide pilgrimage of reconciliation." Participants worship in one another's churches, share scriptural reflection and quiet times together, and often make visits to "places of suffering and hope" in the outlying community.

It is impossible to measure the results of such a pilgrimage, but we know that many small and large walls have fallen down between Christians of different backgrounds, laying the groundwork for a more visible expression of our unity in Christ. In addition to bridging denominational differences, these meetings and visits have helped mend the divisions that arise between members of the same Church, and those between believers and non- or ex-believers. In an issue-oriented society like the United States, where so much energy is spent promoting one cause or another, Christians—even members of the same parish community—often become more attentive to what separates them than to what gathers them together. Simple gestures of sharing help to make the Church a place of visible communion for the entire human family, where even those who do not share our beliefs feel at home.

The lifestyle of the Taizé Community is one example of responding to the call for reconciliation among all Christians. It attempts to live a "parable of community" composed of brothers from different cultures and Christian traditions. To live out a parable does not in any way imply being an example or model to emulate; it means anticipating in our common life a fundamental insight of

Reconciliation Ethic

the gospel, embodying something of what we hope for the whole People of God, something already given in Christ but not yet visible in all its fullness. With some eighty-five brothers from twenty different countries and the major Christian traditions of the West gathered together in a small monastic family, we experience from within something of the diversity of God's people. Our life has made us see how important listening and forgiveness are in realizing a wider communion in Christ. It has meant discovering our identity not in the idiosyncracies of our own background but in the best of the gifts with which God has graced his Body, the Church, in the course of its centuries-long pilgrimage through history.

Even at a time when the passion for unity has cooled down into a benevolent tolerance, when institutional reconciliation among Christians seems as far off as ever, when denominations appear content to move forward on parallel tracks with reconciliation postponed to an indefinite future, it is always possible to achieve an immediate reconciliation within oneself as a means to the larger ecclesial unity. Here is how Brother Roger expressed it in a recent book:

> Where can we find a road to immediate reconciliation, even the smallest way possible, for a time of transition?
>
> This little way forward can only be a personal one, an inner way. It is the way of reconciliation within oneself, in one's own being.
>
> Without humiliating anybody, without becoming a symbol of repudiation for anyone, we can welcome within ourselves the attentiveness to the Word of God, so dearly loved by the Church families born of the Reformation, together with the treasures of spirituality of the Orthodox Churches, and all the charisms of communion of the Catholic Church, in this way disposing ourselves day after day to put our trust in the mystery of the faith.[3]

LEAVEN OF TRUST AND PEACE IN THE WORLD

It can never be an end in itself for Christians to strive to be more fully in communion, to be stronger over against others. The search for reconciliation among Christians enables the Church to live more fully her vocation to be a leaven of trust and peace in the midst of the human family. Reconciliation among Christians calls us to search at the same time for ways of sharing with all, materially and spiritually.

Brother John / Brother Jean-Marie

For our community this has meant living in small groups around the world, especially in places of poverty and division. The brothers do not go to bring solutions to local problems, but simply to share the life of those around them, "to be signs of Christ's presence and bearers of joy" (Rule of Taizé). For example, since 1978 we have been living a small presence of prayer and sharing in "Hell's Kitchen" on the West Side of Manhattan, a changing neighborhood where new residents to the city have always settled. We have become involved in different problems of the area and the city; working as tenant organizers, with the elderly and with homeless people; working with the Center for Seafarers' Rights of the Seamen's Church Institute, which attempts to deal with the growing exploitation of workers on cruise ships. At the center of our life is common prayer three times a day in our tiny chapel on the fourth floor of the tenement where we live. And we attempt to practice hospitality in very simple ways.

Another example arises from the constant presence of young adults in Taizé over the last twenty years, a presence which has made us even more attentive to the universal character of recon-ciliation in Jesus Christ. An aspiration to universality seems to come naturally to the younger generations today. They are put off by discrimination and prejudice of whatever form. They have little patience with the conflicting claims of different Christian denomi-nations; their questions are more basic: Does the living God exist? what answers can the gospel offer to my searching? can I find something worth giving my entire life for? The young are not in-terested in an ecumenism which is just one more department of the institutional churches; they are captivated by reconciliation when it involves an openness to all human beings of good will. But in their desire for unity, they are often discouraged by the great obstacles to peace and reconciliation in the world. Disillu-sionment, a "what's the use?" mentality, is a constant temptation for them. For this reason it is essential to find concrete steps we can all take to make both material and spiritual sharing a reality in the human family.

As an attempt to respond to this aspiration of the young (and many of the not-so-young as well), Brother Roger, accompanied by seven children from different continents, went last year to meet the Secretary General of the United Nations, submitting to him six questions reflecting the hopes of young people that the U.N. be-

Reconciliation Ethic

come a catalyst of trust between peoples. Among other concerns, the questions asked for total disarmament and the recognition of new economic rights to be placed on the same level as all other human rights. Recently, too, a series of world meetings was announced in Taizé for the summer of 1987, to search together for ways of bringing about a civilization founded on trust and sharing.

These projects are not ends in themselves, but rather express the conviction that fostering peace and sharing in the world is one of the great priorities of our time, to ensure a future for all. The question concerns every believer, and the Christian community as a whole: How can the Church, reconciled in itself, be a place of communion for all? How, with the involvement of believers and non-believers, can the Church be "a leaven and, as it were, the soul of human society as it is renewed in Christ and transformed into God's family?"[4] If the Christian ethic is an ethic of reconciliation, this must not be conceived in merely individualistic terms; together, as God's people, Christians can be an irreplaceable leaven of trust and peace in the world.

NOTES

1. Brother Roger of Taizé, *A Heart That Trusts: Journal 1979–1981* (London & Oxford: Mowbray, 1986) 12.

2. Brother Roger of Taizé, *Parable of Community: The Rule and Other Basic Texts of Taizé* (New York: Seabury, 1981) 78–79.

3. Brother Roger of Taizé, *A Heart That Trusts* 107–108.

4. Vatican Council II, Pastoral Constitution on the Church in the Modern World, no. 40.

Brother John/Brother Jean-Marie

Richard M. Gula, s.s.

Sin: The Arrogance of Power

"Sin" is such an abused word, distorted by so many misunder-standings,[1] that it is hard to recognize today. Yet identifying sin is a necessary step before there can be authenticity in the sacrament of reconciliation. For this reason, sin must appear on anyone's agenda of issues for renewing reconciliation in the life of the Church.

No one seems to doubt the presence of evil in the world. We experience it in a variety of ways: national and international con-flict; violence in our streets, schools and homes; political corrup-tion; disorders in corporations; and a host of manifestations of sexism, clericalism, racism, ageism and other violations of justice. All such forms of alienation, brutality or discrimination, when seen from a theological perspective, are rooted in sin. But do we ever recognize the sin?

Sin seems to have lost its hold on us as a way of accounting for and naming so much of the evil we know. Out of many factors, the eclipse of a religious worldview through the rise of the secular spirit stands out as accounting for the loss of a sense of sin.[2] The secular spirit questions the relevance and meaning of all Christian symbols, and even of religion itself. One effect of this secular spirit on the meaning of sin, for example, has been to reduce sin to some form of psychological or social disorder. The therapeutic perspective which pervades the secular spirit looks on behavior as healthily adaptive problem-solving behavior, or as unhealthy, maladaptive and problem-creating behavior.[3] It does not call the latter sin.

Moreover, the secular, therapeutic perspective tends to look on persons more as victims of unconscious or sociocultural influences than as agents of free action. Two leading psychiatrists as Karl Menninger, in his *Whatever Became of Sin?*,[4] and M. Scott Peck, in his *People of the Lie*,[5] want to make full allowance for the condi-tioning factors which cause people to do evil. Yet both insist on a strip of responsibility that cannot be negotiated away to these de-termining factors. While the behavioral sciences provide us with a helpful explanation of human behavior, they do not give a full account. Sin is real, and we need a fresh way to get at it and call it what it is.

Sin is essentially a religious notion, and, as such, has no meaning apart from the divine-human relationship. In this sense, sin is a theological code word or symbol which illumines our refusal to live out of the gift of divine love. How might we be able to interpret this religious symbol so that its connection to our common experience of evil is clear? Does our biblical witness open us to an interpretation of sin which may be the beginning of a fresh conversation about sin in relation to the process of reconciliation? I think it does. I find it to be in the metaphor of sin as the *arrogance of power.*

A consistent theme of contemporary theology has been that we cannot have a proper understanding of sin unless we have a proper understanding of the nature and implications of the covenant God has established with us. *Covenant* and *heart* are the dominant metaphors of biblical faith for understanding the moral life. They provide the biblical horizon against which to recognize sin. The cash value of understanding sin against this horizon is to see sin as the arrogance of power.

Therefore, my intention is to walk around inside these metaphors so that we might be able to see various aspects of sin as the arrogance of power. I will begin with the covenant as the proper biblical context for understanding the offer of divine love and the divine-human relationship which this offer creates. Then I will consider the heart as the center of our response to divine love. Against the horizon of covenant and heart, I hope to show that we can recognize sin as the arrogance of power.

COVENANT

From the biblical perspective, sin is first and foremost a religious, relational reality. This means the biblical experience of sin presupposes a God who is concerned with human well-being and who has taken the initiative to establish a relationship with us. The two frequently used terms for sin in the Old Testament point to violations of relationships. *Hattah* is the most common term. Its meaning, "to miss the mark" or "to offend," points to a purposeful action oriented toward an existing relationship. The existence of the relationship makes the offense or failure possible. *Pesa,* "rebellion," is a legal term denoting a deliberate action violating a rela-

Richard M. Gula

64

tionship in community. The New Testament term for sin is *hamartía*. It, too, refers to a deliberate action that misses the intended mark. Its use in the New Testament adds the connotation of an interior reality which comes from the heart.[6]

These terms acquire theological significance when used in the context of the covenant which expresses the most personal kind of relationship between God and us. The sense that sin involves a broken relationship with God got lost when the law itself was made the absolute object of loyalty. When this happened, the religious foundations of sin were replaced by juridical ones. Then, when taken to the extreme, sin became a transgression of a legal code rather than a failure to respond to God.

At the center of salvation history is the bond of covenant between God and humanity. The primary claim of the covenant is that God loves us without our having done anything to attract God's attention or to win that love. God's covenant is a bond of completely gratuitous love, pure grace. But God's initiative of love (grace) does not destroy our freedom. Unlike *The Godfather*, God makes an offer we can refuse. God's offer of love awaits our acceptance. Once we accept the offer of love we commit ourselves to living by its term.

The terms of the covenant are expressed succinctly in the inseparability of the twofold commandment to love God with all our hearts and our neighbor as ourselves (Matt 22:37–39). This double commandment of Jesus is best read from the johannine perspective of responding to the love we have first received: "Love one another as I have loved you" (Jn 13:34). In this version, we see more clearly that the initiative to love is with God. God's first loving us enables us to love in return and becomes the paradigm of love which we are to imitate. The terms of this commandment and the covenant as a whole may be summarized in a threefold manner: to respect the *worth* of ourselves and others as constituted by God's love; to live in *solidarity* with creation and with one another as covenantal partners; and to develop the virtue of *fidelity* as the proper characteristic of every covenantal relationship.[7] Sin would be to act contrary to these covenantal requirements.

Worth. Our hearts hunger for love. We have a passionate longing to know that we count in the eyes of someone special. We long to know that we are loved, valued and the source of delight to another. The persistent cry of the heart, "Do you love me?" is asked not just of our significant others, but ultimately of God.[8] The covenant responds to this cry of the heart longing for worth with a firm "yes." The covenant insists that grace is the first move. We are not so much searchers as the ones searched out. Because God has taken the initiative to enter into covenant with us, we matter to God in a most serious way. This is what it means to have worth. Our worth comes from God's offer of divine love as a free gift and is not conditioned by our own achievement.

Various biblical passages and images help us to understand divine love as our true source of worth and our only security. In Isaiah, for example, we read of God loving the people of the covenant for their own sakes and not for the sake of their being useful or powerful: "I have called you by name—you are mine . . . . I will give up whole nations to save your life, because you are precious to me and because I love you and give you honor" (Isa 43:1, 4; cf. Isa 41:8-16). Perhaps some of the most powerful texts which communicate our worth being established by divine love are those which use the image of the child to explain our relationship to God. In Hosea, for example, we read of God's love for a rebellious people being expressed through the tender image of the parent for the child (Hos 11:1-9). In the New Testament, one of the favorite images of Jesus for those whose lives are grounded in God's unconditional love is the child. When Jesus is asked who is the greatest in the kingdom of heaven, he reaches into the crowd, sets a child beside him and says, "Unless you become like this, you will never understand greatness" (Matt 18:1-5). What makes the child such a powerful image? The child's worth is constituted not by what it achieves, but simply by the generous love of the parents. That is what we are like before God. We are grounded in a love which desires us out of the abundance of love itself, and not because of anything we may have accomplished.

From within this perspective, therefore, we recognize that our worth and security remain grounded in God and not in ourselves. However, the modern heresy of individualism insists that we generate our worth on our own power. The special temptation of this heresy is to believe that our lovableness is really something we make for ouselves. The covenant, however, is set against every notion of independence.[9] The covenant assures us we are forever

Richard M. Gula

established by God: "I will be your God, you will be my people" (Jer 31:33; 32:38; Ezek 36:28); "I have called you by name—you are mine" (Isa 43:1); "I can never forget you! I have written your name on the palms of my hands" (Isa 49:15, 16).

Sin refuses to believe that we are lovable apart from our virtue. Instead of grounding our worth in divine love, sin attempts to establish worth on the basis of surrogate loves which we create for ourselves and by ourselves to give us the security of being lovable and acceptable. But when we rest our worth on something besides divine love, we create an idol. Creating surrogate loves is the sin of idolatry. These loves may be our talent, our goodness, our efficiency, our charm, our wit, our bright ideas, our wealth, our social position and prestige, or whatever else we might create in order to secure our worth and make ourselves somebody.

When we so fill up our lives with these self-created loves, we have no room for divine love. The beatitudes of Luke (Luke 6:20–26) speak to this condition quite starkly. Luke records the four blessings and the four woes. What is it about being poor, hungry, weeping, and rejected that these should be a blessing, whereas to be rich, filled, happy, and praised receive a curse? To be poor, hungry, weeping, and rejected are blessings of the kingdom because people in these conditions know they cannot establish themselves on any grounds of their own. Rather, they rely totally on being supported by a love which comes to them out of its own abundance and not out of their own boasting or achievement. On the other hand, the rich, the filled, the happy, and the praised have no room in their lives for such love. They are filled already by their own achievements and, hanging on to these achievements as their sole source of security, are unable to surrender to divine love.

Not until we overcome the temptation to regard ourselves as self-sufficient are we able to let go and surrender to the deepest truths about ourselves as being grounded in divine love. But letting go is hard. We hang on to these surrogate loves out of fear that if we let go we will lose our worth, and no longer be valued or valuable. Yet surrendering is the only way to allow God to secure us in divine love.

Perhaps the most challenging of the gospel stories calling us to surrender to divine love is the story of the rich young man in the gospel of Mark (10:17–27). The young man asks Jesus what he

Sin: Arrogance

must do to inherit eternal life. Jesus tells him to keep the commandments, to be loyal to his covenantal commitment. The young man replies, "But I've done that all my life." Jesus then looks at him with love and says, "Then there is one thing more important than all others. Give up all those things on which you have come to rely for status, security, worth, and well-being, and follow me." At this the young man's face fell, and he went away sad, for he relied on much. Now what is it about the rich young man that makes it difficult for him to share in the kingdom of God? It is that he could not let go of his self-made securities which served as his source of worth and loveableness. The challenge of this story is not in trying to make poverty a special virtue. Its challenge is directed to all of those false securities which occupy our hearts and serve as the ground upon which we establish our worth.

Those who establish themselves on their own securities are ultimately not free but are trapped in self-absorbing fears that they are not lovable as they are. This fear and unfreedom drives them to strive for qualities and achievements with which to exalt themselves and oppress others. This only results in the self-righteousness which Jesus singles out as the obstacle to hearing the good news that our worth is grounded in God's love and not our own. We pronounce a judgment against ourselves when we refuse to accept this divine love as our only true source of worth and security. Not until we open ourselves to the source of our worth in God will we overcome our sin of idolatry and be open to the wider values of God's creation and God's people.

Solidarity. The same divine love which calls us into covenant with God and establishes our worth also cultivates the relationship of people with one another and with all creation. In Jesus Christ we affirm all creation as being under the covenantal grace of God and recognize our responsibility to care for all things as related to God (Col 1:12-20). By virtue of the covenant being all-inclusive, we have no other way of relating to God except through our covenantal relationships. These relationships are primarily with one another but also with all of creation.

God's love in the broadest sense is not limited just to us but is also directed toward all creation. We who consciously accept this covenant with God accept responsibility for all that is included in God's love. The lesson this inclusive covenant teaches is the very

Richard M. Gula

one we are learning through our scientific explorations; namely, that every facet of the universe is bound together by an unbreakable bond of relatedness. A metal placard at the beginning of a trail in Yosemite National Park reminded me of this truth with a quote from John Muir: "When we try to pick out something by itself, we find it hitched to everything else in the universe." In short, nothing exists by itself as an independent entity. Everything exists in dynamic interrelationship.

The most important principle governing the working of the universe is a covenantal principle: cooperative community. Patricia Mische, in her book *Star Wars and the State of Our Souls*, has summarized this scientific and covenantal principle and its implications well when she writes,

> Some may call this principle bonding. Some call it electromagnetism. Some call it attraction. Some communion. Teilhard de Chardin looked at this principle and called it love. It may be the most fragile of principles governing the universe, but love, cooperation, communion, is also what makes the universe work. If the whole universe and every cell in our bodies and life itself is possible only through this principle, we may, like Teilhard, wonder why we ever doubted that we were created in love and for love.[10]

However, to see the universe as a community sounds so antithetical to what we experience. We take independence and separation as the norm, and community as the exception. But the covenant, and now scientific understanding, tells us this is to have it all backwards. The covenantal perspective is that we have no life without community and cooperation. But this does not mean we have no individual differences. Diversity, and the tension that comes with it, is part of life. We can enhance our lives to the extent we are able to sustain a high degree of diversity within a cooperative community. But our covenantal commitment, like our scientific discoveries, requires that we develop those modes of cooperation which respect the functional integrity of the universe. Since the universe functions as a unity, any dysfunction imperils every creature.

Sin, from the perspective of an inclusive covenant, affects all the relationships to which we are called. Sin is rooted in radical independence. It adopts simplistically Darwin's perception that only the fittest survive. It fails to respect diversity within a cooperative community. With each competing against the other, sin tries to

Sin: Arrogance

69

eliminate diversity by promoting the domination of one form of life. But, as our lessons from ecology teach us, when one form of life dominates in a region, the whole region collapses. Sin overlooks Darwin's other discovery that only those species survive which learn to cooperate.[11]

The inclusive covenant also creates the human moral community. By calling us into covenant, God calls us to be social. The laws of the covenant express what life ought to look like for those who have accepted the offer of divine love and live in solidarity with one another. The covenant is not fully realized until we live out the covenantal commitment to be responsible to and for one another as covenantal partners. The covenantal laws express the responsibility we have to and for one another by virtue of our sharing in the same divine love. This is the core of the inseparability of the great commandment to love God and others as we love ourselves. The great commandment requires that each of us recognize that the others matter for their own sake and not just as the means to an end.

This has been well illustrated in the famous parable of the Good Samaritan (Luke 10:30–35). Three people notice the man in the ditch. The priest and Levite look at him and pass on. The Samaritan sees him and is moved with compassion. We ask, "Did not all three see the same thing?" When we realize the parable is set within the framework of explaining the meaning of "love your neighbor as yourself," we can understand that they obviously did not see the same reality. Whatever the priest and Levite saw when they looked in the ditch was clearly not themselves. The Samaritan, however, looked in the ditch and saw himself. He is the one "moved with compassion" because he sees himself beaten and lying there wounded. He is the one Jesus holds up as the example of being neighbor and loving another as one loves oneself.

Covenantal solidarity also means that our lives extend beyond a private relationship with God and our neighbor to embrace the whole social order—social structures, institutional order, economic systems. Our lives are inevitably marked by the structural relationships that can act for or against the fundamental worth and well-being of all. The fruit of covenantal solidarity is *shalom*—that peace which is not just the absence of violence, but the peace which is the justice of communal wholeness wherein competing claims achieve a proper balance. Within such covenantal solidarity, sin

Richard M. Gula

70

cannot be limited to breaking the law. Sin is not first and foremost against laws. Sin is against people and, in and through people, against God. Sin is an offense against God, not in the sense of harming God, but in the sense of failing to respect what God loves. Personal sin shows its effects in society and creation as a whole. It shows itself as a violation of the covenant by introducing disorder and strife into the solidarity of the Creator and the created.

Throughout life we have the opportunity to better our world. When we live with indifference, jealousy, envy, contempt, domination, possessiveness, or prejudice and ignore situations of need requiring works of justice, mercy, and love, we are failing to heed the summons of divine-human solidarity. In so doing, we pronounce a judgment against ourselves. One of the meanings of the great judgment scene in Matthew's parable of the sheep and the goats (Matt 25:31–46) is that people did not recognize in the hungry, thirsty, naked, sick, and imprisoned the summons of divine-human solidarity. Our obligations inherent in being social are inseparable from the bond that links us to God. Isaiah's image of true fasting, for example, shows that within the covenant, antisocial behavior cannot be distinguished from irreligious behavior. "The kind of fasting I want is this: Remove the chains of oppression and the yoke of injustice, and let the oppressed go free" (Isa 58:6). Human solidarity is one with our relationship to God. To betray a social commitment demanded by justice is to betray God.

Fidelity. The solidarity of covenantal partners who have responsibility to and for one another awaits fidelity in order to come to its fullest expression. "What I want is loyalty, not sacrifice" (Hos 6:6). Fidelity, trustworthiness, and loyalty are various ways of expressing the central moral virtue of the covenant.[12] From the perspective of virtue, covenantal living asks, "What sort of person should I be?" The answer: be faithful, be trustworthy. Live a life that demonstrates *hesed*, God's faithful love for us. Imitating this faithful love which binds the covenant together is the moral imperative for living in covenant. Fidelity is the very weave of the fabric of the covenant. To rend this fabric through infidelity is to ruin the whole cloth. Therefore, fidelity or trustworthiness—not dominating control by some and subservient submission by others—is the virtue which will bind the covenantal partners together.

Sin: Arrogance

For the covenant to be sustained, each partner must be trust-worthy. Where one cannot trust another to be loyal to the covenantal commitment, the relationship of love breaks down. One of the most bitter moments in the lives of those who join in covenant is to find out that the one who we believed had been committed to us is not being faithful to that commitment. Such moments arouse our moral indignation at the betrayal of trust. When we experience such betrayal, we hedge against any future infidelity by making efforts to defend ourselves against the forces of an imbalance of power. This infects all our relationships with the suspicion and the fear that fidelity is not being practiced in our commitments to one another.

We always know where God stands with us, for God is forever faithful. God's fidelity or trustworthiness is something on which we can rely. We keep covenant with God and with all covenantal partners by being faithful in return. We see this virtue of trust-worthiness or fidelity played out in the contrast of two garden sto-ries in the Bible, the garden of Eden and the garden of Gethsemane. Both can be seen as stories of what we do with our freedom to live as trustworthy creatures.[13]

We look in on the activity of the garden of Eden on the sixth day, when God entrusted the earth to the care of Adam and Eve and entrusted them to each other. The story implies that every-thing comes to us as a gift from a free and gracious God. The story of the garden of Eden is pervaded with the sense that hu-manity is empowered with the capacity to influence creation and one another by being entrusted with gifts, the gifts of creation and the gifts of one another. The serpent enters to sow seeds of dis-trust. The serpent suggests that God cannot be trusted, and so tempts the creatures with power (the knowledge of good and evil). Adam and Eve choose to believe the snake. In this, they missed the mark of their proper role in the covenantal relation-ship. The fall is the result of their abuse of power by seeking self-serving ends.

The moment Adam and Eve refuse to believe God can be trusted and abuse their role in the covenant, they refuse to trust each other also, and so imprison themselves within their own defenses. This is symbolized by Adam's and Eve's hiding in the bushes to protect themselves from God, and by their sewing fig leaves for clothes to hide their nakedness and to protect them-

Richard M. Gula

selves from one another. To stand naked before another is to leave oneself vulnerable. Adam and Eve could no longer afford to do that. They could no longer allow themselves to be vulnerable by saying to each other, "I trust you." From this point, all of life becomes marked by the fear and the suspicion of betrayal. This attitude toward life builds walls of protection and hedges against infidelity with preparations to secure a balance of power.

The story of the garden of Gethsemane, however, is the story of Jesus trusting in God by not abandoning his mission of living to make everyone a friend of God and of one another. Jesus' great act of living by covenantal fidelity was to accept the death on the cross, trusting that his life would not echo into an empty future. Jesus lived his life trusting that he would be sustained by the undefeatable love of God. The resurrection confirms that such trust was not ill-founded.

In the story of the garden of Gethsemane, Judas is an important figure for understanding covenantal fidelity.[14] Judas shows us the real possibility of betrayal. His betrayal provides the contrast to God's faithfulness to Jesus and Jesus' fidelity to God. With Judas in the story, we see more clearly the centrality of fidelity in the lives of those who covenant with Jesus as disciples. To violate fidelity is not only to do something wrong; but it is, above all, to be the wrong sort of person. It is a violation of the call to follow Jesus in the imitation of God's covenantal, steadfast love.

The foundational principle for living in the covenantal community is heard in Jesus' commission to his disciples when he sends them out on mission: "What you have received as gift, give as gift" (Matt 10:8). This is the principle which says the bond of trust which we share with God is to be reflected outward into the affairs that make up the whole of our lives. Our bonding in trust is a commitment to use our power to bring liberation and justice, not to exercise domination and oppression. The parable which most clearly illustrates life in the covenant is that of the unmerciful servant (Matt 18:21–35). The servant who was forgiven a great debt did not forgive even a small debt owed to him. The servant is chastised because he betrayed God's trust in being forgiven by not imitating God and reflecting this trust outward to liberate his own debtor. He did not give freely what he had received freely.

The stories of the garden of Eden and the garden of Gethsemane teach us that we are pursued by the relentless fidelity of

Sin: Arrogance

God. Sin is infidelity. Sin is refusing to believe that God can be trusted and that others are worth trusting. In a covenant, we entrust to one another something of value to ourselves. In God's covenant with humanity, for example, God has entrusted to us divine love, most fully expressed in the person of Jesus. In marriage we covenant with another by entrusting to another our whole selves and our lives. This is symbolized in giving our bodies to each other. In health care, we covenant by entrusting our physical well-being to a health-care professional. In covenants with lawyers, we entrust our legal rights to a legal professional.

In making these acts of trust, we entrust the other with power. We hope that power will not be abused. Sin, however, abuses that power because sin cannot let go of the fear and suspicion that keeps us from coming to know the other as gift. In sin we are unable to live in the freedom of being entrusted by God with personal worth and with the gifts of one another. Sin abuses the power we give to one another when we entrust another with something of value to ourselves: a personal secret, our health, our property, our bodies. Sin abuses this power by not holding in trust that which has been entrusted to us. Rather than living in trust as creatures empowered with gifts to set one another free, we live in suspicion of another's gifts and abuse our power by controlling, dominating, or manipulating these gifts to serve our own self interests. This is sin as the arrogance of power, pure and simple.

HEART

If covenant is the primary metaphor for the biblical context for sin, then heart is an apt metaphor for the personal relationship to God. The heart is what the divine love of the covenant seeks. Divine love is either embraced or rejected in the heart. According to biblical anthropology, the heart is the seat of vital decisions for it is the center of feeling and reason, decision and action, intention and consciousness.[15] This makes the heart the ultimate locale of virtue or sin.[16] The American bishops have expressed this biblical insight in their treatment of sin in the pastoral letter on the moral life, *To Live in Christ Jesus*, ''We sin first in our hearts, although often our sins are expressed in outward acts and their consequences.''[17]

The moral vision of the bible sees good and evil not just in be-

Richard M. Gula

havior but in the heart which promotes good and evil behavior. God complains not so much about perverse actions as about the hardened heart from which such actions arise (Isa 29:13). Jesus continues in this tradition with his concern about the filth on the inside of the cup which shows itself on the outside (Matt 23:25–26). This means that from a person's heart come the evil ideas which lead one to do immoral things (Mark 7:21); whereas, a good person produces good from the goodness in the heart (Luke 6:45). The lucan Jesus aptly summarizes the implications of the unity of the person: "Of what the heart is full the mouth will speak" (Luke 6:45).

The hope of the messianic prophecies is for the people to receive a new heart so that their inmost inclinations will be to live out of divine love in loyalty to the covenant (Jer 31:33; Ezek 36:26). The markan summary of Jesus' proclamation of the kingdom is the call for a new heart (Mark 1:15). The very essence of conversion, or *metanoia*, is to live with a new heart in a new spirit, the spirit of Christ living in us (Rom 8:10; Eph 4:17–24). The radical ethical demands of Jesus stress such interior renewal: "If your eye causes you to sin, pluck it out" (Matt 5:29); "If someone slaps you on the right cheek, give your left as well" (Matt 5:39); "Give to everyone who asks" (Matt 5:42); "Do not store up riches on earth" (Matt 6:19). Imperatives like these are not demands to act in these specific ways. Rather, they are paradoxical figures of speech meant to shock the imagination and to reorient the heart.

The biblical vision of the heart focuses on that dimension of us which is most sensitive and open to others. The essential characteristic of the heart is its openness to God—its capacity to receive divine love. Augustine said that our hearts are by nature oriented toward God. Jesus said "Where your heart is, there will be your treasure as well" (Matt 6:21). When our hearts treasure God, all other treasures will be treasured rightly. The heart properly ordered to God as our single center of value will have a certain instinct for what is good relative to God. Such a properly directed heart yields a life of virtue. The misdirected heart produces sin.

Contemporary theology finds in the notions of covenant and heart the biblical roots for its theory of the fundamental option.[18] The theory of the fundamental option assumes the basic conviction of the covenantal experience, namely, we are born graced. This means God has created us out of love for love. Without destroying our freedom, God's love for us has so affected us in our innermost being (i.e., our hearts) as to give us an orientation toward love and life. Our response is to live out this orientation in freedom. To agree to live in covenant with God is the most self-committing choice we can ever make. Theologians call this basic life choice a fundamental option. The heartfelt rejection of this covenantal love is what we call mortal sin. Any lesser abuse of covenantal love and its responsibilities is venial sin.

SIN: THE ARROGANCE OF POWER

Now that we have walked around inside the metaphors of covenant and heart, perhaps we can recognize more sharply the reality of sin as the arrogance of power. The covenant says we are already established as persons of worth by the gratuitous love of God, nothing else. We live as full partners of the covenant when we live out of the heart accepting the gift of divine love and focusing its loyalty and true desires on God. So the first task of the covenant is not to love but to learn to be one who is loved.

But the heart panics. It does not trust that we are creatures of a gracious God. Life is too ambiguous to assure the heart of being loved without achievement. Since the world we know does not run on unconditional love, the heart finds it hard to accept this gift of love as true. So the heart sets out to secure its lovableness in its own striving. This is idolatry—the strategy of preempting the central place of God in the heart for a surrogate love of some self-made dream, like wealth, fame, or authority. Sin as the misdirected heart takes on some form of idolatry. Our idols are fashioned by the arrogance of power—the imperial "I" living as though it must make itself great.

Rollo May, in his book *Power and Innocence,* provides a helpful schema for understanding sin as the arrogance of power.[19] According to May, all of us have power. But not all of it is demonic. His analysis shatters the commonly held view that the more loving one is the less powerful one is. Love and power, in fact, are not opposites. We need power to be able to love in the first place, since power, as May defines it, is the capacity to influence others and situations for good or ill.

Rollo May distinguishes five kinds of power which can be in all of us at different times.[20] The moral issue becomes the proportion of each kind of power we exercise. *Exploitive* and *manipulative*

Richard M. Gula

76

power are destructive. *Competitive* power can act destructively against another or it can act constructively to bring vitality to a relationship. *Nurturing* power acts for the sake of another by giving care. *Integrative* power acts with another to draw out the best in him or her. The arrogance of power in the misdirected heart seeks a greater proportion of exploitive, manipulative and competitive power over nurturing and integrative power.

What does the right use of power of the properly directed heart look like when compared with the arrogance of power of the misdirected heart? The ministry of Jesus gives us many good examples of power expressive of the properly directed heart. The gospels do not portray Jesus as powerless. In fact, the Gospel of Mark opens with the crowds marveling at his power (Mark 1:22, 27). So the issue that comes out of the ministry of Jesus is not one of power versus powerlessness. It is, rather, always a question of what kind of power to use.

The disciples, as well as the religious and political rulers of his day, often serve as special foils of Jesus' loving use of power. Jesus constantly challenges the use of power that is oppressive and abusive, that does not give life but takes it away. His miracles, for example, are signs of liberating power. His parables are judgments about reversals in power relationships: the first become last; the last, first. Those who make themselves great will be humbled; the humble, made great. The prodigal is celebrated; the dutiful, offended. The publican is blessed; the Pharisee, exposed. The Samaritan is held up as an example of goodness; the priest and Levite, as negligent.

In the life of Jesus, we see what power looks like for one who is loved by God. For this reason, Jesus is the exemplar of covenantal existence. He knew himself to be special in God's sight. This, I believe, is the significance of his baptismal experience: ''You are my own dear Son. I am pleased with you'' (Matt 3:17; Mark 1:11; Luke 3:22). The rest of the gospel demonstrates the practical effect of holding fast to these words of worth received out of the waters of baptism. When we have learned to live as a people who no longer need to strive for greatness, we can be at peace within ourselves and with the world. Because Jesus knew himself to be special in God's sight, he was able to embrace the whole world in love.

Sin: Arrogance

We learn from the actions of Jesus that power is for mediating this divine love and not for preempting it. Consider the conflict between Jesus and his disciples who return to him after meeting a man casting out demons in his name (Mark 9:38–40; Luke 9:40; Luke 9:49–50). The disciples want to stop this man because he is not one of their company. Jesus, however, does not. The arrogance of power wants to control the good and to exalt oneself at the expense of another. For the disciples the fact that someone lives free of demons is insignificant. After all, they are the official "demon-caster-outers." What is important to them is that they were not the ones who worked the wonder. The power unleashed by the divine love in Jesus does not usurp the good. The arrogance of power does.[21]

We can also see this power at work in the scene of the bent-over woman in Luke 13:10–17. In this scene Jesus calls to a woman bent over by an evil spirit for eighteen years. He places his hands on her and she stands up straight. She who was once weak is now strong. Friends of Jesus rejoiced over her liberation, but the officials in the synagogue who observe this are angry about what was done and when it was done. Surely the power that nurtures and liberates by making the weak strong is too challenging to the community. The arrogance of power wants to control the good by keeping some weak while others remain strong. After all, too many strong people in the community would create problems. The power which Jesus expresses is the power which transforms the structures of domination in the community.[22]

This is especially evident in the famous conflict between Jesus and Peter in the footwashing scene in the Gospel of John (13:6–10). Peter resists being washed. He realizes that if he complied with this washing, he would be accepting a radical reversal of the very structures of domination upon which he depends for his use of power. Such a conversion is more than Peter wants to undergo. When Jesus, the master, deliberately reverses social positions by becoming the servant, he witnesses to a new order of human relationships in the community whereby the desire to dominate and establish superiority has no place.[23]

The passion story ultimately brings the issue of power to a climax.[24] In Gethsemane Jesus' opponents come with familiar instruments of arrogant power: betrayal, arrest, swords and clubs. Jesus has no such weapons. Those who appear to be in power, the

Richard M. Gula

Sanhedrin and the Roman procurator, abuse him. Roman soldiers torture him with the very symbols of power—a purple robe, a crown of thorns, the homage of spittle and blows. The ultimate weapon of power inflicted on Jesus is the public execution on the cross. In the crucifixion of Jesus the arrogance of power is raging out of control. Yet the very success of this power is its own subversion. The cross ultimately reveals the emptiness of all oppressive power. As in his ministry so in his death, Jesus exercises a power that gives life: "Just as Moses lifted up the serpent in the desert, so must the Son of Man be lifted up, that all who believe may have eternal life in him (John 3:14–15); and again, "and I, once I am lifted up from the earth, will draw everyone to myself" (John 12:32).

The power revealed in the cross is the power which "takes away the sin of the world." This is the power which takes sin into itself so that others may be free. Sin, the arrogance of power, killed the Son of God and was in turn killed by the Son of God. Jesus, dying on the cross, does not resort to legions of angels to destroy the evil of those who appear to be in power. If he did, then his kind of power and theirs would be the same. The only differences would be the size of the muscle. Jesus resorts to the most powerful reality he knows—divine love—and offers forgiveness.

CONCLUSION

What is supposed to happen to us who follow the way of the cross, tell the story of the Passion, and watch Jesus die in ritual each year, is what happened to the thief who was offered paradise and took it. The purpose of following the way of the cross and watching Jesus die is repentance. What do we see that makes us repent? We see Jesus hold fast to the words of worth he heard in the waters of his baptism and trustfully surrender his life to God. We also see a love powerful enough to transform a crowd from its jeers of mockery to its tears of breast-beating repentance.

Yet watching Jesus die on the cross is not enough. We must take him down. The passion and death of Jesus reveal the steadfast love of God unmasking the arrogance of power which nailed him up. This same steadfast love of God asks for repentant power to take him down. But sin runs deep in us. So long as we strive, deceive, oppress, or control in order to secure our loves and our

Sin: Arrogance

79

lovableness, then the Son of God stays on the cross. The hardness of our hearts resists the outpouring of divine love. When we take him down from the cross, we convert the inner energy of our sin into the life-giving power of redemption. We do this when we surrender to the gracious offer of divine love. The experience of divine love liberates our hearts to live faithfully in solidarity with our partners in covenant.

The true nature of living in covenant is found in the calling of the disciples to be companions of Jesus. Disciples are called to leave all they have and to follow Jesus. To be a disciple means to be dispossessed of all those surrogate loves which we think give us power over our own lives and the lives of others. The more we possess the more violent we must become to protect what we have.[25] Our possessions become the source of our sin, or as we used to say, our near occasions for sin. Our most precious possession is the self we have made by our own efforts. Sin arises out of our need to guarantee that we are lovable and loved. When we set out to protect that at all costs, we set ourselves against God, against nature and against one another. Competing self-serving interests usher in the disharmony of the world which we know as social sin—the cooperation in the continued maintenance of oppressive structures is society.

We will break the dynamic power of sin in our lives when we realize that we are in fact profoundly loved. The only love that will ultimately satisfy our longing hearts is divine love. Divine love disposes us to a power that creates life to transform human relationships and the quality of our institutions and systems. The right use of power remains a central moral issue in our world and in the Church. In accepting the power of divine love, we are taking Jesus at his word: "No longer do I call you servants, . . . I call you friends" (John 15:15). The unfinished agenda of reconciliation is to become one with the mission of Jesus to use our power so that others may have life in abundance.

The pastoral challenge of understanding sin as the arrogance of power is to name the power at work in our personal relationships and in our institutions. Is ours a power that controls, manipulates, dominates and exploits? Or is ours a power that liberates? Being in covenant compels us to take our power seriously, to accept the responsibility we have to use this power to liberate and to give life, and to call others to account for their use of power. When we

Richard M. Gula

80

accept the power that is ours, regardless of the position of authority we may hold in the Church or in society, then we are entering the process of reconciliation in a way that will make a difference for living life in freedom and in peace.

NOTES

1. For a survey of major attempts in the past twenty years to explore the mystery of sin, see James A. O'Donohoe, "Toward a Theology of Sin: A Look at the Last Twenty Years," *Church* 2 (Spring 1986) 48–54.

2. "Secularism" is the first of those listed by Pope John Paul II in his "Apostolic Exhortation on Reconciliation and Penance." The other factors of a non-ecclesial nature which he lists are errors made in evaluating certain findings of the human sciences, deriving systems of ethics from historical relativism, and identifying sin with neurotic guilt. Within the thought and life of the Church, certain trends have also contributed to the loss of a sense of sin. Among these he lists the movement from seeing sin everywhere to not recognizing it anywhere; from an emphasis on fear of eternal punishment to preaching a love of God that excludes punishment; from correcting erroneous consciences to respecting consciences but excluding the duty to tell the truth. Two other ecclesial factors are the plurality of opinions existing in the Church on questions of morality and the deficiencies in the practice of penance. To restore a healthy sense of sin, the Pope advocates "a sound catechetics, illuminated by the biblical theology of the covenant, by an attentive listening and trustful openness to the magisterium of the Church, which never ceases to enlighten consciences, and by an ever more careful practice of the sacrament of penance." See *Origins* 14 (December 20, 1984) 443–444, quotation at p. 444.

3. The research of the team headed by sociologist Robert Bellah which has produced *Habits of the Heart* (Berkeley: University of California Press, 1985), a study of American beliefs and practices which give shape to our character and form to our social order, shows that the therapist is the newest character defining American culture. See chapter 2: "Culture and Character: The Historical Conversation," 27–51, esp. 47–48.

4. Karl Menninger, *Whatever Became of Sin?* (New York: Hawthorn Books, Inc., 1973).

5. M. Scott Peck, *People of the Lie* (New York: Simon and Schuster, 1983).

Sin: Arrogance

6. A helpful, succinct interpretation of the terms of sin in the Bible can be found in S. J. DeVries, "Sin, Sinners," *The Interpreter's Dictionary of the Bible*, vol. 4 (Nashville: Abingdon Press, 1962) 361–376; for the terms, see pp. 361–362, 371.

7. These terms of the covenantal relationship are derived from the analysis of covenant made by Joseph L. Allen, *Love and Conflict: A Covenantal Model of Christian Ethics* (Nashville: Abingdon Press, 1984) 61ff. Allen's analysis is based on the six characteristics of God's covenantal love: "God (1) binds us together as members of a covenant community, (2) affirms the worth of each covenant member, (3) extends covenant love inclusively, (4) seeks to meet the needs of each member of the covenant community, (5) is steadfast, and (6) is reconciling." My threefold subdivision captures the scope of these six.

8. Sebastian Moore pursues this theme to great effect in *The Inner Loneliness* (New York: Crossroad Publishing Co., 1982).

9. This is the central thesis of Walter Brueggemann, "Covenanting as Human Vocation: A Discussion of the Relation of Bible and Pastoral Care," *Interpretation* 33 (April 1979) 115–129. His covenantal thesis is stated on p. 116.

10. Patricia Mische, *Star Wars and the State of Our Souls* (Minneapolis: Winston Press, 1985) 124.

11. Ibid. 125.

12. Allen, *Love and Conflict* 72.

13. The interpretation of these garden stories is inspired by John Shea, *The Challenge of Jesus* (Garden City: Doubleday & Co. Inc., 1977) 93–113.

14. For this interpretation of the significance of Judas in the story of Gethsemane, see Karen Lebacqz, *Professional Ethics: Power and Paradox* (Nashville: Abingdon Press, 1985) 89–91.

15. Hans Walter Wolff, *Anthropology of the Old Testament* (Philadelphia: Fortress Press, 1974) 40–55.

16. DeVries, "Sin, Sinner," p. 364.

17. *To Live in Christ Jesus*, (Washington: USCC, 1976) 5.

18. For a good example of how contemporary theology has situated the theory of fundamental option within this biblical vision of the heart, see Bernard Haring, *Free and Faithful in Christ, Vol. 1: General Moral Theology* (New York: The Seabury Press, 1978) 164–222; for his section on the "heart," as it relates to the theory of fundamental option, see 185–189.

19. Rollo May, *Power and Innocence.* (New York: W. W. Norton & Company, Inc., 1972), esp. chapter 5, "The Meaning of Power," 99–119.

Richard M. Gula

20. Ibid. 105–113.
21. For this interpretation of liberating power, see John Shea, *An Experience Named Spirit* (Chicago: The Thomas More Press, 1983) 255.
22. For this interpretation, see Mary Daniel Turner, "Woman and Power," *The Way Supplement* 53 (Summer 1985) 113–114.
23. For this interpretation of the foot washing scene, see Sandra M. Schneiders, "The Foot Washing (John 13:1–20): An Experiment in Hermeneutics," *Catholic Biblical Quarterly* 43 (January 1981) 76–92, esp. 80–88.
24. For this interpretation of the passion from the perspective of power, see Donald Senior, "Passion and Resurrection in the Gospel of Mark," *Chicago Studies* 25 (April 1986) 21–34, esp. 25–27.
25. For the interpretation of discipleship as the call to dispossession which implies a commitment to non-violence, see Stanley Hauerwas, *The Peaceable Kingdom: A Primer in Christian Ethics* (Notre Dame: University of Notre Dame Press, 1983), esp. chapter 5, "Jesus: The Presence of the Peaceable Kingdom," 72–95.

Catherine Dooley, O.P.

The History of Penance in the Early Church: Implications for the Future

In 1963, Karl Rahner wrote an article entitled "Forgotten Truths Concerning the Sacrament of Penance."[1] This concept of the "forgotten truths" suggests that there is more in the Church's memory than is present at any particular moment in time. "Forgotten truths" does not imply that no one knows these aspects of the Church's tradition; it is simply that they have not been emphasized. They have lapsed from memory.

With regard to penance, Rahner says that the most important truth is that in the sacrament "God forgives us our guilt by the grace of Christ and through the word of the church."[2] The works of God, however, are too rich to be reduced to a single formula. We need to constantly reflect upon them in terms of the tradition and in terms of current pastoral experience.

We do not consider the history of penance in order to restore the past but rather to enrich the present and the future through the interaction of the tradition with contemporary theology and pastoral practice. Moreover, such confrontation implies that the whole of the penance tradition, that is, the authentic witness of every age of the Church, both East and West, needs to be studied and incorporated into current issues. Otherwise, the sacrament is impoverished.

History is also important because it enables us to put the present into larger perspective. For example, it is said that today there is a crisis in the sacrament of penance.[3] A study of the past teaches us that this present crisis is just one among many that have been part of the evolution of the sacrament.

History teaches us about the changes and it also teaches us about the elements that have been a consistent part of the penitential practice of whatever place and time: contrition, confession of sinfulness, conversion and ecclesial forgiveness and reconciliation. The historical and cultural context of a particular era led the Church to place an emphasis on one aspect of the penance process over the others. In the early Church penance centered on penitential works as a sign of conversion. Tariff penance emphasized confession and works of satisfaction. Medieval practice stressed confession and absolution. An almost exclusive focus on one aspect of the sacramental process led to abuse and depreciation of the sacrament in each of these eras. There has never been a "golden age" in the history of this sacrament because the sacramental practice has been in constant evolution. Yet in every age, the Church strived to renew itself.

This essay reviews the historical development of the sacrament in the early Church and indicates some of the "forgotten truths" which are important for the Church today and for the Church of the future.

THE APOSTOLIC CHURCH

The penitential form in the apostolic communities was designed to reconcile individuals who had been excluded from the community because of serious and public sins. The judgement of sin and the authority to exclude was the prerogative of the community (Matt 18:17; 1 Cor 5:3-5) and exercised through its leaders. Separation from the community and from the eucharistic table was based on

Catherine Dooley

84

an understanding of the corporate nature of sin (1 Cor 5:1–5; 2 Cor 5:5–11). Grave sin was not only an offense against God but a contradiction to membership in the Church. Baptism effected the unity of all members in the Body of Christ. Sin destroyed this unity and weakened the bonds of grace that existed among members. Sinners were separated from the community because sin is not only an offense against God; sin is also an offense against the Church. The focus was not so much on the sinner's offense as it was on the change it made in their relationship with other believers. The community, however, viewed the sins of the others with charity. The purpose of exclusion was, first, to bring sinners to an awareness of their wrongdoing; and second, to support the individual in the process of conversion through prayer and charity.[4]

THE TEACHING OF TERTULLIAN

The penitential form in use in the apostolic communities gradually assumed a more consistent ritual. Ecclesiastical penance continued to remain an exceptional form necessary for persons guilty of public or scandalous sins such as murder, idolatry, and adultery. A description of this process is found for the first time in the writings of the African, Tertullian (+225), at the end of the second century. Tertullian describes a threefold process: the individual appears before the community dressed as a penitent in a garment of goat's hair. The penitent begs the community for their intercession (*De paen.* 9, 1) and then sits in the place assigned to penitents. In this way the individual confesses that he or she is a sinner. Second, the penitent is assigned acts of penance in order to insure true conversion. Generally, the penance consisted of fasting, penitential garb, and other mortifications (*De paen.* 9, 4). Third, after the period of penance is accomplished, the penitent is readmitted to the community. There is no explicit description of an official act of reconciliation given by the bishop although it can be assumed from Tertullian's writings that one did exist.[5]

CANONICAL PENANCE

In the fourth century, this ecclesiastical form became more structured because it became regulated by the canons of regional councils and local synods of bishops. Thus it was often termed "canonical penance." The primary characteristics were exclusion

Penance in the Early Church

from the eucharist and reconciliation with the Church. The whole penitential process was a public, liturgical action beginning with the dismissal of the sinners from the Church as a sign of being cut off from the community of believers. This action had its basis in the belief that the Church in its fullest sense is, or should be, a community of saints; whoever grieviously sins no longer belongs to the Church in this fullest sense. The separation from the community found its most painful realization in the exclusion from the eucharistic table. The purpose of this excommunication was to bring about the sinner's conversion and forgiveness. Through the liturgical gesture of the laying on of hands by the bishop, the sinner was enrolled in the order of penitents and bound to certain liturgical and penitential obligations. The primary purpose of these works was not to humiliate the penitent (although the penances were, in fact, humiliating), but rather to demonstrate the sincerity of the individual's conversion and to enlist the prayers of the community. By manifesting contrition and humility, the penitents not only worked out their own salvation but built up the community by their witness. When the penance was completed, the penitents were received back into full communion with the Church in a public ceremony. Prayer and the imposition of hands by the bishop concluded the final stage of the order of penitents.[6]

Throughout the penitential period, the penitents were never without the support of the community. The penitents regularly received a special blessing and the imposition of hands by the bishop in the presence of the whole community. The purpose of this blessing was to assist the penitents to persevere in their penitential works and to obtain the forgiveness of God.

The community's role in the forgiveness of sin was considered an essential aspect of the penitential process. The penance was performed in the presence of the community and had to be supported by the intercession of the Church in order to obtain the forgiveness of sin. Tertullian, preaching on the need to be reconciled with the Church, underlines the role of the community in the process of conversion:

> You [penitents] are living among brothers, servants of the same Lord. Everything we have is shared in common—hope, fear, joy, suffering—for we have the one spirit which comes from the one Lord and the one Father. Why then do you believe that the community is so different from you? The body cannot rejoice when one of

Catherine Dooley

its members experiences suffering and distress. The whole body must share in the affliction of its member and work together for his renewal. Yes, whenever one or two are gathered, there is the church. But the church is Christ. And so when the penitents extend their hands toward the faithful in prayer it is Christ whom they touch. It is Christ whom they implore. And when the faithful shed tears for their brother it is Christ who is suffering in them. It is Christ who is pleading for sinners with the Father. And whatever the Son asks of the Father is quickly granted.[7]

The emphasis on the intercession of the whole community was echoed two centuries later by St. Augustine:

It is not Peter alone who looses but the whole church binds and looses the bonds of sin. You, too, bind; you, too, loose. For whosoever is bound is separated from your community and whosoever is separated from your community is bound by you; and when the sinner is reconciled, he is loosed by you because you, too, pray to God for him.[8]

The role of the community in the forgiveness of the sinner does not diminish the ecclesial act of pardon given by the bishop or presbyter. It points to a deeper and more accurate understanding of the role of the ecclesial leaders in the process of reconciliation.

The bishop, who acts as God's mediator, forgives guilt before God through an official act of pardon. On the one hand, the sinner can obtain forgiveness only through the intercession of the Church because the prayer of Christ's Body is the prayer of Christ himself and is certain to be heard. The intercession of the Church is not simply supportive prayer; it is efficacious in itself and is necessary for the forgiveness of sin. On the other hand, the forgiveness of sin and the reconciliation of the sinner with the Church is the prerogative of the bishop.[9] The intercessory prayer of the community and the reconciling imposition of hands are two phases of the same process. The intercession of the whole Church expresses the profound reality that the Church is the bearer of the Spirit and only in and from the Church can the Spirit be received. The members of the community do not share in the special authority of the bishop but his authority is of the Spirit who exists in the Church. It was this understanding of the presence of the Spirit in the community that led to the conviction that the whole Church mediates grace, remits sin, sanctifies, and offers fullness of life.[10]

Penance in the Early Church

The system of canonical penance began to decline around the fifth century and the ineffectiveness of the institution has to be seen in the context of the sociopolitical situation of the era. The rapid growth of Christianity resulted in the problems of heresy from within and persecution from without. With the conversion of Constantine the Great in the early fourth century, the Church of the persecuted became the Church of the privileged. Many people accepted baptism for political reasons and without genuine conversion. The problem was heightened in the following centuries with the mass baptisms of the Germanic tribes that invaded the Roman Empire. Many of these tribes became Christians when their leaders were baptized. The Church which had previously admitted only convinced believers now became the Church of the masses. The Church found itself in a definite pastoral crisis. In the Church councils convened to deal with dogmatic problems, the canons that concerned penance took on a greater rigidity in order to deal with apostates and to correct the rampant abuses. It was the increased rigidity of the restrictions imposed, together with the rule that penance was a once in a lifetime opportunity, that brought about the decline of public penance.[11] An obvious result of the severe restrictions was that the people simply did not undertake canonical penance. Since there was no recourse for anyone who fell into sin after penance, some pastors began to encourage people to delay penance until their old age or until they were near death.[12] A deathbed penance was considered an abbreviation of canonical penance. The stages were conflated into a single action.[13] If the person recovered from the illness, he or she was bound to enter the order of penitents. Other bishops, in an effort to correct abuses, used alternative means of discipline: exclusion from the eucharist for an assigned period of penance without entrance into the order of penitents, corporal punishment, or, in the case of the clergy, deprivation from office. By the time that ecclesiastical penance reached the height of its liturgical and canonical development in the fifth century, it was irrelevant to the lives of the people.

ORDINARY FORMS OF PENANCE

Canonical penance had to do with those individuals who committed serious and scandalous sins. What means of forgiveness

Catherine Dooley

and reconciliation were available to the ordinary folks during these first six centuries for what Augustine called "daily sins"?

The early Church used a variety of ways to effect forgiveness and to call its members to conversion. In New Testament times and in the first century, baptism was considered *the* sacrament of conversion and forgiveness of sin. The Christian community expected new members to live out the implications of their baptismal commitments.

Forgiveness of sin committed after baptism was accomplished by fraternal correction (Matt 18:15-20), mutual prayer (1 John 5:16; Jas 5:16), and confession to one another (Matt 5:23-24). Charity covers a multitude of sins (Luke 7:47; 1 Pet 4:8), and so prayer, fasting, almsgiving, and works of mercy were the marks of a Christian.[14]

Jesus had summarized his ministry of reconciliation in the words: "This is the covenant of my blood which is poured out for many for the forgiveness of sin . . . ." Participation in the eucharist was the eminent rite of reconciliation since the eucharist was the sign and source of unity.

In the fifth century, Augustine teaches these same forms of daily penance[15]—prayer, fasting, almsgiving, endurance of sufferings, forgiveness of insults, works of service—but he gives first place to the praying of the Our Father in the liturgical assembly. Augustine said: "God has established in his church . . . a remedy which we need to take each day by saying: 'forgive us our trespasses' " (Sermon 352, 8). Augustine included the Our Father in the eucharistic prayer because he understood the prayer to be the sign of repentance and an expression of reconciliation with God and with the community. Thus it is a means of becoming the Body of Christ and a preparation for receiving the Body of Christ.

VALUES OF CANONICAL PENANCE

Despite the serious limitations of canonical penance, there were many values inherent in it, values which have become "forgotten truths" in today's practice. Although the revised Rite of Penance includes many of these principles, they remain, nevertheless, "forgotten truths." In summarizing these aspects, which should form the basis of catechesis and preaching, I include some pastoral suggestions for implementation.

(1) There are several sacraments of reconciliation. Baptism is the primary sacrament of conversion and forgiveness. Baptismal life,

the dying and rising with Christ, is deepened and continued through the sacrament of penance. The eucharist celebrates the very acts by which we are saved and thus is *the* sacrament of reconciliation; penance celebrates an aspect of this mystery of salvation. The eucharist is the preeminent sign and cause of our reconciliation and unity in Christ and with one another. The introduction to the Rite of Penance shows the relationship of these sacraments (no. 2) and in so doing affirms that the entire Christian life is a "serious striving to perfect the grace of baptism" (no. 7b).[16]

(2) The present Rite emphasizes that conversion is a process and puts the sacrament of penance in perspective as *one* aspect of the conversion process (see nos. 1, 3, 4, 6, 8, 11). The stages of canonical penance were aspects of a whole process and each stage took meaning only in relationship to the whole.

(3) At the 1983 Synod of Bishops, Joseph Cardinal Bernardin suggested a sacramental celebration of reconciliation that emphasized conversion as a process and incorporated the principles of the Rite of Christian Initiation as Adults.[17] The proposal, which in effect reinstitutes the "order of penitents," could be used for those individuals returning to the practice of their faith, but it could also be extended to the community as a whole. The proposal includes four stages:

> with the help of spiritual directors and sponsors, the well-prepared penitent approaches the priest to make a full confession of sin;
>
> the penitent begins living a program of conversion and is sustained by the counsel of a spiritual director and events of community prayer;
>
> the penitent joins in the liturgical celebration of penance with full community participation; and
>
> the penitent continues contact with a spiritual director and participation in community prayer to sustain an ongoing conversion, a stage which parallels the mystagogia of the catechumenate.

These stages give proper emphasis both to the sacramental event and to the process which precedes and follows it. Bernardin's proposal states that in regard to penance "exclusive focus on the moment of absolution without appropriate attention to the previous journey of conversion opens the door to a magical view of the sacrament."[18]

(4) Reconciliation is by its very nature a corporate and ecclesial

Catherine Dooley

action. The early Christian communities knew themselves to be the Body of Christ. Their baptismal bonding in Christ was a reality that demanded responsibility to one another because of their solidarity in Christ and their call to give witness to him in their lives. Reconciliation with the community was the effect of the penitential process and thus effected reconciliation with God. The Rite of Penance restores this principle when it states that "the sin of one harms the others just as the holiness of one benefits the others. Penance always entails reconciliation with our brothers and sisters who are always harmed by our sins" (no. 5).

The communal forms of the present rite of reconciliation emphasize the support of the whole praying community. The people listen together to the word of God, calling them to conversion. The act of repentance calls to mind the ways in which the faithful have failed one another. The Lord's Prayer is never omitted. However, it would seem that before the individual confession and absolution, there should be some clear ritual expression or sign of reconciliation with one another. One such adaptation of the rite might be the addition of the greeting of peace in which participants offer the sign of reconciliation to those around them and also seek out those in the assembly whom they have offended. This would be a concrete expression of the petition "forgive us our trespasses as we forgive those who trespass against us."

(5) Perhaps the strongest value to be learned from the early Church is that reconciliation is the ministry of the whole community. In canonical penance, the intercessory prayer of the community played an essential role in the forgiveness of the sinner.

Today, even with the reforms of Vatican II, we still have little understanding of the value of communal prayer and little awareness of the rationale for communal penance celebrations. One author suggests that elements of the old parish mission can be reinterpreted or reintroduced into quarterly seasons of repentance in order to foster an ecclesial environment of conversion.[19] Seasonal celebrations also develop a rhythm of regularity necessary for the development of conscience. The week-long process begins at the Sunday eucharistic assembly with the proclamation of and preaching on the gospel of forgiveness. The people are invited to fast and abstain. The parish plans a variety of events for the week; discussion and reflection groups, celebrations of the word which focus on repentance and conversion, and opportunities for service. Toward the end of the week, ample opportunity is made available for the sacrament of penance. Finally, the eucharist of the following Sunday is an occasion to celebrate the mercy of God evident in the lives of God's people. Such a pastoral practice underlines the responsibility of members to each other. There are a variety of ministries and a variety of gifts. They all play a part in reconciling the world to Christ.

(6) There are a variety of forms of forgiveness and reconciliation that take place within the life of the community. The Rite of Penance states that the people of God become a sign of conversion in the world by enduring the difficulties of life, carrying out works of mercy and charity, and adopting ever more fully the outlook of the gospel message (no. 4). The people of God become a sign of reconciliation whenever they confess their sinfulness and ask the pardon of God and of their brothers and sisters. This happens in penitential services, in the proclamation of the word of God, in prayer, and in the penitential aspects of the eucharistic celebration.

The penitential celebrations (which are nonsacramental in the Rite of Penance), are not frequently used in the United States. These celebrations foster a spirit of penance, prepare people for sacramental confession, help in the formation of conscience, support catechumens in their conversion, and are useful in areas where no priest is available to give sacramental absolution. They are a means of reaching that perfect contrition which comes from love. The 1983 Synod of Bishops[20] and the report of the International Theological Commission of the same year[21] promoted the use of these services. The Synod document acknowledged that the celebrations have a certain salvific value. The International Theological Commission stated that with regard to daily sins they can become a true occasion of pardon, provided that there is a real spirit of conversion and contrition.[22] Perhaps the greatest value in the penitential celebrations is an experience of repentance as an action of praise and thanksgiving.

CONCLUSION

Today we face a situation that is very similar to the early centuries in the sense that the official form of penance is largely ignored. It is essential that, first, we acknowledge the fact that the revision of

Catherine Dooley

92

the Rite of Penance has not effected a great difference in the attitude of people to the sacrament.[23]

Second, we need to recognize that the revision has not had the desired effect. Is it because the Rite has never really been implemented? Is it because there has been a lack of good catechesis on the nature and the purpose of the sacrament? Is it because there has been a lack of good liturgical experience? Is it because parishes lack a sense of community?

Finally, what happened in the early centuries must happen now. We need to draw up a plan of action in response to these questions. This will involve systematic, effective catechesis and good liturgical experience. The "forgotten truths" need to be brought to greater consciousness. The restoration of these forgotten truths must lead the way to legitimate adaptations of the Rite in order to insure a future for the sacrament of reconciliation.

NOTES

1. Karl Rahner, "Forgotten Truths Concerning the Sacrament of Penance," *Theological Investigations*, vol. 2 (London: Herder, 1963) 135–175.

2. Ibid. 136.

3. Pope John Paul II, "Apostolic Exhortation on Reconciliation and Penance," no. 28, in *Origins* 14:27 (20 December 1984), 449.

4. Jerome Murphy-O'Connor, "Sin and Community in the New Testament," in *Sin and Repentance*, ed. Denis O'Callaghan (Dublin: Gill and Son, 1967) 18–50.

5. Karl Rahner, *Theological Investigations*, vol. 15, *Penance in the Early Church*, (New York: The Crossroad Publishing Company, 1982) 135.

6. For the liturgical function and theological significance of the imposition of hands, see James Dallen, "The Imposition of Hands in Penance: A Study in Liturgical History," *Worship* 51 (1977) 224–247.

7. Tertullian, "Treatise on Penance," *Ancient Christian Writers* 28, trans. W. P. LeSaint (Westminster: The Newman Press, 1959) 33.

8. Augustine, *De Sabbato Octavarum Sanctae Paschae*, II in *Miscellanea Agostiniana: Testi e Studi*, vol. 1, *Sermones post Maurinos reperti*, ed. G. Morin, (Rome: Typis Polyglottis Vaticana, 1930) 492.

9. In the writings of Cyprian of Carthage (e.g., *Epistles* 15:1, 16:2, 17:2, and 15:9) in the early third century, there is evidence that other clergy reconciled by the imposition of hands.

Penance in the Early Church

10. Rahner, *Penance in the Early Church* 130–141 passim.

11. Bernhard Poschmann, *Penance and the Anointing of the Sick,* trans. Francis Courtney (New York: Herder and Herder, 1964) 106.

12. Caesarius of Arles, *Sermon* 56:3. Henry G. Beck gives a thorough presentation of deathbed penance in *The Pastoral Care of Souls in Southeast France During the Sixth Century,* Analecta Gregoriana 51 (Rome: Gregorian University, 1950).

13. Cyrille Vogel, "An Alienated Liturgy," in *Liturgy: Self-Expression of the Church,* Concilium 2, ed. Herman Schmidt (New York: Herder and Herder, 1972) 22.

14. Some authors include the anointing of the sick (see Jas 5:15, "And if he has committed sins, he will be forgiven.") as one of the forms of forgiveness in the apostolic Church. For example, Jean Dauvillier states that the anointing of the sick is the first rite of remission of sins practiced by the Church even before public penance was organized (see Gabriel LeBras, ed., *Histoire du Droit et des Institutions de l'Eglise en Occident,* vol. 2, *Les Temps Apostoliques* (Paris: Sirey, 1970) 559. Some authors such as Origen, Chrysostom, Bede, and Caesarius of Arles, as well as the Council of Trent, see a relationship here to the penitential discipline of the Church. This is an open question, but in the context of the entire passage it would seem that the anointing is a remedy which acts upon the entire person, involving bodily healing for the sake of spiritual life.

15. A. M. LaBonnardiere, "Pénitence et reconciliation des pénitents d'aprés S. Augustin, I," *Revue des Etudes Augustiniennes* 13 (1968) 47–53.

16. The precise nature of the relationship of eucharist to penance remains a matter of theological discussion. See F. Sottocornola, "Les nouveaux rites de la pénitence. Commentaire," *Questions liturgiques* 55 (1974) 104; and J. M. Tillard, "The Bread and the Cup of Reconciliation," in *Sacramental Reconciliation,* Concilium 61, ed. E. Schillebeeckx (New York: Herder and Herder, 1971) 52. Charles Gusmer states that the eucharist is "the paradigm of all sacramental encounters with the living God which result in healing and reconciliation. Penance has but a single specific modality, namely the forgiveness of sin, serious sins after baptism, to which one could also add a secondary tradition which provides for confessions of devotion." See *New Catholic World* 227 (1984), 38.

17. *Origins* 13 (20 October 1983) 324–326.

18. Ibid. 324.

19. Mary Collins, "Culture and Forgiveness," *New Catholic World,* 227 (1984) 12–15.

Catherine Dooley

20. "Reconciliation and Penance in the Mission of the Church," the working document of the Sixth General Assembly, Synod of Bishops, 1983, no. 32.

21. *Origins* 13 (12 January 1984) 514–524.

22. Ibid. 522.

23. The Notre Dame Study of Catholic Parish Life is one of the most recent studies in support of this statement. See *Origins* 15 (13 June 1985) 53–54.

James Dallen

Recent Documents on Penance and Reconciliation

The fear is sometimes voiced that Church officials are retreating from the "spirit of Vatican II." The fear is as vague as the reference point: the nebulous character of the "spirit of the Council" means that it can meander in almost any direction, with the boundaries dependent on the viewer's perspective. Yet in the area of the sacrament of penance and reconciliation there is a clear evidence that the trends apparent throughout the twentieth century and given official status in the Council and in conciliar reforms have, to some extent, been suspended, minimized, or reversed in recent documents.

TWENTIETH-CENTURY TRENDS, THE COUNCIL, AND REFORM
The theology of penance began to depart from the conventional theology of the Counter-Reformation period during the 1920's. It did so in order to retrieve long-forgotten elements of the tradition. Pastoral practice, however, generally maintained the Counter-Reformation outlook until the 1950's. Since then it has tended to be more in line with the dominant theological trends. The major theological and pastoral trends can be loosely grouped into three interrelated categories stated in the form of conclusions which stand in strong contrast to the Counter-Reformation perspective: (1) the sacrament of penance is social and ecclesial in its nature as well as its effects; (2) the sacrament of penance is an act of ecclesial worship; (3) the deepest meaning of penance is conversion,

and this conversion goes beyond ritual to the whole of the Christian life.[1]

With the exception of Pius X's statement on children's confession[2] and Pius XII's defense of the practice of frequent and devotional confession,[3] the papal magisterium prior to Vatican Council II took little note of these theological and pastoral developments. The major development in Church law had been, in the context of the world wars, a broadened understanding of causes excusing from integral confession: first in emergency situations where death threatened and individual confession was impossible,[4] and then, in the 1944 instruction of the Sacred Penitentiary, in other situations of grave urgent necessity proportionate to the requirement of integral confession.[5] The 1944 instruction stated that long deprivation of sacramental grace *and* holy communion because of an inability to observe the Tridentine requirement was an example of such necessity.

The Council did take these theological and pastoral developments into account. It did so by adopting as its own the characteristic perspectives of the contemporary theology of penance and calling for a reform that would more clearly express them.

Nevertheless, several controversies developed during the preparation of the Rite of Penance. The issues were primarily theological and doctrinal, though undoubtedly complicated by political and personal factors. The major source of controversy within the Congregation of Rites (known after 1969 as the Congregation for Divine Worship), and between it and the Congregation for the Doctrine of the Faith, was a tension between the Counter-Reformation perspective and a pastoral perspective comfortable with the twentieth-century trends accepted at Vatican II. The Counter-Reformation perspective held rigidly to Trent's teaching on individual auricular confession and absolution and insisted on retaining the juridical formula of absolution in the current format. The groups promoting broader reform claimed to situate the Tridentine teaching in the context of the broader tradition retrieved in and through the contemporary developments.[6]

The confusion that came to surround the preparation of the reformed Rite of Penance contrasts with the clear criteria officially set for the reform: (1) sin as an offense against both God and the Church; (2) reconciliation with both God and the Church; (3) the whole Church's involvement in sinners' conversion; (4) penance's

James Dallen

value in fostering the Christian life.[7] The Consilium and the responsible committee also agreed that the reformed rite needed to express the communal dimension by providing for communal celebrations, including one with general absolution.

These criteria expressed the dominant trends adopted at the Council. Nevertheless, the Congregation of the Doctrine of the Faith countered. A 1966 letter to the heads of episcopal conferences expressed reservations on the emphasis being given in theological reflection and pastoral action to the social function of reconciliation with the Church. In the opinion of the Congregation this was to the detriment of reconciliation with God and personal confession.[8] After delaying the approval of the draft rite for two and a half years, the Congregation in 1972 issued norms which restricted the reform by setting limits for communal celebrations, particularly those with general absolution.[9] Although these 1972 norms meant the rejection of the 1969 draft rite, they also represented several significant developments, especially the acceptance in principle of the value of communal celebrations and, in particular, of communal celebrations where general absolution was no longer simply a grant of forgiveness after a private act of contrition but was part of an act of communal worship.[10]

In the meantime, the apostolic constitution *Paenitemini*[11] had *1967* reformed penitential discipline with the hope that Christ's call to continual conversion would be heard and answered more clearly and effectively in everyday life. The apostolic constitution emphasized the social dimension of sin, conversion, and penance; in particular it stressed the link between penance and social responsibility. It affirmed that in the sacrament of penance the gift of *metanoia* or conversion, first received in baptism, is restored and strengthened, and insisted that ways beyond the traditional self-restraint of fasting and abstinence must be found to express that gift in everyday forms to benefit the neighbor. *Paenitemini* brings into prominence the penitential orientation of Christian life as ongoing conversion, relates it to baptism and penance, and insists that its social and ecclesial character is evident. Without denying aspects of the late medieval and post-Tridentine understanding of mortification and self-denial, the apostolic constitution places social action alongside personal asceticism as the underlying motive and dynamic of penitential practices (social action may even have an edge over personal asceticism in this document).

Recent Documents

It should be added that failure to implement *Paenitemini* can now be seen as a sure sign, twenty years ago, that the institutionalized structures of the Counter-Reformation Church would not easily be converted and transformed. The document applied implications of Vatican II's acceptance of the trends in contemporary theology. The half-hearted implementation was a hint that under the surface there were still conflicting crosscurrents that would interfere with the reform of penance.

Nevertheless, the reformed ritual which was finally promulgated on 2 December 1973 did follow the main lines of twentieth-century developments, the conciliar teaching, and the criteria set for the reform. This is clear both in its doctrinal introduction and in the form and content of the rites provided.

RECENT DEVELOPMENTS

The tensions that accompanied the preparation of the reformed rite—from its beginning in 1966 to its completion in 1973—seem due primarily to the conflicting perspectives of the Counter-Reformation era and twentieth-century trends which retrieve the broader tradition. Although the understanding of penance found in the documents of Vatican Council II and in the 1973 Rite of Penance does reflect the dominant trends of contemporary theology, the tensions remained and surfaced again in the 1983 Code of Canon Law, the 1983 Synod of Bishops, and the post-synodal exhortation of Pope John Paul II.

The 1983 Code of Canon Law

Pope John Paul II has emphasized that Vatican II, not the previous Code, is the criterion for interpreting the 1983 Code of Canon Law, since it reforms Church law to conform with Vatican II.[12] However, the thoroughness with which this was done in the case of penance can be questioned. In several cases the new Code seems not only to maintain the clerical, aliturgical, and individualistic outlook of the 1917 Code but also to deliberately revert to the Counter-Reformation perspective.[13]

1. *The Social and Ecclesial Character of Penance.* The Code fails to express clearly the social and ecclesial nature of the sacrament. The terminology used is revealing. The definition of the sacrament in canon 959 mentions reconciliation with God and Church—it fails, however, to mention Christ, the Spirit, or God's mercy—and

James Dallen

98

canon 960 does likewise, but the term "reconciliation" does not appear again; instead, the preconciliar "confession" is the preferred term for the sacrament.[14] What goes unmentioned—communal celebrations—is also revealing, although the restrictions placed on general absolution clearly have them in view. The rewording of the 1973 Rite of Penance required by the 1983 Code seems at times deliberately intended to minimize the social and ecclesial dimension of the sacrament and the penitent's participation.[15]

2. Ecclesial Worship. The canons on penance make no mention of worship in connection with the sacrament.[16] By not mentioning communal celebrations, by speaking generally of "confession," and by being concerned over the use of general absolution, the Code returns to a preoccupation with integrity that focuses on past sin and ignores praise and thanksgiving to God. Except for the canons restricting general absolution (961–963), legislation concerning the penitent (987–991) is concerned only with individual confession and absolution. The statement of the priest's ministry in canon 978 reverts to the words of the 1614 ritual, giving priority to the role of judge and ignoring the expanded understanding of this ministry in the Rite of Penance. The required availability of the confessional screen (canon 964, 2), to be used at the penitent's option, does not affect the worship character, although the implicit encouragement of its use does.

On the surface, canon 961 appears to restate earlier norms on general absolution. In fact, it is more restrictive than the 1972 norms of the Congregation for the Doctrine of the Faith (which were incorporated into the 1973 Rite of Penance) since general absolution may not be used except in imminent danger of death when confession is impossible—and when a communal celebration would likewise be impossible[17]—or in another situation of grave necessity; only the diocesan bishop may determine such a situation, but he is given little leeway.[18] Rather than continuing the development that has taken place in penance legislation during this century, a development based on response to pastoral needs, the Code returns to the letter of the 1944 instruction of the Sacred Penitentiary and its criterion, the impossibility of complying with the Tridentine discipline. In fact, it is even more restrictive, considering the theological and liturgical development that has taken place since then and the conciliar preference for communal celebration of sacraments.[19]

3. *Conversion Spirituality*. The canons on penance make no attempt to link the sacrament to continual conversion of life or growing in likeness to Christ. Though canon 987 mentions the penitent's conversion to God, this seems to refer more to the penitent's disposition in the ritual than to conversion of life, as is likewise the case in canon 962. The statement that confession is to precede first communion (canon 915) also seems more concerned with ritual than life.[20] Similarly, the penances assigned seem to be understood more as punishment or satisfaction than as conversion of life (canon 981). The confession of grave sins is required, that of venial sins is recommended (canons 988–989). The call to holiness mentioned in canon 210 seems more concerned with avoidance of sin than with growth in likeness to Christ. Canons 1249–1253, which deal with days of penance, do so without stressing their social, ecclesial, or liturgical character—a significant change from *Paenitemini*, particularly when coupled in practice with a renewed emphasis on the obligatory character of external penitential observances.

The 1983 Synod of Bishops

The 1983 Synod of Bishops indicated even more clearly that the tensions that surrounded the Council and subsequent reforms have not yet been resolved.[21] The working paper for the Synod, "Reconciliation and Penance in the Mission of the Church,"[22] viewed the sacrament within the context of the Church's life and mission in a divided world. To that extent it was in continuity with the pastoral thrust of Vatican II and its social consciousness. But several positions taken in the document—a negative view of the world, personalization and socialization as opposing tendencies, little appreciation of communal celebrations—were more in accord with another orientation. The understanding of the sacrament itself was individualistic, clerical, juridical, and aliturgical.

The same ambivalence was present in the document prepared by the International Theological Commission,[23] though not so obviously, and in the discussions at the Synod. If press reports can be believed and if the published interventions are representative, curial officials (particularly Cardinals Oddi and Ratzinger) presented in the synodal discussions the Counter-Reformation position based

James Dallen

on the teaching of Trent, and diocesan bishops upheld the results of twentieth-century developments adopted by Vatican II and the postconciliar reforms. The disagreement centered on the nature and character of the varied sacramental forms provided in the 1973 Rite of Penance and on norms restricting general absolution and requiring subsequent confession. In his closing address Pope John Paul II hinted at the disagreements and stressed his own conviction about the "profoundly personal character" of the sacrament.[24] Although the propositions developed by the Synod were not published, their themes appear to be in line with the direction approved at Vatican II.[25]

The Post-Synodal Apostolic Exhortation

Pope John Paul II had stated that the decisions of the Synod would have binding juridical authority and serve as the base for a subsequent document.[26] In February 1984 the Council of the General Secretariat of the Synod gave him a draft document developed from the Synod's propositions. The pope's post-synodal apostolic exhortation, *Reconciliatio et paenitentia*, was issued on 2 December 1984.[27] Not surprisingly, there is a close correspondence between the penance canons in the 1983 Code and the papal document.

The exact relationship of the papal document to the synodal draft is unclear. It is stated to be Pope John Paul's response to the Synod and "something produced by the Synod itself." Its contents are said to be from the preliminary documents, the Synod discussions, and the propositions which summarized the Synod's position. Its general lines are said to have been indicated by the Synod secretariat (no. 4). The third part in particular, on the pastoral ministry of penance and reconciliation, is called the contribution of the Synod fathers (no. 23). Nevertheless, though the topics dealt with were discussed in the Synod, the exhortation does not clearly present the positions taken or the relative importance given various themes in the Synod.[28] The issues discussed in the exhortation are clearly Pope John Paul's concerns and are reminiscent of those which surrounded the preparation of the new rite, beginning with the 1966 letter of the Congregation of the Doctrine of the Faith.

Loose structure, occasional repetitiveness, awkward transitions, internal inconsistencies, and some basic shifts in perspective sug-

Recent Documents

gest that the papal document has more than one source, that it probably incorporates and/or revises material from earlier documents, including the draft prepared by the Synod secretariat. A few explanations of what the Synod really meant (by social sin in particular, no. 16), and positions which seem to be at variance from those of the Synod (on general absolution and on outreach to alienated groups in the Church), suggest that the document is more John Paul's than the Synod's and "corrects" views expressed in the Synod and/or the draft document prepared by the Synod secretariat.[29]

It is important to establish the source and nature of the document before analyzing its content. It is clearly a papal, not synodal, document, though it claims to represent the views and teaching of the Synod. It falls in a new category of papal documents, that of a "post-synodal apostolic exhortation." Apostolic exhortations are normally, as the title suggests, exhortative in nature rather than legislative or doctrinal and are addressed to a particular group.[30] In this case, the document is a call to penance and reconciliation (no. 35) addressed to all members of the Church and to those who look to the Church for guidance, with bishops, priests, deacons, and religious singled out (no. 4). Its intention is to present the doctrinal and pastoral message of the Synod (no. 4). Its "indications, suggestions, and directives" (no. 35) break no new ground in doctrine or legislation but rather encourage the members of the Church, particularly the clergy (to whom the exhortation seems actually to be addressed),[31] to receive and implement the norms of the 1983 Code.[32] In terms, then, of its source, nature, and contents, it represents Pope John Paul II's personal pastoral views on the subject and lays no claim to a binding doctrinal or legislative character except insofar as it repeats existing teaching and canonical regulations.

In his closing address at the Synod Pope John Paul made reference to disagreements within the Synod and showed where his sympathies lay when he emphasized the "profoundly personal character" of the sacrament of penance and reconciliation. This emphasis on the personal dimension determines the doctrinal points considered in the document (especially nos. 30–31). These points are those characteristic of Counter-Reformation theology, although the exhortation states that the intent of Vatican II's recommendation for reform was precisely to express these points of

James Dallen

Tridentine doctrine more clearly (no. 30).[33] This emphasis also effects the presentation of the Synod's message[34] and means that the trends of twentieth-century theology, the teaching of Vatican II, and the characteristic features of the 1973 Rite of Penance receive little attention.

1. *The Social and Ecclesial Character of Sin and Penance.* In the apostolic exhortation, the social and ecclesial character of sin, conversion, and the sacrament of penance is present but not prominent. *Social effects* are indicated, but the overall stress on the *personal nature* of sin, conversion, and the sacrament is more in line with Counter-Reformation perspectives than with the twentieth-century trends that shape the teaching of Vatican II and the reformed Rite of Penance.

Human solidarity in sin and the divisive character of sin is treated at length and, in some instances, with interesting creativity.[35] Concern that the sense of sin has been lost is evident. Though the exhortation is unlike other recent documents in preferring "mortal" rather than "grave" sin, it is careful to present sin and its distinctions in terms of relationships (nos. 14–17) in order to maintain sin's religious and covenantal reality (no. 17) and social effects (no. 16). It is dubious about a threefold distinction of sins and cautions against any use of "fundamental option" that changes the traditional concept of mortal sin. While discussing sin in terms of relationships avoids the dangers of an excessively individualistic, objective, and impersonal understanding, in the exhortation these are relationships of one individual to another—humanity seems identified with individuality and social life is something added on. In discussing what "social sin" might mean, the document is concerned to correct any impression given by Synod discussions that would diminish the personal character of sin and responsibility (no. 16) by emphasizing human relationships to the detriment of the individual's relationship with God (nos. 7, 13).[36]

As a consequence, personal conversion is the path to reconciliation (no. 4) and catechesis and the sacraments (especially individual confession) are the Church's principal means of promoting penance and reconciliation (no. 24).[37] Though the Church's social teaching is an element in catechesis on reconciliation (no. 26), the document does not stress changing society and its sinful structures as John Paul's other documents have and as did the Synod.

Recent Documents

Everything seems to take place between the solitary individual and God (no. 31), both in life and in the sacrament. The individual needs to be alone with God (no. 31). Reconciliation with God in the individual's heart does lead to other reconciliation (no. 31), but the reconciled individual is already a "reconciled world" (no. 31). Thus fidelity to Christ, obedience to Church law, and pastoral concern for the rights and duties of the faithful require that individual confession and absolution be the ordinary way to be reconciled (no. 33) because the nature and function of the sacrament is judicial and medicinal (no. 30). The communal celebration with individual confession and absolution is described as equally normal, since it is a ceremonial enhancement of individual confession and absolution, but the need to have a sufficient number of confessors restricts its practical value and use (no. 32). The communal celebration with general confession and absolution is dealt with only in terms of the restrictions on its use (no. 33). Thus the social nature of the sacrament is ultimately identified with the official character of the priestly minister, who is the witness and representative of the ecclesial nature, as well as judge and healer (no. 31), because of the transmitted power to forgive sins (no. 29).

The social and ecclesial dimension, so characteristic of twentieth-century trends and of the reform initiated by Vatican II, is hardly present in the document. The Liturgy Constitution's emphasis on communal celebrations is absent. *Lumen gentium* 11 is cited only to emphasize the certainty of forgiveness through absolution (no. 30) and reworded to indicate that other reconciliations—with self, neighbor, Church, creation—follow from reconciliation with God (nos. 31, 4, 8). The priest, judge and healer, witnesses and represents the ecclesial dimension (no. 31); the document refers to his ritual gestures and the juridical words of absolution to illustrate a point of doctrine (no. 31). That obscuring the social and ecclesial dimension has consequences is merely mentioned (no. 18), while the dangers of exaggerating it are repeatedly warned against.

Because of the preference for the personal character of penance, as articulated at Trent and interpreted in the post-Tridentine manuals, the social and ecclesial dimension is barely noted in the exhortation. That other reconciliations follow from the reconciliation with God—often expressed in terms of divine forgiveness—is evidenced by the inner conversion of heart, interior repentance.

James Dallen

Reconciliation with the Church is thus an effect secondary to divine forgiveness; it is neither simultaneous with it nor is it the *res et sacramentum* of penance. The ecclesial role of the penitent is not singled out for attention. Communal celebrations seem more tolerated than encouraged. Their values are relatively unimportant; the presence of the priest, who has power to forgive sins, expresses the ecclesial dimension of the sacrament, which is judicial and medicinal in its nature and function.

2. Ecclesial Worship. It is not surprising, then, that the document gives little attention to the sacrament as ecclesial worship. The resurgence of sacramental individualism and clericalism and liturgical minimalism is evident here as well as in the permission to use the Tridentine Mass in certain circumstances. In considering the various sacramental forms, the community's presence in the sacramental celebration is relatively unimportant, if not superfluous; the features of the second rite are meaningful but nonessential preparatory ceremonies, so values of the third form go unmentioned, and the (nonsacramental) penitential celebrations are ignored.[38] Only the individual confession of sins is described as a liturgical act (no. 31). The 1973 Rite of Penance is rarely cited, although ritual elements are used to illustrate doctrine[39] or as means to prevent formality and routine.[40] The only liturgical text cited is the concluding juridical statement from the absolution formula.[41]

There is a natural correlation between the social character of penance and the community character of ecclesial worship. Conversely, emphasis on the personal character of penance as judgment and healing necessarily means that community worship receives little attention. Worship, of course, is the community's response of joy and gratitude to God. Since the joy of being saved that is regained through contrition and conversion is regarded as something that most people cannot experience today (no. 31), this, as well as uneasiness with the ecclesial nature of the sacraments, may help explain the lack of attention to worship.

3. Conversion Spirituality. Although the post-synodal apostolic exhortation shows little interest in the social and ecclesial dimension of the sacrament or in its worship character, there is a strong emphasis on penance as conversion and as a basic orientation of the Christian life. This conversion is always, however, an interior personal conversion and reconciliation—perhaps more accurately an individual conversion and reconciliation—which then goes on to have social effects and consequences. The description of the acts of the penitent goes beyond the scholastic contrition, confession, and satisfaction to include rectitude and clarity of conscience; each is integrated within a process of conversion (see no. 31). But whereas the Rite of Penance describes the examination of conscience as comparison with Christ, *Reconciliatio et paenitentia* puts first the interior moral law and evangelical norms proposed by the Church (no. 31). Penance is linked with scriptural *metanoia*, described as an inner change of heart; this leads to changing one's life to be in harmony with the interior change and makes a person's life penitential, a continuous striving for what is better, expressed in deeds and acts of penance (no. 4).[12] Such acts of penance are satisfaction, signs of commitment and mortification countering the wounds and sources of sin and expiating the temporal punishments imposed by the confessor (no. 31).[43] Interior transformation is thus the base for reconciliation with God, self, and others (no. 4). This conversion is heavily dependent on forgiveness of sins in the ritual of confession; its beginning in baptism and continuation in a growing likeness to Christ is often lost sight of.

Although other means of conversion and reconciliation (no. 8; elsewhere referred to as means of forgiveness and grace, no. 32) and varied forms of penance in the past (no. 28) are noted, the frequent celebration of the sacrament of penance seems to be the way to conform more closely to Christ. Interestingly, the ecclesial dimension of sin and penance can be a motive for devotional confession (no. 32), although it was not mentioned as a value of the individual form (no. 32).

Because of this stress on the personal character of penance, Pope John Paul does not present the Church's social teaching as forcefully as he usually does. The Church's mission of reconciliation is presented here primarily in terms of calling and assisting individuals to conversion: to reconcile individuals with God, self, neighbor, and creation (no. 8) by personal conversion (no. 12). The Church's mission is to be a reconciling community (no. 8) by itself being a reconciled community (no. 9)—thus a sacrament (no. 11)— and by prayer, preaching, individual contact, and witness (no. 12).[44] Although this applies to the whole Church, only the pastoral

James Dallen

106

ministry of the hierarchy is given specific attention. The laity are not mentioned, not even in connection with catechesis. Their ecclesial role is apparently little more than acceptance and obedience and their sacramental role merely confession of sins and reception of absolution.

The link between the sacrament and the Church's social mission appears to be only an extrinsic one. The social dimension of Church mission is evident, in the recognition of the social consequences of sin and situations of sin (no. 16)—even though little attention is given to structural sin and work toward structural reform (no. 16; cf. no. 23)—but the ecclesial dimension is most apparent in warning against differences in opinion in the Church (nos. 2, 18) which lead to doctrinal and pastoral pluralism (nos. 2, 5) and in calling for close adherence to the magisterium (nos. 25, 18, 9). The biblical images of the prophet and the Good Samaritan were prominent in the Synod's report to the pope and integrated its reflections on the Church's mission; they are not used in this document.[45] The Synod's call for an outreach to the divorced and remarried, to priests who have left the active ministry, and to all the alienated—in order to be a credible sign of reconciliation—is noted with the statement that this cannot happen sacramentally until the required dispositions are present (no. 34).

CONCLUSION

Twentieth-century trends have emphasized the social and ecclesial dimension of penance, the worship character of the sacrament, and a conversion spirituality that goes beyond ritual to the whole of ecclesial life and mission. These trends countered post-Tridentine views that emphasized penance as an individual encounter with God mediated by the priestly exercise of the power of the keys, a ritual and external means of forgiveness and sanctification. The teaching of Vatican II and the shape of the reforms that followed reflected these contemporary trends and nuanced the teaching of Trent by situating it in a new context.[46]

Tensions, however, accompanied this acceptance of contemporary trends. The Congregation of the Doctrine of the Faith warned against overemphasizing the ecclesial dimension and at all de-emphasizing personal confession; in its 1972 Pastoral Norms it grudgingly accepted communal celebrations in principle but restricted the growing use of general absolution. The 1973 Rite of

Recent Documents

Penance does not always successfully integrate a biblical and contemporary understanding of reconciliation with a medieval and Counter-Reformation understanding of forgiveness, but its intention is clear. On the other hand, the 1983 Code of Canon Law gives primacy to the Tridentine view of the sacrament. Disagreements in the 1983 Synod suggest that diocesan bishops are more likely to be in sympathy with the twentieth-century trends than are curial officials.

Seen against this background, the post-synodal apostolic exhortation of John Paul II must be viewed as no more than part of the continuing discussion of penance. It is not a definitive resolution of tensions. It is, in fact, evidence of how deeply unresolved tensions are in this time of transition. It expresses his personal pastoral concerns and his own misgivings regarding some directions in contemporary theology and pastoral practice, even though these directions were accepted at Vatican II and in the 1973 Rite of Penance and are valued by many bishops and the Church at large. Despite his overall concern with human solidarity and social justice, he gives little attention here to the social and ecclesial dimension of the sacrament, the focus of the Council's reform, or to the sacrament as other than a means for individual forgiveness and personal sanctification. Despite his deep piety, social consciousness, and pastoral dedication, there is little attention to community worship or ecclesial life; conversion is primarily an individual interior transformation, a reconciliation with God which then leads to other reconciliations, though the individual is already a "reconciled world."

Such an individualistic preoccupation when dealing with the sacraments contrasts with Pope John Paul's deep social consciousness in other areas. Such a focus on individual forgiveness is an understandable historical outcome of the early medieval effort to relieve individual anxiety and guilt and of the scholastic emphasis on contrition and interior repentance as mediating divine forgiveness. Nevertheless, it clashes with his realization, expressed elsewhere, that the ecclesiology of Vatican II requires more than these, and that work for peace and justice is a constituent element of the gospel for our time. Such a focus also clashes with other spoken values, for example, that the ministry of salvation is religious and, at the same time, "service to humanity—the person and society—to his and her spiritual and temporal needs, fun-

James Dallen

damental human rights and human and civil life in common.''[47] Integrating sacramental piety and social mission means that it is no longer enough for the sinner to feel forgiven by God: penitents must experience and strive for reconciliation with their brothers and sisters as sign of reconciliation with God because the sacramental symbol only then provides an experience of the reality that it proposes as ultimate goal.

As in the penance controversies of the third century, ecclesiological differences are probably at the root of the contemporary tensions surrounding penance. Then it was a clash between an elitist ecclesiology with a rigorous view of penance discipline and a more flexible, compassionate, and pastorally-minded ecclesiology.[48] Today the differences are less rigid, more of nuance and emphasis, but they are still divisive as the Church, always in need of reform, hesitatingly follows the path of conversion away from the beleaguered institutional model of the Counter-Reformation era.

NOTES

1. I have analyzed the theological development and the 1973 Rite of Penance's relationship to them in much greater detail in ''A Decade of Discussion on the Reform of Penance, 1963–1973: Theological Analysis and Critique'' (S.T.D. diss., The Catholic University of America, 1976). See the chapter ''Theological Foundations of Reconciliation'' for how these three statements contrast with the preceding views and were incorporated into the conciliar documents and the reformed Rite of Penance.

2. *Quam singulari*, Decree of the Sacred Congregation of the Sacraments, 8 August 1910. *Acta Apostolicae Sedis* 2 (1910) 577–583; hereafter cited as AAS.

3. Devotional confession began to be questioned in the 1920's and criticized in the 1930's. Pius XII reacted angrily, asserting the values of devotional confession: ''genuine self-knowledge grows, Christian humility develops, bad habits are corrected, spiritual neglect and lukewarmness are countered, the conscience is purified, the will is strengthened, healthy self-control is gained, and an increase of grace is obtained by the very fact the sacrament is received'' (*Mystici Corporis*, 86; AAS 35 [1943] 235). It was during his pontificate, in the 1950's, that the frequency of confession peaked—and then began to decline.

Recent Documents

4. See *AAS* 7 (1915) 72, 282; 31 (1939) 710–713; 32 (1940) 541.

5. *Instructio circa sacramentalem absolutionem generali modo pluribus impertiendam*, 25 March 1944, *AAS* 36 (1944) 155–156.

6. I have described the reform process in more detail in *The Reconciling Community: The Rite of Penance*, (New York: Pueblo, 1986) 209–215.

7. See *Notitiae* 4 (1968) 183.

8. *Epistula ad venerabiles praesules conferentiarum episcopalium*, *AAS* 58 (1966) 660–661.

9. *Sacramentum paenitentiae*, *AAS* 64 (1972) 501–514.

10. They also extended the possible use of general absolution by requiring only a "grave" rather than a "grave and urgent necessity," by envisioning the situation of necessity as one where penitents were deprived either of communion *or* of sacramental grace, and by permitting priests to give general absolution, under certain circumstances, in situations not foreseen by the bishop. Papal indults in the 1960's had gone further by dispensing from the requirement of subsequent confession.

11. *AAS* 59 (1967) 177–198.

12. In a January 26, 1984, address to the Roman Rota; see *Origins* 13 (1984) 584.

13. For a discussion of penance in the new Code, see Ladislas Orsy, "General Absolution: New Law, Old Traditions, Some Questions," *Theological Studies* 45 (1984) 676–689.

14. This is particularly apparent in the canons of chapter two (regarding the minister), which regularly refer to "hearing confessions" (canons 967–974, 976, 978, 984–986). The canons are obviously concerned with the celebration (or administration) of the sacrament, not the narration of sinfulness (which can be made to anyone). Similar usage is found in canons concerning the penitent (988–991).

15. Rite of Penance, no. 31, for example, uses the plural for "faithful" and the active voice; canon 960 changes this to the singular and the passive voice—the individual passively receives absolution rather than a community being actively involved in reconciling themselves with God and the Church. See *Emendations in the Liturgical Books Following Upon the New Code of Canon Law* (Washington, D.C.: United States Catholic Conference, 1984) 17–20.

16. Canon 2, however, explicitly states that the canons are but incidentally concerned with liturgical law and canon 840, dealing with the sacraments in general, does state that they are acts of worship.

17. Rite of Penance, nos. 64–65 provides a form of emergencies.

James Dallen

18. The 1972 norms—incorporated into the Rite of Penance—were stated positively rather than negatively, gave the bishop wider latitude, and permitted the priest to act in circumstances not foreseen by the bishop.

19. It is important to remember that the 1972 norms were not intended for wartime emergency but the contemporary pastoral situation. The 1973 Rite of Penance, with its well-developed introduction, set higher standards for celebration and its rite with general absolution is clearly not intended for an emergency. For further analysis of this development, see my *The Reconciling Community* 376-378.

20. The "requirement" must, however, be understood in light of canon 988.2: it obliges only children conscious of grave sin.

21. I have examined the 1983 Synod in "Church Authority and the Sacrament of Penance: The Synod of Bishops," *Worship* 58 (1984) 194-214.

22. "Reconciliation and Penance in the Mission of the Church," *Origins* 11 (1982) 565-580.

23. "Penance and Reconciliation," *Origins* 13 (1984) 513-524.

24. *Origins* 13 (1983) 376.

25. For a summary released by the Vatican, see *Origins* 13 (1983) 371-373.

26. *Origins* 13 (1983) 307.

27. The English translation, prepared by the Vatican, was released on 11 December 1984. See *"Reconciliatio et Paenitentia:* On Reconciliation and Penance in the Mission of the Church Today" (Vatican City: Libreria Editrice Vaticana, 1984). The text is also in *Origins* 13 (1984) 432-458. References are to the Vatican edition. I have examined the background and contents of *Reconciliatio et paenitentia* in more detail in "Reconciliatio et Paenitentia: The Postsynodal Apostolic Exhortation," *Worship* 59 (1985) 98-116. For a positive assessment, which sees the exhortation as the summit of conciliar and postconciliar development, see P. Gervais, "L'Exhortation apostolique 'Reconciliatio et Paenitentia,' " *Nouvelle Revue Théologique* 108 (1986) 192-217.

28. See especially the summary of the propositions (*Origins* 13 (1983) 371-373) and the final statement of the Synod (*Origins* 13 (1983) 369-371).

29. The vast majority of references in the exhortation are to scripture (122). Next in number are references to John Paul II's documents and addresses (21); the documents of Vatican II (18); the early fathers, especially Augustine (8); Paul VI (7); Trent and the Rite of Penance (6 each); Thomas Aquinas (4). Synod discussions are frequently referred to but never quoted.

30. Francis G. Morrisey, "The Canonical Significance of Papal and Curial Pronouncements" (Canon Law Society of America, n.d.) 3.

Recent Documents

31. See nos. 26, 29, 31, 33.

32. As did *Veterum sapientia*, John XXIII's 22 February 1962 document on Latin. This, however, was an apostolic constitution, normally the most solemn papal legislative document.

33. Although the manner of presentation shows little influence from contemporary theology, the exhortation does note the polemical context of the Tridentine statements (no. 30). See below, note 46.

34. Thus the Synod is said to have called for an "analysis of a theological, historical, psychological, sociological and juridical character of penance in general and of the Sacrament of Penance in particular" (no. 28). The failure to mention the social and ecclesial character is striking.

35. This has been analyzed in detail by Norbert Rigali, "Human Solidarity and Sin in the Apostolic Exhortation *Reconciliation and Penance*," *Living Light* 21 (1985) 337 344. Rigali sees a notable advance over a previous privatized understanding of sin. While conceding that John Paul's discussion of sin tries to avoid individualism and is more balanced than Trent's, I do not think that the exhortation as a whole is as successful as Vatican II or the Rite of Penance in this regard.

36. The discussion of social sin parallels that in the "Instruction on Certain Aspects of the Theology of Liberation" (*AAS* 76 [1984] 885–889; *Origins* 14 [1984] 193–204.) It should be complemented by the more recent "Instruction on Christian Freedom and Liberation," *Origins* 15 (1986) 713–728.

37. Confession and catechesis were the subjects of curial reports by Cardinals Ratzinger and Oddi. See *Origins* 13 (1983) 331–332, 373–376. The treatment of these subjects in *Reconciliatio et paenitentia* is in line with these reports.

38. The discussion of "reasons which order the celebration or Penance in one of the first two forms and permit the use of the third form" (no. 32–33) indicates only doctrinal, disciplinary, and pastoral reasons for the first two forms (the second is stated to be the same as the first). Values of the third form and reasons permitting its use are not given, only restrictions on its use. The impression is that something from a source document has been omitted.

39. The apostolic exhortation refers to the imposition of hands and the sign of the cross and quotes the juridical words of absolution (not the full form) in no. 31 to highlight the priest's ministry and the certainty of divine forgiveness.

40. This is the reason given for the use of scripture in no. 32, although no. 32 mentions that the word, when listened to together, has greater effect and emphasizes the ecclesial character of conversion and reconciliation.

James Dallen

41. In no. 31. There is also a reference to Eucharistic Prayer III in no. 7.

42. However, no. 26 seems to consider *Paenitemini* as mitigation of discipline rather than stress on personal responsibility for continual conversion.

43. Temporal punishment is here explained in contemporary terms; in no. 17, expiation of temporal punishment is mentioned in traditional terms.

44. The Church here is more sign than sacrament. The document sees the Church's role in responding to humanity's needs (no. 2–3) and social evils (nos. 16, 25) as showing the path to reconciliation through conversion of heart and offering the means for achieving it through the word, prayer, and the sacraments (no. 8). See also nos. 12, 23, 25.

45. See *Origins* 13 (1983) 372. The concepts of evangelization and service to humanity in the 22 March 1986 "Instruction on Christian Freedom and Liberation" parallel these images.

46. Cf. *Reconciliatio et paenitentia,* no. 30, which sees this as a transferral from one time to another and a translation of terms. This classicist sense of history also characterizes the understanding of the historical development of sacramental forms which is mentioned in no. 30. This historical development seems to be regarded as no more than the changing ceremonial context of the priest's exercise of his power to forgive sins.

47. This was most recently expressed in his April 1986 letter to the bishops of Brazil. See *Origins* 16 (1986) 12–15, where the quotation is found on p. 13. Similar perspectives were evident in the 22 March 1986 "Instruction on Christian Freedom and Liberation."

48. See my *The Reconciling Community,* pp. 50–52.

Kathleen Hughes, R.S.C.J.

Reconciliation: Cultural and Christian Perspectives

There are three tasks this paper will try to accomplish. The first, and by far the most difficult, is to describe the ways that people experience and ritualize reconciliation in ordinary life individually, with those around them, and in society at large. I need to propose at the outset, however, that I believe vast numbers of people do not experience reconciliation at all and consequently have nothing to ritualize. We will therefore touch on several sides of this question, examining experiences of both reconciliation and rupture in ordinary daily life. I will devote the major part of my presentation to this first topic.

The second task, after looking at contemporary culture, is to suggest the relationship of these daily life experiences to sacramental rituals.

And the third is to glean whatever insights I can about the way cultural experiences of rupture and reconciliation might influence Christian celebration. I intend to combine parts two and three in brief concluding remarks.

CULTURAL PERSPECTIVES

First, then, cultural perspectives.

How is it possible for any of us to gain enough distance from our culture in order to achieve a "wide-angle" view of contemporary human experience? The lens I have chosen is that of the chroniclers of society, those people who offer us social commentary through anthropological accounts, surveys of opinion, novels, plays, fairy tales, even comedy. These social critics will provide us simply with a variety of snapshots of contemporary life. Arranged as a collage, these snapshots in turn will yield some hints about our present cultural experience of the process of coming to reconciliation.

I begin by describing two rituals: the first an extraordinary ritual of reconciliation; the second, an equally curious contemporary ritual of excommunication. Neither of these rituals are part of our daily experience, yet both may shed light on some of our attitudes and values.

There is a ritual of reconcilation which takes place annually in a delta area of Nigeria among a people known as the Ijaw. One day a year, everyone in the tribe wades into the local river, stands in 3 or 4 feet of water, and lets fly with scornful abuse on one another. Perhaps they have prepared their lists well in advance. Everyone in the river is shouting at each other; perhaps a few are listening, too. Each one hurls insults and accusations as well as mud and water for the grievances and the slights and all the "debris" that has piled up between and among people in the course of the year. This mutual vilification goes on for as long as necessary—maybe for an hour or so—and there may be some humor and teasing; but mostly it is high drama.

When each person has gotten everything off his or her chest (and such an experience is definitely cathartic), all the people duck under the water and are totally submerged. When they come up they bring with them a handful of mud from the riverbed, and walk out to dry land. Near the river there is a large cloth spread on the ground and as each member passes it, he or she throws mud and stone from the river into the cloth. Then they stand around as the designated leader ties the four corners of the cloth into a knot. The cloth is hung between the horns of a goat tethered nearby, and the animal is driven into the bush with the dirt—and the filth and garbage of the year. Only after that can the festivities begin. The accusations are over and if there is anything anyone forgot, it is too late. Nothing from the previous year can ever again be said. There is no redress for what goes on in the river. In the water there is a total leveling, a quite amazing chapter of faults, a ritual purging and the annual beginnings of new life.[1]

I am captivated by this story, an experience of reconciliation and a ritual pattern so foreign to our own experience. But perhaps precisely because it is unusual it helps to highlight a variety of ritual features we need to explore. There is, for example, the ritual pattern repeated year after year, the sheer length of the ceremonies, the layering of ritual elements. There is the emphasis on sin as disruptive of relationships, as essentially social, and thus the need for a prolonged communal ritual of rupture and resolution. There is a fresh start for everyone by mutual agreement, and a great and joyful celebration when the purging is complete. There is an interesting designation of leadership chosen on an *ad hoc* basis, sometimes from the socially unfit, sometimes from those with physical imperfections, either men or women, but chosen often because they are the meek and humble with whom each member, in some measure of weakness, is able to identify.

There are numerous analogues in the literature of Africa; rituals of healing, rituals to settle moral conflicts, rituals of transformation of individuals and of whole societies. What stands out most in such literature is the emphasis on social sin and social rituals of redress and renewal, of regularly recurring patterns, of the completeness of the events because of the time given over to full celebration. Perhaps these patterns are not practices easily transferred in detail—however much it appeals to us to wade into a river with a few of our acquaintances and confess *their* sins—but still cultural patterns not our own can be instructive and might stretch our categories and add to our repertoire.[2]

What of a ritual closer to home? The next story I want to relate is not about reconciliation but its opposite, excommunication. I find the questions that this ritual has raised for me to be very disturbing. Let me tell the story and then raise the questions.

This is a hypothetical account of a very real practice in this country in this century by the Amish community. We shall call our character Joseph, a boy who grew up in a very strict Amish home, under the guidance of orthodox parents. Joseph was baptized at the age of twenty. Three years later, he was formally excommunicated and shunned. Charges laid against Joseph included: attending a revival meeting, associating with excommunicated persons, purchasing an automobile, and attending a Mennonite church. Joseph was excommunicated with the counsel of the whole assembly and was so informed in their presence.

At home the young man was shunned: he could no longer eat at the family table, but had to eat separately, either with the younger children, or after the baptized persons were finished eating. Joseph was urged to mend his ways, to make good his baptismal promise. His normal work relations and conversations were strained. When friends came to his home for conversation, Joseph's parents headed them off at the gate and turned them away. Soon his father and mother asked him to leave home so that they could continue to take communion. They were also

Kathleen Hughes

afraid the younger members of the family would be led astray. Joseph was no longer welcome.

The excommunication service itself is a painful and sober procedure as the following description attests:

> The excommunication of members was an awful and solemn procedure. The members to be expelled had been notified in advance and were present. An air of tenseness filled the house. Sad-faced women wept quietly; stern men sat with faces drawn. The bishop arose; with trembling voice and with tears on his cheek he announced that the guilty parties had confessed their sins, that they were cast off from the fellowship of the church and committed to the devil and all his angels. He cautioned all the members to exercise shunning rigorously.[3]

Excommunication among the Amish is generally for life unless there is repentance on the part of the individual. Shunning is an effective means of dispensing with the offender. The act of shunning in all social relations minimizes the threat of this person to other members of the community and to the community as a whole.[4]

This is a most extraordinary ritual in the twentieth century. In our own church history, of course, we have known the practice of public canonical penance and severe forms of excommunication which prevailed from the third to the sixth century. But public canonical penance and the excommunication it implied were very rare; they were harsh, they were arduous, and they fell by the wayside.

Or did they? That's the question I want to raise. The story of Joseph got under my skin. I had every intention of focusing on experience and celebrations of reconciliation until "Joseph" prompted me to wonder whether it might not be "the practice of shunning" which has emptied our churches of penitents these last several years. Joseph opened my eyes to another reality.

In his intervention at the 1983 Synod on reconciliation Archbishop John Roach discussed the chronic rejection and alienation felt by some people in our community which they might easily ascribe to the Church or even to God, namely those who are minorities because of race, low income, psychological and physiological problems, minimal social skills, disordered family environments, and other factors which separate them from society's mainstream. He says:

Such people sometimes carry a diffused sense of guilt, stemming not from personal sin but from judgments rendered by the majority culture. Some cultures, for example, subtly regard personal prosperity and social success as signs of God's favor. The absence of such achievements can impose unrealistic burdens of guilt and a sense of divine rejection on numbers of people. Pastors must attempt to dispel such guilt and self-depreciation, for it is unrelated to personal sin. The pastor's acceptance of all penitents as sinners like himself is essential in reconciling the socially alienated Catholic.[5]

Is it possible that the Church communicates, in ways that are sometimes subtle and sometimes not so subtle, that we are a community of the saved and that broken people have no home with us? In the fairy tale *The Wizard of Oz*, there is a chapter which describes a perfect kingdom where there is no room for broken people or mended lives. Dorothy, the Woodman, the Scarecrow and the Lion come upon a country made entirely of china, a country that they must cross to continue their journey. All the inhabitants shy away from Dorothy and her friends—shun them, in fact—afraid of being damaged by contact. As the princess of the china kingdom says, "One is never so pretty after being mended."[6]

It is curious that they knock over the china church in their haste to escape, and the church smashes into a million pieces. The quartet discovers that everything is brittle in this perfect china city, and most fragile of all is the perfect china church. Breathing a sigh of relief, the Scarecrow speaks for them all: "I am thankful I am made of straw and cannot be easily damaged. There are worse things in the world than being a Scarecrow."[7]

There are, indeed, worse things in the world than being a scarecrow. There are worse things in the world than being broken and mended and broken yet again. There are worse things, of course, unless we live in a society or a church which only has room for the perfect and practices "shunning" as a matter of course.

It may be that "shunning" has been going on in our preoccupation with number and species, and with the sixth and the ninth commandments. It may be that we communicate that the community embraces only certain of its members, members who have the good fortune to remain in stable marriages, members who abide by Western cultural values, members who are codifiable in canon law, members whose religious constitutions are approved.

Kathleen Hughes

118

In whatever measure we communicate to one another that there is a hierarchy among us because of vocation, sex, values, lifestyle, we suggest that the shadow of public canonical penance remains, although it is off the books. In whatever measure there is a lack of equality in the community, and a less than enthusiastic welcome at the eucharistic table, we participate in the ritual of shunning.

But the difficulty is this: there can be no reconciliation until there is recognition of need, of rupture, of alienation, of sin, of being drawn to conversion and a new life. If you are a member of the perfect society you have no need of conversion and little need for adequate rituals to express healing. Who needs healing if you aren't broken? How difficult it is to experience conversion when numbers of people feel they do not need it. How difficult it is to stand in need of the mercy of God if some in the community think they are able to define it and mete it out. Reconciliation cannot happen in a community where the majority believe that they don't need it and that the minority don't deserve it. Shunning follows logically from such a posture.

Graham Greene's *The Heart of the Matter*, a morality play set in West Africa during World War II, expresses how much of life is a posturing and describes the need to see through such pretensions and to live without disguises. Major Scobie, stationed in a remote backwater, wonders to himself:

> Why do I love this place so much? Is it because here human nature hasn't had time to disguise itself? Nobody here could ever talk about a heaven on earth. Heaven remained rigidly fixed in its proper place on the other side of death, and on this side flourished the injustices, the cruelties, the meannesses, that elsewhere people so cleverly hushed up. Here you could love human beings nearly as God loved them, knowing the worst: you didn't love a pose, a pretty dress, a sentiment artfully assumed.[8]

Scobie loved the place and the people as they were, offering this advice: "You'd forgive most things if you knew the facts."[9]

But Scobie, who believed in God's mercy and love for everyone else, could not believe in it for himself. Torn between fidelity to his wife and love of his mistress, Scobie commits suicide. Greene gives the conversation between the righteous widow and the weary priest. Mrs. Scobie begins:

> "He was a bad Catholic."
>
> "That's the silliest phrase in common use," Father Rank said.

Perspectives

"And at the end, this—horror. He must have known that he was damning himself."

"Yes, he knew that all right. He never had any trust in mercy—except for other people."

"It's no good even praying . . ."

Father Rank clapped the cover of the diary to and said, furiously, "For goodness sake, Mrs. Scobie, don't imagine you—or I—know a thing about God's mercy."

"The Church says . . ."

"I know the Church says. The Church knows all the rules. But it doesn't know what goes on in a single human heart."[10]

Scobie's inability, faced with the facts, to forgive himself or to believe in God's mercy is matched by William Kennedy's character Francis in the novel *Billy Phelan's Greatest Game*. Francis holds himself responsible for the accidental death of his child. As the child's mother explains to the other children years later:

> He had just come home after the car barns and a few jars at the saloon, and he wasn't no different from the way he was a thousand other nights, except what he did was different, and that made him a dead man his whole life. He's the one now that's got to forgive himself, not me, not us. I knew you'd never forgive him because you didn't understand such things and how much he loved you and Gerald and loved me in his way, and it was a funny way, I admit that, since he kept going off to play baseball. But he always came back. . . .
>
> Sweet Jesus, I never thought he'd come back and haunt you both with it, and that's why I'm telling you this. Because when a good man dies, it's reason to weep, and he died that day and we wept and he went away and buried himself and he's dead now, dead and can't be resurrected. So don't hate him and don't worry him and try to understand that not everything that happens on this earth has a reason behind it that we can find in the prayer book. Not even the priests have answers for things like this. It's a mystery we can't solve any more than we can solve the meaning of the stars. Let the man be, for the love of the sweet infant Jesus, let the man be.[11]

Without forgiveness Francis, though alive, had died as surely as Major Scobie. Perhaps the heart of the matter is this: just as we are given life daily, so we need to be forgiven into new life daily.

Kathleen Hughes

120

The playwright, Herb Gardner, captures the dailiness of our need to forgive and be forgiven in his work, *A Thousand Clowns*, in a passage which is both poignant and funny. It is the second act, and Murray is walking down the street rehearsing how he is going to apologize to a friend he is about to meet. This is what happens in Murray's own words:

> I shall now leave you breathless with the strange and wondrous tale of this sturdy lad's adventures today in downtown Oz. Picture, if you will, me. I am walking on East Fifty-First Street an hour ago, and I decided to construct and develop a really decorative, general-all-purpose apology. Not complicated, just the words "I am sorry," said with a little style. (Sorry for what? you ask.) Anything. For being late, early, stupid, asleep, silly, alive. Well, y'know when you're walking down the street talking to yourself how sometimes you suddenly say a coupla words out loud? So I said, "I'm sorry," and this fella, complete stranger, he looks up a second and says, "That's all right, Mac," and goes right on.
>
> He automatically forgave me. I communicated. Five-o'clock rush-hour in midtown you could say, "Sir, I believe your hair is on fire," and they wouldn't hear you. So I decided to test the whole thing out scientifically, I stayed right there on the corner of Fifty-first and Lex for a while, just saying "I'm sorry" to everybody that went by.
>
> (Abjectly) "Oh, I'm so sorry, sir . . ."
>
> (Slowly, quaveringly) "I'm terribly sorry, madam . . ."
>
> (Warmly) "Say there, miss, I'm sorry."
>
> Of course, some people just gave me a funny look, but I swear, seventy-five percent of them *forgave* me.
>
> "Forget it, buddy" . . .
>
> "That's O.K., really."
>
> Two ladies forgave me in unison, one fella forgave me from a passing car, and one guy forgave me for his dog. "Poofer forgives the nice man, don't you, Poofer?"
>
> It was fabulous. I had tapped some vast reservoir. Something had happened to all of them for which they felt *some*body should apologize. If you went up to people on the street and offered them money, they'd refuse it. But everybody accepts apology immediately. It is the most negotiable currency. I said to them, "I am sorry." And they were all so generous, so kind. You could give 'em

Perspectives

love and it wouldn't be accepted half as graciously, as unquestioningly.

I could run up on the roof right now and holler, "I am sorry," and half a million people would holler right back, "That's O.K., just see that you don't do it again!"[12]

Why is it this story of Murray is so appealing? Perhaps the playwright is correct in suspecting that we have each experienced some rupture, not of our making, for which we long to hear an apology. Perhaps the author hints that all of us, at one time or another, have been the minority to some other majority. All of us have experienced "shunning" in one form or another.

Yet perhaps it is Murray's extraordinary presence to others and his becoming vulnerable there on the street corner in Manhattan that touches us most. It is tantamount to wading into the river and, in the presence of all of the people, choosing to accuse only oneself.

Bette Midler describes the flip-side of the character of Murray. She hopes, whether in the river or out, to remain in disguise. She says:

I was walking forty-second street and this amazing thing happened to me. It was July. It was about 89 degrees. It was hot, hot for New York, you know, and I was walking East and this humongous person was coming west and she had this big blue house dress on papered all over with white—with little white daisies, you know. She was almost bald, but sitting on top of her head, forehead you know, on her forehead was this fried egg, which I thought was really unusual because in New York City the ladies with the fried eggs on their heads don't generally come out until September or October. But here was this lady, this demented lady with a fried egg on her head in the middle of July—Oh God what a sight, and ever, ever since I saw that lady not one day goes by that I don't think of her and I say to myself, Oh God, don't let me wake up tomorrow and want to put a fried egg on my head. Oh God! Then I say, real fast, I say, Oh God . . . if by chance I should wind up with a fried egg on my head—cuz sometimes you can't help those things, you know,—*You can't*, I say to myself, don't let anybody notice, and then I say real fast after that, if they do notice, that I'm carrying something that's—that's not quite right, and they want to talk about it, let 'em talk about it, but don't let 'em talk so I can hear—I don't want to hear it. Because the truth about fried eggs, you can call it a fried egg, you can call it anything you like, but

Kathleen Hughes

everybody gets one. Some people wear 'em on the outside. Some people—they wear them on the inside.[13]

Now let's get very concrete about "fried eggs." How do people talk about their experience of sin and of holiness, of betrayal and forgiveness, of brokenness and weakness and need and the mediation of God's grace through daily events? We've heard already from Scobie and Murray, from Francis and Father Rank and Bette Midler, but what of ordinary folk? Is there the same convergence of brokenness, of brittle lives in china churches, of posturing and disguises, of daily death, of a constant and insatiable need for forgiveness? Is there the same longing, on page after page of the lives we ordinary folk are writing, for the experience of reconciliation?

A number of years ago staff members of the Notre Dame Center for Pastoral Liturgy conducted a series of dialogues to attempt to discover how ordinary people of today talked about God in their lives.[14] An important finding was that brokenness and healing were focal religious experiences. When asked to identify God's presence in their lives, a significant number of participants had prefaced their remarks by recounting an experience of isolation, lack of identity, illness, a hurting relationship, nonacceptance, need for reconciliation, painful decisions, and so on. They then related how, through these experiences, they had known God's touch and presence. Here are some excerpts from their testimony:

> After the death of my child I felt surrounded by the love of my friends; everyone who came took some grief and replaced it with peace;
>
> At one time the sense of my own inadequacy almost swallowed me up and then someone said to me: "you have been a sign of faith to me";
>
> Reconciliation unbinds and frees people; I forgave my father; "I have forgiven you and I love you" I said and I hugged him; he's now smiling and he's free; forgiveness is so essential;
>
> God's presence is not in a building; we only know him and share him in experience with other people;
>
> I had an alcoholic father and when I was younger I hated him for it and hated myself for hating him; I was so guilty all of the time; at age 17 I was able to understand and forgive him and then forgive myself—it was a real healing;

Perspectives

I have a friend with whom I can bare all, everything both good and bad; she is a healing presence to me like the sacrament of Penance;

How important it is to share our pain, to realize that I'm not different or unique; we all share the same problems, struggles, wounds, headaches, hang-ups, weaknesses—and we need help on the way;

I was the perfectionist, Mrs. Clean; I was so uptight and nervous, no fun, always proving myself, pretending, impressing others and having no time for them; but closing minds and hearts to the people around us denies God's entry into the world—that was my blessed revelation; I feel released from the need to live up to images; I'm free to be;

Someone has to be the absorber of the violence; I remember living with my grandparents and they were not close; they argued and there was sometimes violence; there was no love expressed between them, no touch in our family; I decided I would be the absorber of the violence; I shed many tears alone and kept it all inside; a friend's mother became mother to me and loved me into life;

Healing is a long slow process which involves support, tolerance, acceptance, breakthrough, understanding, friends, people-love, hugs, gestures, conversation;

When our son ran away, three persons had the courage to say: "we know you have trouble, is there something we can do?" You know there wasn't anything they could do but sit with us in our grief. It took courage to come; why are we so afraid to reach out that way just to be with and for each other;

I agonize over my mission experience with the Indians when I realize I helped to deny their culture; I was the representative of the rubricized Church; they had to do it my way; it was all so oppressive;

After I had moved I was so alone; I had no roots—it was a real loss of identity; slowly the forming of new friendships restored me with a sense of confidence again;

We need first to learn to love ourselves; yet, that is intertwined with knowing we are loved and cared for as who we are;

Sometimes the expectations of others are an insupportable burden;

Healing is needed when we know ourselves to be responsible and at the same time helpless, in different forms of sickness, in the midst of misunderstanding, in coping with death; healing comes from people being there, sharing feelings, helping, letting go;

We often put people in boxes and don't appreciate them or allow them to change; we say: "You know what so and so is like" even if

Kathleen Hughes

so and so hasn't been like that for years; we sometimes set ourselves up as judges rather than forgiving healers;

For me the phone is a real symbol; I have a ministry of the tele-
phone, calling friends, asking how they are, willing to listen, bringing joy or consolation—I think you could call that a ministry of
healing; (the other day I talked forty-five minutes on one call which
was a wrong number).[15]

These testimonies are the manifold ways that men and women
identified their "fried eggs": limitations, alienation, suffering,
pain, death, hurting, aching, disintegration, broken self, burdens,
guilt, denial, rejection, indifference, darkness, doubt, being out of
touch, grief, violence, inadequacy, lack of peace, failure, neglect,
misunderstandings, helplessness, false values, struggles, defeats,
anxieties, pretending, and certainly not least, sin. At the same
time, their words give evidence of the experience of reconciliation:
healing, patient and constant dialogue, presence, encouragement,
acceptance, overcoming, care, forgiveness, understanding, unbinding, freeing, release, breakthrough, unmasking, repairing what is
broken, process, conversion, letting go, helping, being with, journey, time.

Let me offer a brief summary of the results of these dialogues.
The data gathered in the Notre Dame study suggests an understanding of sin, both in itself and in its consequences, as an experience of inner division, turmoil and conflict. The experience of
sin as alienation from others is no less profound an experience.
This is consistently mirrored in the naming of broken relationships; hate, rejection, indifference, violence, pretending, neglect,
alienation, aloneness, being out of touch—all of them constituting
the many forms of death which were experienced. Perhaps the
word "sin" was infrequently employed, but the reality of sin was
a universal reference. Refusal to love, to be present, to encourage,
to care, to heal, causes rupture within and without. It is death.

In face of this experience of rupture in human life, how does
reconciliation happen? It does not happen easily, or quickly, but is
a long process. The participants in the Notre Dame study named
it journey, being on the way, long torturous struggle, overcoming,
waiting, conversion and continuous reconversion. The participants
spoke of their lives in dynamic terms, as a continuous process of
becoming, a continuous movement from death to life, from bondage to freedom.

Perspectives

Perhaps the primary symbol of reconciliation for these participants is that of community. Reconciliation is not only a process. It is a mediated process. We heard both in their words and in the previous series of stories a common desire for reconciliation in the midst of the ruptures which mark our lives. There is a yearning for healing from pain and grief, from a pervasive sense of loneliness, from daily anxiety, from the experience of rejection, from a personal sense of inadequacy, from self-pity, from the manifold ways that sin dominates human life. Frequently it is this very awareness of personal weakness and need which opens us to the needs of those around us. As the participants noted, they had sometimes been able to reach out and heal one another because they had been there themselves, which empowered them to reach out to others, to be absorbers of violence, to say the liberating word. In examining this data for patterns and meaning, one might be reminded of the story of Lazarus as an image of the community as mediating *locus.* Jesus calls Lazarus forth from death to life, but it is the community which rolls away the stone and the community which is charged with unbinding him.

Did these participants think of themselves as channels of grace? Surely not in those words. But they did describe themselves as instrumental in mediating God's gracious presence to others. And other persons were for them graced presence which broke the spell of death and summoned them to life.

But in the end, what is quite startling in all of the data gathered during this study is one significant omission. The sacrament of penance was mentioned only once and that by way of analogy. What, then, is the relationship between these daily life experiences and the sacramental rites of the Church?

CONCLUSION: SHAPING AN AGENDA

That question, finally, brings us to a few conclusions and a few insights about the way cultural experiences of rupture and reconciliation might influence Christian celebration.

Where is Christian sacrament in all that we have been discussing? It all depends, of course, on your definition of "sacrament." I believe that the sacrament of reconciliation extends over time in the midst of the community, all of whom are sinners in need of forgiveness and reconciliation yet also called to be ambassadors of Christ's healing and peace. Reconciliation is a process and a way

Kathleen Hughes

of life, and as such, the sacrament may be understood to be coextensive with the journey of conversion which is our life. The various phases of the process, the various moments on the journey, participate in the reality of sacrament. That suggests for our developing agenda that we need to help one another recognize and name as sacramental those genuine experiences of reconciliation in daily life.[16]

Second, there are many ministers of reconciliation that we encounter in our lives, only some of whom are ordained to that ministry in the Church. All of us have been entrusted with the ministry of reconciliation in our world. We experience certain persons among us, both women and men, as ambassadors of reconciliation because of the evident wisdom, grace, and holiness of their lives, and because they acknowledge their own sinfulness and are able to welcome other sinners. The Christian community should not be denied the gift and grace of these "soul friends" in our midst. That suggests for our agenda that we must stop driving a wedge between the reconciling ministry of the ordained and the laity, and instead recognize and rejoice in the many ways Christ's healing presence is celebrated in the community.

Third, in whatever ways we participate in that subtle form of excommunication by the shunning of one another, we need to stop it, lest we lose all credibility as God's ambassadors. When I heard all the brouhaha over whose feet could be washed this year in Pittsburgh, it reminded me of the first and only time the mandatum made sense to me. It was at Notre Dame, in Sacred Heart Church, where the ceremonies are perfect all of the time—but even more so during the high holy days of the Triduum. As the twelve to be washed approached the altar, a derelict staggered down a side aisle and took his place on the steps of the sanctuary. Time stopped; people froze in their tracks—except for one deacon who went over to the man and helped him take off his shoes. For our agenda: do we have room for derelicts? how about for people with their "fried egg" on the outside? Let us shatter the dainty china church once and for all, and make room for broken people.

Fourth, rituals need to develop over time. Rituals are a complex interplay of many elements and they take root in a culture, not by decree from on high, but because they are able to express the life and religious experience of those for whom they are celebrated. Many reasons have been put forward to explain why the sacrament of reconciliation is disappearing. I suggest for our continuing agenda that we shift the focus of our concern from the frequency with which people approach the sacrament, to the depth of their experience once there. T. S. Eliot has a line that is perfect in this instance: "We had the experience but missed the meaning." Let us shift our concern to that of preventing people from celebrating reconciliation prematurely, lest they miss its meaning.

Finally, I believe genuine conversion and reconciliation is a celebration of God and grace and future, not of me and sin and past. Reconciliation is the experience of a God who rescues me and heals me and grants me new life. Mrs. Scobie wanted to know from Father Rank if he knew her husband very well. "Not well," he said, "only the unimportant part, the sins. Nobody speaks of their virtues." What a wonderful new focus that could be for the celebration of reconciliation and the promotion of holiness as a way of life.

The reform of reconciliation has only just begun. The questions and the ideas that we need in order to shape our agenda for the future cannot help but surface in our imaginations if we continue to listen to the Scobies and the Murrays and all the ordinary folk in this world who long to know Christ's pardon and peace.[17]

NOTES

1. I received this oral history from Anthony Gittins, an anthropologist and missiologist on the faculty of the Catholic Theological Union at Chicago, who worked for a number of years in Africa.

2. For further reading in the area of healing rituals and rituals of transformation from an anthropological perspective, see: Richard Katz, *Boiling Energy: Community Healing Among the Kalahari Kung* (Cambridge: Harvard University Press, 1982); Ari Kiev, ed., *Magic, Faith and Healing* (New York: The Free Press, 1962); Benjamin C. Ray, *African Religious: Symbol, Ritual, and Community* (Englewood Cliffs: Prentice-Hall, Inc, 1976).

3. John Umble, "The Amish Mennonites of Union County, Pennsylvania," *Mennonite Quarterly Review* (April, 1933) 92.

4. "The Punishment of the Disobedient" in John A. Hostetler, *Amish Society* (Baltimore: The Johns Hopkins University Press, 1963/1968) 62–65.

Kathleen Hughes

5. John R. Roach, "Are Christians Free?" in Synod of Bishops, *Penance and Reconciliation in the Mission of the Church* (Washington: National Conference of Catholic Bishops, 1984) 31–32. For another approach to cultural perspectives on reconciliation, the various speeches of this Synod, particularly those from bishops of Third World countries are insightful. Many of these speeches are published in issues of *Origins* from the Fall of 1983.

6. "The Dainty China Country," in L. Frank Baum, *The Wizard of Oz* (New York: Grosset and Dunlap, 1900/1963) 163.

7. Ibid. 167.

8. Graham Greene, *The Heart of the Matter* (New York: Bantam Books, 1948/1967) 26.

9. Ibid.

10. Ibid. 243–244.

11. William Kennedy, *Billy Phelan's Greatest Game* (New York: Penguin Books, 1983), 248–250.

12. Herb Gardner, *A Thousand Clowns* in *Best American Plays*, 5th series, 1957–1963 (New York: Crown Publishers, Inc., 1963) 447.

13. Bette Midler, from the show *Live at Last*, 1977. Tape available from Atlantic Recording Corporation, 75 Rockefeller Plaza, New York, 10019.

14. The source of the data offered in this section of the paper is a research project sponsored by the Murphy Center for Liturgical Research (now: Center for Pastoral Liturgy) at the University of Notre Dame. It was stated in the *Third Instruction on the Proper Implementation of the Constitution on the Sacred Liturgy* that liturgical renewal need be studied in both its theoretical and its practical aspects so that liturgy may become for the Christian community a living and meaningful experience. It was the question of what constituted a living and meaningful experience of worship which led the Center to undertake the study named "Partners in Dialogue." For further information on the "Partners in Dialogue" program, methodology, and interpretation, see *Ritual Signs, Liturgical Celebrations, and the Faith of Contemporary North Americans,* May 1976, and *Ritual Signs, Liturgical Celebrations, and the Faith of Contemporary U.S. Catholics,* December 1976. Both of these reports are unpublished materials prepared by the staff of the Center. In addition, L. Kenneth Hannon used the data gathered in this study as the focus of his dissertation, *The Rooting of Ritual: A Study of the Liturgical Reform as Exemplified by a Select U.S. Population* (University of Notre Dame, 1985).

15. All excerpts presented here are from verbatim notes taken during the dialogue phase of the "Partners in Dialogue" research.

Perspectives

16. See Mark Searle, "Faith and Sacraments in the Conversion Process," in *Conversion and the Catechumenate,* ed. Robert Duggan (New York: Paulist Press, 1984) 64–84.

17. For further reading: Kevin Condon, "The Sense of Sin," *Irish Theological Quarterly* 49 (1982) 155–171; Paul DeClerck, "Celebrating Penance or Reconciliation," *Clergy Review* 68 (1983) 310–321; Everett Diederich, "Recovering the Interior Moments of Christian Repentance," *Review for Religious* 43 (1984) 688–698; Catherine Dooley, "Developments of the Practice of Devotional Confession," *Questions Liturgiques* 64 (1983) 89–113; Peter Fink, "Investigating the Sacrament of Penance: An Experiment in Sacramental Theology," *Worship* 54 (1980) 206–220; John Gilbert, "The Reconciliation Service: A Reflection on Pastoral Experience as a Theological Source," *Worship* 59 (1985) 59–65; Robert Hater, "Sin and Reconciliation: Changing Attitudes in the Catholic Church," *Worship* 59 (1985) 18–31; Monica Hellwig, "Sin and Sacramental Reconciliation," *The Way* 24 (1984) 217–223, 305–311; Kathleen Hughes, "Liturgical Reconciliation and Spiritual Growth," *Spirituality Today* 30 (1978) 211–224; Kevin McNamara, "Penance: Sacrament of Reconciliation," *The Furrow* 36 (1985) 3–17; Ladislas Orsy, "General Absolution: New Law, Old Traditions, Some Questions," *Theological Studies* 45 (1984) 676–689; Clare Wagner, "Reconciliation: Can We Live Without It?" *Spirituality Today* 36 (1984) 355–364.

Kathleen Hughes

Robert J. Kennedy

The Rite for Reconciliation of Individual Penitents: Celebration of the Church

This paper is about what we already have in the Rite for Reconciliation of Individual Penitents, not what we would like to have. I puzzle (I am sure many pastoral ministers and theologians do) about the problems, ambiguities, contradictions, and form of this rite in trying to implement its practice by both confessors and penitents. This rite will be with us for a while, however—certainly during the time it will take us to rediscover the value of the sacrament of penance at the practical level of Church practice. And so we need to put the best face on the rite as we can—or better, to mine its riches—to see how it can serve the Church's celebration of reconciliation.

IS IT LITURGY?

The rite of individual penance as we have practiced it in recent centuries, and to a large extent still do practice it, has lost its ecclesial connection; that is, it has become a highly individualized, private practice. The history of penance reveals some reasons for this: the individual form itself has its roots in the private practices of manifestation of conscience and spiritual direction; the understandings of sin, of the requirements for forgiveness and reconciliation, and of the ministry of reconciliation focused progressively more on the individual acts of the penitent and the priest; and the emphasis on the juridical side of penance over the last four centuries minimized the liturgical, and therefore the social, dimensions.[1] In fact, we have become so removed from the social and ecclesial connections of the individual form of penance that we must ask whether the rite is liturgy at all.

Liturgy, in the Christian context, is an act of the Church, the community of believers, the Body of Christ, which employs ritual gestures, symbols, and stories of faith in order to praise God for the wonderful works done for us in Christ and to be renewed in the continuation of that saving presence and activity of grace. Can individual penance be understood in terms of this (working) definition?

Penance as an act of the Church. Although it is clearly a minimal assembly of faith ("where two or three are gathered"), the encounter of penitent and priest in individual penance constitutes a worshiping community in which Christ is present. The Introduction and texts of the Rite of Penance[2] clearly affirm that the celebration of this rite is "always" a liturgical act of the Church (nos. 7, 8, 11). They describe the ecclesial, and especially baptismal, context of penance (nos. 2, 4–8, 44), and declare that the goal of reconciliation is a renewed community at the eucharist (no. 6d). The absolution formula asks God to grant pardon and peace "through the ministry of the Church" (no. 46).

In addition, the ministries of reconciliation are presented in their relation to the action of the Church. The first ministry named, in fact, is the ministry of the "whole Church, as a priestly people, [which] acts in different ways in the work of reconciliation which has been entrusted to it by the Lord" (no. 8, cf. no. 5). The work of reconciling sinners is clearly a community effort. Of the second-named ministry of priest-confessors the Introduction says that they "act in communion with the bishop and share in his power and office of regulating the penitential discipline," and that "the competent minister of the sacrament of penance is a priest who has the faculty to absolve in accordance with canon law" (no. 9). In light of our human and gospel understanding of the reconciling act, we may groan at these hierarchical connections and questionable criterion for competency. But it means that the priest-confessor is accepted as a minister of the local church and acts in its name—a radically ecclesial connection and function. We will explore the dimensions of this more fully below. The third-named ministry/office of penance is the penitent, who is described as sharing in the actions of the sacrament and celebrating it with the priest (no. 11). This "concelebration," as already noted, makes for a worshiping community and enables the Church to renew itself. Even in an unreconciled state, the penitent ministers to the Church by calling it to be continually converted to the Lord, and to offer the Lord's forgiveness and mercy.

Penance as ritual/symbol. The reconciliation celebrated in individual penance is already symbolized in the gathering, the encounter of the Church's minister and the penitent moving toward each

Robert J. Kennedy

other (no. 16). The sign of the cross at both the beginning of the rite and in the absolution recall the baptismal life of grace and the Trinitarian nature of reconciliation (nos. 5, 6d, 16, 19). The reading of the word, the confession of sins, and its reception by the Church's minister are the symbolic dialogue of God, the Church, and the penitent (nos. 17–18), which is continued and deepened in the prayer of the penitent and the absolution with the imposition of hands (no. 19). This polyvalent gesture of imposing hands offers the penitent renewed incorporation in the faith community and recommissions him or her as an ambassador for Christ's sake (2 Cor 5:20). The dismissal sends the reconciled one out upon this mission, as well as encouraging continued personal conversion (no. 20). This rich repertoire of symbolic language—gathering, signing, dialogue, touching and sending forth—while basic to any liturgical celebration, contains and expresses the mystery of reconciliation in which those ''who were once far off have been brought near'' by the cross of Christ (see Eph 2:13).

Penance as praise and prayer. There are specific times of prayer in the individual rite such as the prayer of the penitent after confessing and the brief proclamation of praise at the end (nn. 19/45, 20/47). There is also room for spontaneous prayer on the part of either the priest or the penitent or both, and for silent prayer, especially after the reading of God's Word. But apart from these particular instances within the rite, the whole context of the rite is prayer, an encounter in love with the merciful God who earnestly desires the integrity of heart and unity of spirit of all people. The root meaning of the term ''confession'' speaks of grateful acknowledgement of God, the humble response of unworthy creatures who have discovered that their Creator's mercy endures forever. So at heart penance magnifies in a unique way God's merciful act of reconciling us and the whole world in Christ by proclaiming its faith in that mystery with gratitude, and by renewing the power of that mystery in the life of the Church and of the penitent.

Individual penance, therefore, is liturgy *theologically* because ''the celebration of this sacrament is . . . always an act in which the Church proclaims its faith, gives thanks to God for the freedom with which Christ has made us free, and offers its life as a spiritual sacrifice in praise of God's glory, as it hastens to meet the Lord Jesus'' (no. 7). It is liturgy *ritually* because, employing a

Individual Penitents

rich symbolic language, it follows the pattern of all sacramental liturgies: introductory rites, the reading of God's Word, the celebration of the particular sacramental symbols, and the dismissal to serve. It is liturgy *pastorally* because in it "the Christian dies and rises with Christ and is thus renewed in the paschal mystery" (no. 44). As liturgy, individual penance may be more informal, more dialogical, than other liturgies, but it is liturgy nevertheless.

IN WHAT SITUATIONS?

If we say that individual penance is an act of worship, we must go further and say that this act of worship is situated within a sacramental *process* of conversion and reconciliation in the life of the individual Christian, "the follower of Christ who has sinned" (no. 6). The very celebration of the rite presumes that a great deal has happened in the penitent's faith life by way of conversion: comparing one's life with the gospel, recognizing and acknowledging one's sins and God's mercy, and moving toward God through the agency of the Church. It presumes a continuation of conversion and a renewed gospel lifestyle after the celebration. In other words, it presumes a direct connection with one's life in the world.

The rite itself suggests two life situations for the individual form: "those who by grave sin have withdrawn from the communion of love with God" and "those who through daily weakness fall into venial sins" (no. 7). While it is not clear from the text what "grave" or "withdraw" mean, it is clear that grave sinners stand in need of deep conversion. They have so seriously ruptured their relationship with God and their brothers and sisters in Christ that a thoroughgoing change of heart is what the sacrament of penance would call them to and celebrate in this situation. It calls the other members to an ongoing conversion that will strengthen them to gain the full freedom of the children of God, a "serious striving to perfect the grace of baptism so that, as we bear in our body the death of Jesus Christ, his life may be seen in us more clearly" (no. 7b).

But here we run into one of the several problems that trouble the individual rite for reconciliation. The *content* of this rite seems geared to the reconciliation of grave sinners. For example, contrition/conversion are described as "a profound change of the whole person" (no. 6a), and the rite (and sacrament) are required only

Robert J. Kennedy

134

for those in grave sin (no. 7a). Yet the *form* of the rite favors those who confess venial sins—the weaker members seeking ongoing conversion—and emerges from the tradition that fosters deeper growth in the holy life.

In both life situations—that of grave sin and that of venial sin—it is important to note that they describe and presuppose sin as the occasion for conversion and the celebration of reconciliation. Since sin is a religious and theological category, we can eliminate some situations as not falling within the bounds or purposes of the sacramental ritual per se. These would include spiritual direction (concerned primarily with the discernment of spirits and growth in the holy life), pastoral counseling (concerned primarily with guidance on life issues in the light of faith), and psychological counseling or therapy (concerned primarily with healing the illnesses of mind, spirit, and emotion). It is true of course that all of these do occur in the sacramental encounter or at least overlap with the same concerns as the sacramental encounter. But they would seem more properly considered as support ministries in the sacramental process (much the same way that the Rite of Pastoral Care and Anointing of the Sick describes doctors, nurses, therapists, social workers, technicians, and aides as ministers of that sacrament).[3] It is also true that the priest-confessor is encouraged to give "suitable counsel" to the penitent (nos. 18, 44), but in what does that consist? If sin is the occasion for conversion and celebration of reconciliation, the "suitable counsel" consists in breaking open the Word of God, applying the dimensions of the Christian mystery of reconciliation to the life of the penitent, and exploring the meaning of fidelity to the Christian life. If this sounds like a homily or an instruction at marriage or ordination—good! That is exactly what it is, only more informal, more dialogic. In the face of sins great and small, and in the face of the penitent's conversion great and small, "suitable counsel" is holding up the mirror of the gospel and the gospel standards of the Catholic Christian community—and doing so in terms of the particular penitent's life, with the heart of the Father's mercy.

THE PENITENT

Let us look more closely however at the penitent who enters into this act of worship. The primary self-identity here is that of a sinful but beloved member of the Church. Whether the penitent is

Individual Penitents

broken from the community or merely a weak member, she or he has discovered the two-edged sword of God's word challenging her or his sin, and has recognized the still greater mercy of God. This discovery and recognition lead the penitent to contrition/repentance and to thanksgiving and praise.

The penitent also recognizes the Church as the community of Christ's hospitality, and herself or himself as finding life's meaning with that community. One of the most frequent questions and biggest pastoral problems is "why should I confess to a priest?" Yet presenting oneself as sinner to the Church's minister is the most consistent symbolic gesture in the entire history of penance. What did that long line of penitents see then that we do not see now? It seems to me that they recognized that the bishop or priest embodied the focus of the Church's desire to offer welcome and peace to the sinner: here is the host of the welcoming community standing at the door to greet in understanding and love, not to judge. But there is something in the penitent which stands behind the gesture of approaching the Church and the Church's minister. When tax collectors, prostitutes and sinners sat at table with Jesus, it was not because they were looking for cheap grace: they knew the challenge of his teaching. They came to his hospitable table ready to surrender their lives to the direction he would give them. A similar attitude and response is necessary in the penitents, so that the sacrament "may take root in their whole lives and move them to more fervent service of God and neighbor" (no. 7).

To approach the sacrament in order to be directed by the gospel of Christ is a pretty high ideal for the penitent, and we recognize that people approach the sacrament from many directions. There is a small number of neurotics and psychotics (to be welcomed with the greatest compassion and realistic love); there is perhaps an equally small number who see the sacrament in the terms I am trying to describe it. There are many who expect the formal mechanical style—and who may need it because they cannot yet manage a more relaxed, personal and celebrative style. Some will come open to the present rite, but hesitant and confused about it; some who will come seeing themselves much more as sinful than as beloved; some will come who will need a greater sense of their own sinfulness. Some will be alienated, some agitated, some suspicious, some already at peace. Yet all must be met *where they are*

Robert J. Kennedy

with the compassion of Christ, and brought to the worship of God in the best way possible.

What does the penitent "confess"? Confession (in Greek, *exomologēsis*) was "not merely the verbal admission of sin; it was an act of worship, a recognition of the reality of God and of what that demands of us . . . , at once the expression of what we are before God and of the contrition we have already conceived in our hearts."[4] Thus the penitent acknowledges his or her sin in the context of professing faith in the God who reconciles and saves: it is a personal act of contrition, credo, and eucharistic prayer rolled into one.

By thus entering into this act of worship, the penitent is a concelebrant of the sacrament with the Church and the Church's minister. The penitent needs to be confident that it is his or her religious experience which is the "matter," the reason, for the celebration. (This is met by the Church's reason for celebrating, the return of one of its own.) The penitent can then choose texts consistent with that experience (scriptural reading, prayer of sorrow, act of penance) and grow comfortable in praying with the priest-confessor and entering into dialogue with him.

THE CONFESSOR

Who is the Church's minister who presides at this act of worship? The primary self-identity of the priest-confessor is that of sinful minister of the Church. There are other identities and images described in the rite of penance. He is spiritual physician, an image taken from the monastic tradition of penance, manifestation of conscience, and spiritual direction; the spiritual physician is one who understands the disorders of souls and applies the appropriate remedies to them (no. 10a; cf. nos. 6c, 18). He is also judge, in two senses. First, in the post-Tridentine view of "the tribunal of penance," a courtroom analogy, the priest "pronounces his decision of forgiveness or retention of sins in accord with the power of the keys" (no. 6b), "imposes an act of penance or satisfaction on the penitent" (no. 18), and "helps the penitent to make an integral confession" (no. 44). Second, he can also be judge in terms of discernment of spirits, having a deep knowledge of God's actions in human hearts (no. 10; see Phil 1:9–10). For this kind of judging the priest must have wisdom, knowledge, prudence gained through serious study of scripture and human life, and

Individual Penitents

137

must be guided by the Church's teaching and prayer; he must have the ability to distinguish between penitent and penitent by "recognizing the vast diversity of moral capacity, commitment to the Lord, response to God's gifts, intellectual background, psychological sensitivity."[5]

The rite also speaks of the attitudes the confessor should have: he should be always ready and willing, and he should be compassionate: revealing the heart of the Father and the image of the Good Shepherd who seeks out and saves the lost (no. 10). The compassionate discerner of spirits comes closest to describing who we want as the presider at this sacramental celebration, but it is not quite adequate yet.

Richard Gula introduces another image. The confessor is "not the judge of the convicted sinner, but the host of the reconciling community welcoming the penitent home again, . . . both the instrument through which God communicates forgiveness and the representative of the whole community of faith granting pardon and peace. . . ."[6] The image of host is most appropriate for presiding at liturgy, and, although it is not specifically named in the rite, the spirit of this image can be found there. It is in the verbs which describe the confessor's action in the rite: the priest *welcomes* warmly and with kindness, *urges* confidence, *invites* trust in God, *helps* a complete confession, *encourages* complete sorrow, *offers* suitable counsel.

The person of the minister is the symbol of the whole community, but in terms of incarnation, not function. The person of the minister reveals the compassion and forgiveness of Christ offered through the community. Thus the qualities of any good host are the qualities of the presider at the rite of penance: joy in the presence of the penitent, reverence and respect for the penitent, one who is relaxed and sets the penitent at ease, one who is open and makes room for the other—what Henri Nouwen calls "the hospitality of receptivity."[7] The presider-confessor does not dissolve or deny himself, however, but serves and confidently enters into dialogue with the penitent. This is Nouwen's "hospitality of confrontation," offering an articulate presence, a presence within boundaries, not hiding behind neutrality but showing our ideas, opinions, and lifestyle clearly and distinctly. This the confessor offers by his own transparency of faith, the gospel-inspired "suit-

Robert J. Kennedy

able counsel," and the remembrance of his self-identity as *sinful minister of the Church.*

There are at least five resources the presider-confessor can draw on for this sacramental ministry in penance. The first is his own experience of sin, conversion and reconciliation; he cannot lead others where he has not gone. The second is the experience of the hurts of others. He is not a voyeur into the miseries and vulnerabilities of others, but he must learn the ways of compassion and the meaning of life-from-death from those situations which inevitably come his way. The prayerful reflection on the woman faced with a decision about abortion or the young executive struggling to control masturbation or the family struggling with an alcoholic member will go a long way toward making a compassionate discerner of spirits who presides at the celebration of penance. The third resource for the confessor are the scriptures since it is the biblical standards—both in terms of its challenges and of its promise of God's mercy—that are key to this celebration.

> [The confessor] is best suited for that role by letting the Bible form him (the Spirit, that is to say) in the image of Christ. This does not mean spouting the Bible glibly or proof-texting a defenseless laity to death. It means letting the sacred text seep into his being so that he tells its stories and recounts its New Testament forays into theory as familiarly as any rabbi might in telling a thousand Talmudic tales without repeating once.[8]

The fourth resource is his own prayer, so that his own exploration of the heart and mind of God will make his (perhaps struggling) faith apparent and consoling to the penitent. And fifth is the confessor's continued study in the processes by which spirits are discerned and conscience is formed. Presiding at individual penance requires the doing of homework.

CONTINUING PASTORAL NEEDS

If we consider the rite of individual penance as the meeting of a sinful yet beloved member of the Church and a sinful minister of the Church in a liturgical celebration, there are certain issues or pastoral needs which have to be met in order to open up the full impact of the sacramental sign. I want to suggest six of these needs as part of the continuing agenda of reconciliation.

First, if the recognition of sin great and small is central to this liturgical rite, then *we need to renew our understanding of sin.* Here a

Individual Penitents

few questions might move us in the right direction. What is the gospel framework for Christian moral living; what are the gospel norms? What are the standards of the Catholic Christian community; what are the norms of its welfare, holiness, integrity, and membership? How is the understanding of sin related to the baptismal commitment of each believer and the whole process of living the baptismal life? How do we account for the communal/social dimensions of sin and individual responsibility? The answers to these questions are not easily found and tentative responses are hotly debated. Yet they remain urgent pastoral questions as we continue to implement the rites of Christian initiation and reconciliation.

Second, *we need to reintroduce the virtue of penance as part of the Catholic Christian identity* (or, if that phrasing seems too negative or old-fashioned, we need to develop a practical spirituality of reconciliation in each Christian who is by baptism an ambassador of Christ's work of reconciliation). Prayer, fasting, and the works of mercy and justice remain valid means of accomplishing this. In addition to the personal prayer which seeks to love the world with God's heart, there are penitential celebrations which invite people to conversion and renewal of life (nos. 36–37), and additional times of penitential prayer in the spirit of ember days and Rogation Days. (Do we not need repentant prayer on the anniversaries of the bombing of Hiroshima and Nagasaki, or on the day our Jewish brothers and sisters remember the Holocaust?) Fasting fills us with Christ and a sense of solidarity with our brothers and sisters in need: what are the holy uses or non-uses of food, drink, time, money, and talent that would be appropriate forms of fasting in today's world and lifestyles? Closely connected to the answer to this question is an understanding of the works of mercy as not only private acts of charity but social acts of justice. For example, "feed the hungry" asks not only grain for the starving of Africa but also the construction of irrigation systems which will help reclaim the land for farming; "cloth the naked" requests not only donations for the Thanksgiving clothing drive but also the elimination of the destructive attitude of "consumerism" in our society; "shelter the homeless" demands not only soup kitchens and overnight shelters but also educating the President and Congress of the United States to the reality of poverty and the value of government assistance programs.

Robert J. Kennedy

In addition to these "traditional" ways of practicing penance, the study of the Scriptures will enable progress in putting on more and more the outlook of the gospel, which forever challenges us to be sure that we are fulfilling the law of Christ.

Third, *we need renewed efforts of conscience formation and catechesis on the mystery of reconciliation*, especially with adolescents, young adults and parents. Preaching in all its forms and settings, first-penance parent meetings, confirmation and marriage preparation programs, retreats, infant baptism preparation programs, adult education and many other normal parish settings are all times when these efforts can take place.

Fourth, *we need the signs of the rite of penance to foster and nourish faith*. The statement of the U.S. bishops in *Music in Catholic Worship* applies here: "good celebrations foster and nourish faith, poor celebrations may weaken and destroy faith" (no. 6),[9] I would suggest four such signs in penance for our special consideration.

(1) It is the presider-confessor who embodies the community's hospitality for the sinner, and the burden still falls on him to form himself in and preside over the ritual of penance. Thus attention to body language (posture, facial expression, bodily movements), personal appearance, tone of voice, cadence of speech, choice of words, eye contact, and his own comfort with silence, tears, and touch will make him a gracious host in the name of the Church.

(2) Despite the title of paragraph 43 of the Rite of Penance and the present sins of omission in this regard, the reading of the Word of God is not "optional." The following statements emphasize its importance:

> Through the word of God the Christian receives light to recognize his [or her] sins and is called to conversion and to confidence in God's mercy (no. 15).

> The sacrament of penance should begin with a hearing of God's word, because through his word God calls men [and women] to repentance and leads them to a true conversion of heart (no. 24).

To underscore the importance of the reading of God's Word the lectionary of the rite provides 110 options from the Old and New Testaments! The reading in this context, as always, should be prayerfully done with preparation and care.

(3) Is the reconciliation room or confessional a place to worship in well? Do they speak of the hospitality of the community?

Individual Penitents

141

(4) Is the scheduled time hospitable? Confessors need to ask themselves for whom the scheduled times are convenient: a consultation of the parish council and other parish groups might suggest convenient times other than Saturday afternoon or evening.

Fifth, *we need to continue to assess the adequacy of the present individual rite.* Again, some questions. Can this rite serve well both the situations of grave sin and ongoing conversion? Do the liturgies of exorcism and scrutinies in the RCIA process offer us *models* for the latter situation? Do the language and ritual adequately contain and express the mystery of Christian reconciliation being celebrated? How can the communal/ecclesial dimensions of the individual rite be better expressed?

Finally, *we need an individual rite adapted to children,* and perhaps teens, and prayers, as in the Anointing of the Sick, adapted to the various circumstances of sin and reconciliation being celebrated in the rite. These will enrich the present texts, and enable the rite to be better expressive of the experience of sinful members of the Church.

NOTES

1. For a recent general treatment of the history of penance, with a fine and helpful emphasis on its ecclesial dimensions, see James Dallen, *The Reconciling Community: The Rite of Penance* (New York: Pueblo Publishing Company, 1986) 1–201. For excellent studies of the roots of the individual form, see Catherine Dooley, O.P., "Development of the Practice of Devotional Confession," *Questions liturgiques* 64 (1983) 89–113; "A Theology of Devotional Confession," *Questions liturgiques* 66 (1985) 109–123; and "From Penance to Confession: The Celtic Contribution," *Bijdragen, tijdschrift voor filosophie en theologie* 43 (1982) 390–411.

2. *The Rites of the Catholic Church* (New York: Pueblo Publishing Company, 1976) 335–446.

3. The Rite of Anointing and Pastoral Care of the Sick, no. 33, in *ibid.* 571–642.

4. J.D. Crichton, *The Ministry of Reconciliation: A Commentary on the Order of Penance 1974* (London: Geoffrey Chapman, 1974) 23.

5. Frederick R. McManus, *Rite of Penance: Commentaries, Volume One: Understanding the Document,* with Ralph Keifer (Washington: The Liturgical Conference, 1975) 40.

Robert J. Kennedy

6. Richard M. Gula, s.s., *To Walk Together Again: The Sacrament of Reconciliation* (New York: Paulist Press, 1984) 230.

7. Henri Nouwen, *Reaching Out* (Garden City, NY: Doubleday and Company Inc., 1975) 69–70.

8. Gerard Sloyan, "The Confessor As A Man of Scripture," *The Rite of Penance: Commentaries, Volume Two: Implementing the Rite,* ed. Elizabeth McMahon Jeep (Washington: The Liturgical Conference, 1976) 106.

9. Bishops' Committee on the Liturgy, "Music in Catholic Worship," rev. ed. (Washington, D.C.: United States Catholic Conference, 1983) 1.

Edward Foley, O.F.M. CAP.

Communal Rites of Penance: Insights and Options

One of the hazards in liturgical preparation is to think that "pastoral" liturgy means "practical" liturgy, or that good worship is attainable with the right technique. Practitioners of the art such as Austin Fleming, however, offer an important corrective to these views. He suggests that the task of pastoral liturgists is not to *plan*—not to create or devise entertaining ritual—but to *prepare* for a liturgy which is already given to us.[1] Worship in this perspective is not merely an exercise in aesthetics or an effective means for social bonding. Rather, it is acknowledged as something beyond our invention, initiated between Jesus Christ and the one we call the Father, into which we are invited.[2]

This essential viewpoint cautions us. Any consideration of options for communal rites of penance could degenerate into a summary of recipes and resources. The resulting worship from such a venture might be well structured and aesthetically pleasing, but would also be artificial and ultimately unconnected to life. We are, however, concerned with the real here: with worship that respects its divine initiation and touches people's lives. It is this concern which convinces us, therefore, not to begin with techniques or recipes but with the broader questions about reconciliation.

What are the various ways the Church has enabled the forgiveness of sin in the past? Who are the people who wish reconciliation, and what are their expectations? What are the capacities of the current rites to incorporate these traditional means and address this variety of needs? Are there any principles from the tradition or current rites which should inform our liturgical preparation?

These are the kinds of questions which provide the appropriate context for preparing communal rites of reconciliation. Though our exploration of them will by necessity be limited, it is only after such groundwork that we can suggest specific scenarios for implementation. These scenarios, however, are not of primary importance here. More compelling, we believe, are the principles for reconciliation drawn from our tradition and experience, which must shape any adaptation of contemporary penitential practice.

OUR RICH PENITENTIAL VOCABULARY

The introduction to the Rite of Penance reminds us that reconciliation was foundational to the ministry of Jesus Christ and his Church (nos. 1-2). It was through Jesus' life, death, and resurrection that the world was reconciled to God. In the spirit of this same Jesus Christ the Church has been empowered to call all to conversion and show the victory of Christ over sin.

This reconciling ministry has assumed a myriad of shapes and forms over the centuries, and manifold are the ways believers have been invited into Christ's victory over sin. Chief among these are certain sacraments of the Church. It is first in baptism that we are "freed from all sin, given . . . a new birth by water and the Holy Spirit, and welcomed . . . into his holy people."[3] In the eucharist we are invited to share the gifts of the new covenant, poured out for us so that sins may be forgiven. In the sacrament of penance our hearts are cleansed and our sins forgiven, that we might "proclaim the mighty acts of God who has called [us] out of darkness into the splendor of his light" (no. 62). Finally, the anointing of the sick "provides the sick person with the forgiveness of sins and the completion of Christian penance."[4]

Besides these sacraments, however, believers of every age have found numerous other ways to express their sorrow and encounter reconciliation. The patristic writer Origen (+253), and many after him, recognized that sin was remitted by martyrdom, alms-

Edward Foley

144

giving, mutual forgiveness, assisting in the work of another's conversion, and charity to the needy.[5] Though there existed a rite of public canonical penance in the early Church, its impracticality

> . . . led some bishops, like Caesarius of Arles (+552), to encourage their people to *avoid* seeking admission into the order of penitents. . . . (and) to seek forgiveness through prayer, fasting, or works of charity and mercy like visiting the sick and the imprisoned.[6]

The Carolingian reform Council of Chalon-sur-Saône (813) noted approvingly that confession to God alone (*confessio Deo soli*) was an alternative and effective means of reconciliation.[7] Confession of sins to a lay person was accepted during the Middle Ages as an ordinary means for the forgiveness of "venial" sins.[8] Furthermore, entry into the monastic life, pilgrimages, and some forms of physical punishment were all recognized forms of penance, and employed as useful substitutes for more formal rites of reconciliation.[9]

Though not specifically recommending any of these to the modern penitent, this brief sampling reminds us that our tradition knows a rich vocabulary for reconciling sinners.[10] It is not only the sequence of contrition-confession-satisfaction-absolution which mediates Christ's victory over sin. As the Introduction to the Rite of Penance reminds us,

> The people of God accomplishes and perfects this continual repentance in many different ways. It shares in the suffering of Christ by enduring its own difficulties, carries out works of mercy and charity, and adopts ever more fully the outlook of the Gospel message (no. 4).

A VARIETY OF NEEDS

Besides acknowledging the various modes of reconciliation which have marked our tradition, we need also reckon with the differing needs of the people who submit themselves to penitential discipline in the Church. It is not overstating the obvious to note that every penitent is a special individual, and unique are the experiences of sin and brokenness which need to be healed. This diversity of need places great demands upon the liturgies of penance, and a brief sampling of this diversity can be instructive. For the sake of discussion, we will explore the categories articulated by three recent authors.

Communal Rites

Speaking at the 1983 Synod on Penance, Archbishop John Roach of St. Paul-Minneapolis remarked that any reflection on reconciliation necessitated a concurrent consideration of alienation.[11] He went on to suggest that at least three dominant types of alienation from the Church exist in contemporary Western culture: 1) those alienated by *anti-institutionalism,* perceiving the Church primarily as an institution more concerned with its own self-maintenance than with its mission; 2) those alienated through *narcissism,* promoting self-fulfillment at any cost, which isolates the individual from commitment and self-sacrifice; and 3) those alienated through *secular humanism,* who reduce religion to politics, and regard gospel faith as a palliative which perpetuates inequitable social structures.

In presenting his vision for a new order of penitents in the Church,[12] James Lopresti suggests another way of understanding the alienated in our midst. In his view, the alienated include (1) the *unawakened,* or those who have never heard the personal call to be an apostle, and have yet to recognize that a place has been prepared for them at table; (2) the *truly alienated,* or those who have heard the call of the gospel and responded with a life commitment, but at some point have rejected the call or the life response; and (3) the *prophetically alienated,* or those who absent themselves from the table because they believe that others who gather around the table do so inauthentically or invalidly.

Finally, Francis Mannion begins his discussion of various types of penitents by distinguishing between "penance" which serves a believer's ongoing conversion, and "reconciliation" which overcomes a radical, post-baptismal break between a believer and the community and God.[13] In light of this distinction, Mannion believes that the current rites are serving three quite diverse groups: (1) those to be reconciled *after grave sin,* (2) those involved in the journey of *ongoing penitential transformation,* and (3) those engaged in the process of *spiritual purification and growth.*[14]

Though certainly not exhaustive, this sampling demonstrates that penance or reconciliation is offered to a variety of people with a variety of needs. It is not, and never has been, a simple remedy for a single ill;[15] it is, rather, a broad ministry responding to innumerable situations. As the Introduction to the Rite of Penance itself notes, "Just as the wound of sin is varied and multiple in the life of individuals and of the community, so too the healing which penance provides is varied" (no. 7).

Edward Foley

Given this broad context of the Church's rich penitential vocabulary as well as the varying needs of penitents, it is now for us to look at the rites. Specifically, we will consider the structure and content of the Rite for Reconciliation of Several Penitents with Individual Confession and Absolution (= Rite II), and the Rite for Reconciliation of Several Penitents with General Confession and Absolution (= Rite III). Our concern is to ascertain some of the strengths and weaknesses of these rites in light of the broad context discussed about communal rites of penance, which we will attempt to incorporate into the three scenarios at the end of this paper.

In outline form we can see a fundamental similarity between these two rites:

Rite II	*Rite III*
Introductory rites	Introductory rites
song	song
greeting	greeting
opening prayer	opening prayer
Celebration of the Word	Celebration of the Word
reading	reading
response	response
second reading	second reading
gospel acclamation	gospel acclamation
gospel	gospel
homily	homily
	Instruction
Examination of Conscience	Examination of Conscience
Rite of Reconciliation	Rite of Reconciliation
general confession	general confession
individual confession/	general absolution
absolution	
proclamation of praise	proclamation of praise
prayer of thanksgiving	
Concluding rites	Concluding rites

There are numerous facets of these rites which have been praised since their appearance in 1973. Sottocornola, for example,

Communal Rites

offered an early commentary in which he outlined many of their basic strengths.[16] First among these is the new ecclesial emphasis which reconciliation receives, as well as the clear social dimension of these rites. Here we are dramatically reminded that sin is not merely a private failing, but a collective experience which affects the entire Body of Christ. Sottocornola also commends the rites for their attention to Scripture, returning the word to its proper place in the sacrament. It is precisely through the word that God calls us to repentance and leads us to a true conversion of heart (no. 24). Finally, he believes the development of Rite III and the introduction of general absolution is a most important innovation, with wide pastoral possibilities. Sottocornola summarizes by suggesting that this reform is not so much a passage from one rite to another, as a transformation of a mentality and style of celebration, ultimately moving from a reform of rites to a reform of life.[17]

Given these positive aspects of Rites II and III, there are also substantial theological-liturgical problems with these sacramental forms. Specifically speaking of Rite II, William Marrevee has noted that, though there is a concern to blend personal and communal dimensions in the rite, the elements surrounding individual confession and absolution are rather circumstantial. Ultimately he concludes that this rite "very awkwardly isolates the individual encounter between the confessing penitent and the absolving priest."[18]

Concerning Rite III, Marrevee underlines as problematic the exceptional nature of general absolution. Noting that the Rite of Penance makes it clear that individual confession and absolution are the norm, he believes that the basic preoccupation of Rite III (like Rite II) is individual confession and absolution.

This criticism has grown since the publication of the Pastoral Norms on General Absolution in 1972.[19] These norms require that, except for a good reason, those who receive general absolution are to experience private reconciliation before any further reception of absolution, and are required to go to a confessor within one year. Marrevee's belief that this rite is basically preoccupied with individual confession and absolution is confirmed in these norms.

A further difficulty with Rite III, arising from the implementation of the Pastoral Norms, concerns the confession of sin after absolution. Pierre-Marie Gy and others have noted the "incontestable difficulty" of trying to explain that a serious sin

Edward Foley

can be truly forgiven, and at the same time needs to be individually confessed at a later date.[20] Again, the preoccupation with individual confession and absolution dominates.

As both rites, therefore can be criticized for their emphasis on individual confession and absolution, so could both rites be criticized for their structural monotony and verbosity. Structurally, these two rites (as well as Rite I) are virtually identical. Moreover, the fundamental outline for Rites II and III is the same as the eucharist: with confession and absolution replacing the eucharistic prayer and communion rite. The overuse of this structure is certainly problematic. Furthermore, these rites are long on text but short on symbolic action. "It is almost as though the persons who composed the rites felt sin could be eliminated by talking it to death."[21] Yet the symbolic act is as fundamental to the experience of reconciliation as the taking, blessing, breaking and giving of bread and wine are to eucharist.

Finally, at the heart of the criticism, there is deep concern these rites do not attend to the process of reconciliation, which by definition takes place over time. As James Dallen has summarized, this view of penance as a process extending over time was at least implicit in the contemporary theology during the period of preparation for the new Rite of Penance.[22] Since the appearance of the Rite, this awareness has grown explicit.[23] Like the Rite of Christian Initiation of Adults, which understands initiation as a gradual incorporation into the community punctuated by rites, so is true reconciliation a gradual reincorporation into the same community, requiring the same ritual punctuation.

PRINCIPLES FOR COMMUNAL RITES OF PENANCE

Given our summary discussions of the wider context of the Rite of Penance, as well as the specific critique of Rites II and III, we are now in a position to extract a few principles about the rites which can inform our preparation. Following the statement and explanation of these principles, we will offer three variant examples of how they might be applied.

Our discussion of the Church's rich and varied penitential vocabulary suggests our first principle: *the sacramental forms found in the Rite of Penance cannot bear the weight of the entire reconciliation process.* Just as the eucharist cannot be the only rite in our liturgical vocabulary for giving thanks and constituting ourselves as the

Communal Rites

living body of Christ, so we cannot expect the various forms in the Rite of Penance to be our only ritual encounters in forgiveness. It is true, to continue the analogy, that the eucharistic liturgy is the focal way in which we are constituted as the Body of Christ, and enjoys a clear primacy in this regard.[24] The eucharistic liturgy, however, cannot be the only worship experience which enables this. Such limitation does not do justice either to the rich liturgical and theological traditions of the Church—or to people's real need for a wide range of liturgical experiences which will allow them to enter the eucharist more completely.[25] In the same way, though the various "sacramental" forms in the Rite of Penance are focal and assume a clear primacy in the Church's penitential vocabulary, they cannot be the only such moments and means. To confine forgiveness to these three rites is to ignore the good wisdom of the ages and the real need of the faithful.

A second principle flows from the first. Since the various "sacramental" forms in the Rite of Penance cannot bear the weight of every need, yet hold a central place in our penitential vocabulary, then *we need to integrate other penitential practices into the given sacramental forms of reconciliation.* It is important to encourage a wide range of traditional practices such as works of charity, mutual forgiveness, fasting and almsgiving. Given the special place, however, which the formal rites of penance hold—especially as they culminate in absolution—it seems essential to integrate these with the ongoing practices of the faithful. This integration not only validates normal penitential practices as an integral part of the reconciliation process, but it also serves to play down the almost magical emphasis given to absolution.

Third, we have recognized that there are numerous needs, various kinds of alienation, and many expectations for the rite of penance. This suggests that *there should be flexibility in the rites of reconciliation, and the possibility for particularizing the rites to suit various expectations and needs.* This does not necessarily imply that every form of reconciliation must be able to respond to every penitential need. It is quite possible, instead, that some forms could be structured to respond to specific kinds of alienation and sin. The principle does suggest, however, that adaptability of the rites to the particular needs of each penitent or group of penitents is a value.

Fourth, our critique of Rites II and III surfaced the realization

Edward Foley

that reconciliation is not fundamentally a verbal experience. It is the enacted ritual and the embodied embrace of the community which best articulates and effects reincorporation. Consequently, *rites of reconciliation need to be marked by rich symbolic action, which must be integral to the ritual.*

Finally, our summary of the strengths and weaknesses of the current rites also reminded us that reconciliation is fundamentally a process of reincorporation into the Body of Christ. Two elements seem essential here. First, just as sin alienates us from God, other, and self, so does reconciliation strengthen or reestablish this tripartite bond. Second, such reincorporation takes time. It is not a moment event, though it might be culminated in a powerful ritual moment. Consequently, *the rites which serve this reincorporation must respect both the process and the ecclesial dimension of reconciliation.*

APPLICATIONS

Having discussed the expansive penitential vocabulary of the Church, admitted the various needs people have for reconciliation, critiqued Rites II and III, and extracted certain principles for the preparation of communal rites of reconciliation, we now arrive at the final stage of application. In a sense, this is the most artificial part of our discussion, because reader and author share no real community experience in which to ground these pastoral suggestions. What we offer, therefore, should be taken as theoretical scenarios which cannot be indiscriminately imposed upon a community. These "models" must, instead, be adapted to local needs, traditions and capacities.

The three following scenarios will address different pastoral situations. Needless to say, there are many more. Hopefully these samples will indicate some of the possibilities for adapting Rites II and III.

Scenario I: a weekend retreat. A weekend retreat holds great potential for crafting a reconciliation service which would respect the diverse needs of the individuals and the process of the Rite. This could especially be true if the celebration focused on a specific kind of alienation or brokenness like divorce or chemical dependency. In this Friday evening to Sunday afternoon experience, a complete process of reconciliation is not possible. The weekend could be so structured, however, so that the process might begin or be strengthened; it would then need to be continued after the weekend was over.

Communal Rites

One reason the weekend retreat offers such rich possibilities is because of its natural movement from the day of the cross (Friday) to the day of resurrection (Sunday). This cyclic progression is a weekly icon for the Good Friday to Easter Sunday journey. Its potential in reconciliation should not be overlooked. Furthermore, Sunday as the primordial day for eucharist, which is the ritual finale to authentic reincorporation, offers rich direction to the entire process.

It would be necessary in this scenario to prepare the participants before their arrival. To be led in an intense process of reconciliation requires preparation. A retreat so envisioned would not only have to be appropriately advertised (e.g. "A Journey in Forgiveness"), but participants would also need to come prepared to face their own alienation or brokenness.

As a variation on Rite II, the ritual structure for the three days could entail the following components:

1. gathering in hope, and acknowledgement of alienation and/or sinfulness (Friday evening);

2. proclamation of God's mercy and invitation, in the word (Friday evening);

3. reflection on our common holiness and need for purification (Saturday morning);

4. individual sharing with presbyter, retreat staff, spouse, friend, etc., on one's personal alienation or sin (Saturday afternoon);

5. communal gathering, reiteration of the word, space for individual sharing of reflections, prayer, or experiences (Saturday evening);

6. prayer service, incorporating individual gestures of return, laying on of hands, and the Church's declaration of forgiveness (Saturday night);

7. eucharist (Sunday morning);

8. festive meal (Sunday noon);

9. mystagogia on the reconciliation encountered, and the journey yet ahead (Sunday afternoon).

Recalling our principles, this scenario does not put all the emphasis on "absolution," but gives equal weight to elements of

Edward Foley

word, sharing, and reflection, with pride of place given to eucharist. There could be great flexibility in the scenario, as for example, in the choice of presbyter, retreat staff, or other in the sharing of personal alienation or sin. Integration of the various elements could be achieved not only by the prepared reflections by the retreat staff which naturally accompany such a weekend, but also by echoing previous ritual elements in each succeeding step, or by a single continuous word, symbol, or song throughout the weekend. This scenario also acknowledges that reconciliation is a journey over time, for which the weekend serves as a paradigm. Two of the challenges of this model are calling the participants to properly prepare for the weekend, and to continue the reincorporation after the retreat is over.

Scenario II: a single parish gathering in Advent. Often the local community can only gather a single time for a celebration of penance. It is yet possible, however, to prepare this single gathering so that it respects the process of reconciliation. Preparation is again an essential component. It is important to know what scriptures will be proclaimed, the focus of the homily, and whatever symbolic gesture or music will be employed. These elements, well planned in advance, will serve both the preparation for the gathering and the actual ritual.

The service would need to be contextualized in the wider movement of the Church year. This will allow integration of the basic motifs and symbols which give direction to the whole of a season's worship into the reconciliation service. During Advent, for example, the season turns on the image of the solstice, and the triumph of Jesus the light over all darkness. This motif could find resonance in a journey to reconciliation which invites us to consider where we are the light of Christ, or how we cast shadows on the message of the Gospel.

The Advent wreath, potentially present in the church and in the home, could serve as a symbolic focus for this seasonal journey. During the entrance rites for the First Sunday of Advent the wreath could be blessed with a text which recalls our baptismal commitment to walk as children of the light. This text could be related to prayer for ("Lord, have") mercy for the times as individuals and community we have chosen the darkness, e.g.,

> Blessed are you, Wisdom of the ages, for your goodness has
> revealed itself from the dawn of time and your salvation
> is made known in Jesus the Christ.

Communal Rites

Bless us in this season of waning light. Increase our
longing for your son and our willingness to grow in his
love.
As we light this candle [these candles] in expectation
of his final return,
Give us strength to shun the darkness, and witness to your
glory,
That the dawn of his presence may find us rejoicing in his
word and welcoming his truth.
We ask this in the name of Jesus the Lord.

This same lighting of the wreath could be done in each household
of the community. In preparation for the daily lighting of the
wreath, members of each household could be invited to share
what area of their life they wish to be enlightened. A familiar
song like "O Come, O Come Emmanuel," with its textual images
of ransom and liberation could accompany both the eucharistic entrance rites and the family wreath lighting.

Three weeks of light and blessing, confessing and family
penitential practices could punctuate this special season of charity
and almsgiving. These would also prepare for the communal service of reconciliation, which could take the following shape:

1. Begin with the same opening rituals around the wreath,
   employing variations on the same musical setting and a
   variation on the same opening prayer;

2. proclaim the word of promise in Christ who is the light to
   the nations;

3. invite two or three individuals, or members of a single
   household, to speak of their advent reflections or journey
   toward the light;

4. confess publicly our individual and communal failure to
   prepare the way of the Lord;

5. offer general absolution;

6. as a symbol of reincorporation and recommitment, light
   candles off the Advent wreath and share with all members
   of the community while singing "O Come, O Come Emmanuel";

7. dismissal.

It is also possible to integrate a parish's option for the poor into
this reconciliation journey. Households could be invited to share

Edward Foley

154

one simple meal each week, which would serve as a special focus of prayer and sharing. The food that they would normally eat, or expenditures for that food could be given over to the poor. Some kind of food or monetary collection could be taken from the people as they enter the church for the reconciliation service.

It is further possible to extend the ritual journey beyond the Advent season, by using the lighting of candles as an opening rite during the Christmas season. Therein recall the baptismal commitment made to Christ who is the never-fading light, and invite the community to recommit itself to the mission of incarnating this same Christ into the world.

The possibilities are endless; the task is to rely on the seasonal movements in prayer, symbol, and activity, and choreograph them into a coherent ritual movement which encourages a process of reconciliation, and integrates it with life and mission.

Scenario III: multiple parish gatherings during Lent. A final scenario for communal reconciliation is composed of multiple gatherings of the community during the premier season of purification and enlightenment, Lent. The ritual hinge for these gatherings could be the three scrutinies for the baptismal elect, which occur on the Third, Fourth and Fifth Sundays of Lent. These scrutinies have a twofold purpose, "revealing anything that is weak, defective, or sinful in the hearts of the elect, so that it may be healed, and revealing what is upright, strong and holy, so that it may be strengthened."[26] This dual purpose is quite applicable to the post-baptismal reconciliation process. Whether or not a community has candidates for Easter initiation, the rehearsal of these scrutinies during Lent could be a valuable ritual guide for the entire community.

The "rehearsal" of each scrutiny could take place on a weeknight before the designated Sunday. The scrutiny which normally occurs on the Third Sunday of Lent, for example, would serve as the basis of a penance service on Wednesday of the second week. The structure of this service could be:

1. gathering;
2. proclamation of the gospel for the coming Sunday;
3. catechesis on the journey to baptismal recommitment during Lent, and the role of the scrutinies in that journey;

Communal Rites

4. prayer for the community, adapted from the scrutiny's prayer for the elect;[27]

5. prayer of exorcism, adapted from the exorcism prayer in the scrutiny;[28]

6. a prayer of blessing;

7. end of communal ritual, and opportunity for individual prayer with parish staff, with options of private confession, anointing (adapted from catechumenal anointings), laying on of hands, etc.;

8. fellowship.

Three such services during the second, third and fourth weeks of Lent could prepare the community for the scrutinies in the Sunday assembly, encourage a communal awareness of the post-baptismal Lenten journey, and invite people into a process of reconciliation. Absolution, at least in its communal form, should be postponed until Wednesday of the fifth week.[29] This service could revolve around the presentation of the profession of faith or the Lord's Prayer, which are also proper to the journey towards Easter initiation.[30] Employing basically the same structure of the three previous weeks, this final reconciliation service would end with general absolution, and singing the Lord's Prayer as a common penance.

The proclamation of forgiveness (absolution) should not, however, be presented as the culmination of the Lenten journey. Every effort should be made to lead people into the Triduum, which is the ultimate celebration of the reincorporation of sinners (Thursday), the encounter with the crucified one poured out for us (Friday), and the final victory over sin (Easter Vigil).

Ritually these individual segments are easily connected through the use of common symbols, e.g., a continuous piece of music. The weekly reiteration at the Wednesday services and through the Triduum of a song like "We Remember"[31] jogs the memory, invites connections, and leads to closure. Parishes which are used to a Lenten series or mission could invite a special preacher to these four Wednesday evenings for continuous catechesis on the season's rituals. Whatever the traditional strengths of a parish community during this Lenten season, they should be respected and integrated into this process of reconciliation.

Edward Foley

As cautioned in the beginning, authentic liturgical preparation is not a scramble for the newest technique or structural innovation. Rather, it is acknowledging the relationship of worship which exists in Godself, and enabling believers to encounter the same. Adapting the communal rites of penance requires no less. Respect for individual needs in this encounter is paramount. It is in the context of this respect, and in view of the rich and varied tradition of the Church, that our reconciling ministry must continue.

NOTES

1. Austin Fleming, *Preparing for Liturgy* (Washington, D.C.: The Pastoral Press, 1985) especially 31–41.

2. See Pius XII's *Mediator Dei* no. 20, echoed in the Constitution on the Sacred Liturgy no. 7.

3. Optional prayer for anointing after baptism, Rite of Christian Initiation of Adults (RCIA), no. 224. This and all subsequent quotations of the rites are taken from *The Rites of the Catholic Church* (New York: Pueblo Publishing Co., 1976).

4. Introduction to the Rite of Anointing and Pastoral Care of the Sick, no. 6.

5. *In Lev. hom.* 2.4 = PG 12:417–418.

6. Nathan Mitchell, "The Many Ways to Reconciliation: An Historical Synopsis of Christian Penance," *The Rite of Penance: Commentaries*, vol. 3, ed. Nathan Mitchell (Washington, D.C.: The Liturgical Conference, 1978) 30.

7. Canon 33, in Mansi 14:100. This ancient tradition continued to be recommended for centuries, as by the reformer John Calvin (+ 1564) in his *Institutes* III:4.

8. Bede, *Expositio in Epis. Jac.* 5.16 = PL 93:39–40.

9. See Bernard Poschmann, *Penance and the Anointing of the Sick*, rev. and trans. by Francis Courtney (New York: Herder and Herder, 1964) 151–154.

10. For further discussion of this topic, see W. Kasper, "Confession Outside the Confessional?" in *The Sacraments: An Ecumenical Dilemma*, Concilium 24, ed. Hans Kung. (New York: Paulist Press, 1967) 17–22.

11. This is a summary of his address, "From Alienation to Reconciliation," published in *Penance and Reconciliation in the Mission of the*

Communal Rites

Church, Synod of Bishops: Rome, 1983 (Washington, D.C.: United States Catholic Conference, 1984) 45–48.

12. See his "RCIA and Reconciling the Alienated" in this volume, and his monograph *Penance: A Reform Proposal for the Rite,* American Essays in Liturgy 6 (Washington, D.C., The Pastoral Press, 1987).

13. M. Francis Mannion, "Penance and Reconciliation: A Systemic Analysis." *Worship* 60 (1986) 98–118.

14. For a recent discussion of "devotional" confession, see C. Dooley, "Development of the Practice of Devotional Confession," *Questions Liturgiques* 64 (1983) 89–113; *idem,* "A Theology of Devotional Confession," *Questions Liturgiques* 66 (1985) 109–123.

15. As early as the third century we have evidence of clear gradations between different types of sinners. In his so called "Canonical Epistle," for example, Gregory the Wonderworker (+ c. 270) enumerates the different classes of sinners, each with their own place in the church: 1) mourners who cannot even enter the church, 2) hearers in the narthex, 3) fallers, in the nave, 4) bystanders who can stand with the faithful, and 5) participants who are admitted to full communion. *Canonical Letter,* canon 11 = PG 10:1048.

16. Franco Sottocornola, "Les nouveaux rites de la pénitence: commentaire," *Questions Liturgiques* 55 (1974) 89–136.

17. Sottocornola 89.

18. William Marrevee, "The New 'Order of Penance'—is it adequate?" *Église et Théologie* 7 (1976) 130.

19. The Congregation for the Doctrine of the Faith, "Pastoral Norms," 16 June 1972, in *Documents on the Liturgy* 1963–1979 (Collegeville: The Liturgical Press, 1982), nos. 3038–3056.

20. Piérre-Marie Gy, "Le Sacrement de Pénitence," *La Maison-Dieu* 139 (1979) 136.

21. Cora Marie Dubitsky and Nathan Mitchell, "The New Rite of Penance: Its Value for Religious Education," *The Rite of Penance: Commentaries,* vol. 3, 102.

22. See his summary in James Dallen, "A Decade of Discussion on the Reform of Penance, 1963–1973: Theological Analysis and Critique," (S.T.D. Dissertation, The Catholic University of America, 1976) 202–221.

23. See, for example, Joseph Cardinal Bernardin's "Proposal for a New Rite of Penance," which attends to this process, in Synod of Bishops, 1983, *Penance and Reconciliation* 41–44.

24. Constitution on the Sacred Liturgy, no. 10.

Edward Foley

158

25. The Directory for Masses with Children makes this clear when discussing the introduction of children to the eucharist (nos. 8–15). I would suggest that most of the principles articulated in this document are applicable to adults as well.

26. RCIA, no. 25.1.

27. RCIA, no. 163.

28. RCIA, no. 164.

29. People experiencing "individual confession" should also be encouraged to postpone absolution until this final service, though absolution cannot be denied them if they so desire it.

30. See RCIA nos. 183–193.

31. "We Remember" from the collection *With Open Hands* by Marty Haugen (Chicago: G.I.A. Publications, Inc., 1981).

James Lopresti

RCIA and Reconciling the Alienated

If the RCIA has taught us anything about pastoral practice, it is the value of process in sacramental life and pastoral care. In the RCIA, initiation is experienced, not as an isolated event, but as an ongoing development punctuated by a series of privileged moments. Put another way, the catechumenate is not a preparation for initiation; it is an integral part of initiation. Furthermore, since the RCIA is not a classroom instructional model, the decision about the right time for the celebration of initiation is not based on completion of a program—six months of classes with baptism (graduation) at the end. Rather the celebration is the outcome of a process of discerning the candidate's readiness for the particular rite to be celebrated, for example, the rite of becoming a catechumen, or the rite of election. The value of the process in the prac-

This essay first appeared in *Church* 1:2 (Summer, 1985). Published here by arrangement with National Pastoral Life Center, 299 Elizabeth St., New York, N.Y. 10012.

tice of initiation is beginning to affect other kinds of sacramental experience, most notably, within certain contexts, the sacrament of penance. In parish communities where the RCIA has flourished, Catholics who are separated from the church are asking to be included in the catechumenal process. In addition, a number of parishes and dioceses are developing programs such as "Come Home for Christmas" to integrate newly reconciled members into the community. In these efforts, the need for process is strongly evident. Perhaps these local efforts at re-evangelization are signaling the need for a fuller reform of the sacrament of penance than we have seen so far.

My purpose in this essay is not to offer a new form for the rite of penance, but some foundational principles for its reform. I want us to think more deeply about penance by taking a closer look at the process of reconciliation itself as it appears in the church's life and worship. Then I want to trace out some of the lines a reform of the rite might follow. My thesis is quite simply this: there are different kinds of alienation from the church, and each kind calls for a specific approach to reconciliation. I want to describe three: alienation of the unawakened, true alienation, and prophetic alienation. This is not an exhaustive typology, but this threefold division will help us to be clear about the varieties of human experience we must understand when we receive people "back" into the church.

In each instance—alienation of the unawakened, true alienation, and prophetic alienation—estrangement or distance from the church is the common element. We need to be more specific about the meaning of that distance. From the perspective of a liturgical spirituality, we can say that this estrangement is a kind of "excommunication"—not meant necessarily in canonical terms, but as a distancing from the eucharistic table. In some forms of alienation, the alienated do not gather at the community's table at all. Others may be physically present in the assembly, but do not really participate in the life of the community. When someone validly and authentically assumes a place at the table, that person is fully incorporated into the community. It is a matter of engaging the heart and the mind, of inspiring action and conviction. To gather validly and authentically at the community's table means an acceptance of the life of the community. This acceptance is not merely a passive consent; it is an active involvement in the com-

James Lopresti

mon life of apostles and witnesses who recognize the risen Lord in the breaking of bread.

The goal of reconciliation, then, is not mere reactivated membership, but active participation in the common life of apostles and witnesses. This goal ought to give rise to those processes that will end the estrangement of the alienated. What does it take to gather validly and authentically around the table as apostles and witnesses? The answer to that question defines the process of reconciliation. The process will be different for different people. Let us look at each form in its turn.

Alienation of the unawakened. Some may never have heard the personal call to be an apostle or witness. Theirs is an alienation of the first order. They have yet to recognize that a place has been prepared for them at the table. Because they have not yet heard his invitation to the table, they can be said to be "estranged" from a God not yet discovered. They await a first hearing of the gospel. Strictly speaking this description applies to the potential catechumen rather than to the already baptized. The catechumenate itself is a process of "reconciliation" to the table precisely because it is a means of awakening people to the gospel call. But it also applies to the situation of those who carry their membership card in the church but who have never "realized," that is, both discovered and made real, their inheritance and responsibility as followers of Jesus in the life of Christian community. The young adult who disappears from the church for a number of years may be the best example of the alienation of the unawakened. It is not so much that he/she left the church as that he/she never validly and authentically assembled at the table as an adult member with a unique call and gift to contribute to the life of the church.

True alienation. True alienation is a term I reserve in this essay for those who have heard the call of the gospel and at some point have rejected it. In the ancient church true alienation was recognized in the complete rupture of common life effected preeminently, but not exclusively, in acts of apostasy, adultery, and murder. The first Christian communities, so deeply aware of the Holy Spirit present in their assembly, experienced such alienation as a violent wrenching of their corporate life. Some of Paul's most anguished writings (Rom 6:12–20; 1 Cor 11:17–22) showed his own

Reconciling the Alienated

mystical awareness of the deeply rooted unity of Christian corporate life and the brutal violation it suffered when members chose to return to the slavery of sin from which their baptism, their first reconciliation, had originally freed them. He was not only outraged; he was dumbfounded by the possibility of such a choice. In later ages, this forceful testimony hardly appears in the abstracted descriptions of the differences between mortal and venial sin. Yet the intent is the same. Mortal means rupture, true alienation.

Prophetic alienation. Some absent themselves from the table for reasons that appear to be exactly the opposite from "true alienation." The prophetically alienated claim that those who do gather around the table are doing so inauthentically and/or invalidly. The issue is not whether or not their claim is unwarranted. To understand this form of alienation, we need only be able to discern their stance in relation to the community. The prophetically alienated take a stance over against the community because of what they claim to be the community's own failure or sin. In classic forms such alienation resulted in schism, the separation of the churches. In contemporary forms, while schism may not be publicly acknowledged, that is the private experience of the prophetically alienated. In the past, doctrinal or jurisdictional questions may have caused the separation. Today it is usually a matter of disagreement about moral principles, acceptability of variant lifestyles, and disputes over roles of church leadership.

No one is likely to be a pure representative of any of these three categories. The experience of the alienated person would probably be a mixture of any or all of them. The young adult who was never fully engaged in the life of the church may also vehemently oppose the magisterium's teaching on sexual ethics or its inattentiveness to particular social ills, while at the same time surrendering to a life of ruthless competitive consumerism, sexual manipulation, and violent egoism. While argument is possible about the details of any such analysis, it should be clear that the valid and authentic gathering at the table would take a different route to cover the distances implied in each kind of alienation.

There are, I would suggest, four specific markers for closing the distance in each journey: (1) hearing the gospel announced; (2) responding to the gospel announcement; (3) acquiring a new set of relationships to God and the world; and (4) celebrating the recon-

James Lopresti

ciled life. Let us look at these four markers for the three categories I have described: first for the unawakened, namely, the potential catechumen; then to the reconciliation of the truly alienated in what is essentially the penitential process; third, and briefly, in relation to the prophetically alienated. Finally, in the last section, I will develop in some detail a way to think about the rite of reconciliation in light of the RCIA experience.

THE UNAWAKENED

1. Hearing the gospel announced. Evangelization in the RCIA is meant to begin the process of nurturing conversion. When the candidate has heard the gospel, when he/she is said to have received "elementary faith" (RCIA, no. 68) and to have undergone "initial conversion" (RCIA, no. 15), then, according to the RCIA, it is time to celebrate, that is, manifest and effect, or "realize," the new Christian life already his/hers in the rite of becoming a catechumen. "Elementary faith" and "initial conversion" are vague terms to describe the goal of evangelization. In the implementation of the RCIA, those responsible for the catechumenate have to determine what these two dispositions look like in practice. It seems to me that one could equate "elementary faith" with an act of discovery. One is gifted with an awareness that Jesus is more than a character in history or a good model for behavior. Correspondingly, "initial conversion" implies at least the rudimentary desire to act on that discovery. More precisely, we could say that evangelization has the goal of stimulating the discovery that the Christian story as lived in this community is one's own story (elementary faith), and that there is the desire to follow up on the discovery (initial conversion). Thus, that discovery and desire, expressed in a prayerful act of realization, make one a Christian in the order of catechumen. One becomes an apprentice Christian, as it were. That determines the shape of the process to follow, namely catechesis.

2. Responding to the gospel announcement. Catechesis, in its fourfold shape, doctrinal formation, moral formation in the experience of life in Christian community, liturgy of the word, and apostolic involvement (RCIA, no. 19) should lead to a fuller development of the dispositions first conceived at the time of becoming a catechumen (RCIA, no. 19). Catechesis is intended to produce "enlightened faith" (RCIA, no. 134) and "conversion of attitude and

Reconciling the Alienated

behavior" (RCIA, no. 23) beyond elementary faith and initial conversion. One way to appropriate the meaning of these two terms is as descriptions of the skilled apprentice's accomplishments. One knows through at least some limited experience what is at stake in being an apostle and witness in the world, and while aware of his or her personal limitations, still hears the call to live an active Christian life in identity with other Christians. Therein lies a certain satisfaction, in the sense of a gifted certitude that this always unfolding Christian way of life is the only one that will satisfy a growing hunger to live well. Then it is time to "realize" (manifest) this call in the rite of election.

Undoubtedly the new self arising from the baptismal rebirth is not the product of an instant, unprepared change. Catechesis alone is not enough to lead to this transformation; something of a more passionate nature is required. Those elect to the font and the table are first illumined and purified in the Lenten "retreat," nurtured in the center of the community itself on the same retreat, with prayers of exorcism, laying on of hands, and anointings in prayerful assembly.

3. *Acquiring a new set of relationships.* When the process surges to its ritual climax at the Easter Vigil, truly the baptismal bath and the sealing by the spirit to this common life mark and effect a new set of relationships to God and the world. The initiate, stranger and alien no longer, is grafted onto the Body of Christ, relating to God as daughter or son and heir, to the community as part of the whole, to the world as agent of transformation. One is now a member of the order of the faithful, an order of apostles and witnesses to the Resurrection.

Just as this is true for the newly baptized, so it is, or should be, true for those who renew their baptismal promises at the Easter Vigil. While the Church has never permitted rebaptism, neither did the Church intend the renewal of baptismal vows to become an anemic and perfunctory ritual act. Now is the time to recapture the full significance of that renewal. "Unawakened" Catholics would do well to join in the catechumenal process in some way, at least during the Lent-Easter season. If that be the case, then the act of renewal of baptismal promises could manifest and effect a hitherto unknown level of participation in the full apostolic life of the community. In fact, for some people this renewal would constitute a special case of what scholastic theologians called "revivifi-

James Lopresti

cation," a coming to life of a mystical reality celebrated at an earlier time in the manner of a pledge. That is to say, someone baptized earlier into the Christian life now consents to that immersion and claims participation in the church's apostolic mission of witnessing to the death and resurrection of Jesus. This acceptance marks a new relationship to the church, to God, and to the world.

4. *Celebration.* The goal of the process is a valid and authentic gathering at the table in celebration of these new relationships. Here the people assemble and realize their unity with God and each other; each voice is part of the unity. In that sense the eucharist is not merely the sum of individual actions. Put another way, the eucharistic liturgy is more a corporate act of prayer than the occasion for private prayers. That is seen in the unity of many voices raised in one song, the unity of movement in procession to the one table, the unity of resolve to proclaim and live the gospel. Eucharist is the event that announces reconciliation more than any other. This celebration of apostolic witness is as much the goal of penance as it is of initiation.

Having examined the process of first reconciliation, or the awakening, we can now turn to reconciliation of those who have turned away, the truly alienated, and begin to hear the call to return to the faith community.

THE ALIENATED

1. *Hearing the gospel announced: reevangelization and confession.* As elementary faith and initial conversion are the marks of the acceptance of the gospel announcement to the awakening new Christians, so "sorrow" and "intent to lead a new life" mark the new hearing of the gospel as noted in the rite of penance (RP nos. 6, 6a). Sorrow appears in this context not as remorse, but as another kind of "discovery." It is made of the same stuff as elementary faith, a simultaneous discovery of one's distance and estrangement and of the real and valued divine invitation and empowerment to cross that distance and bridge that estrangement. That is, the discovery ("sorrow") gives rise to the desire ("intent to lead a new life"). That intent is akin to initial conversion, a desire to follow on the path opened up to the traveler. As the initiation journey realizes this accomplishment in the rite of becoming catechumen, so the penitential journey, in an analogous way, realizes this stage in the rite of confession. When I speak of confession here I mean

Reconciling the Alienated

only that. I do not mean to include absolution. The act of confessing God's abundant mercy encountering the human heart in its impoverished condition, weakened and held captive by sin, estranged and isolated by fear, is in itself deeply transformative, expressing its own reality and having its own effect preliminary to any consideration of absolution.

Just as the rite of becoming catechumen initiates a person into an apprentice membership in the church and marks the beginning of a process of formation through catechesis, illumination, and purification, so the rite of confession establishes one as a penitent, or "returning member" undergoing a special process of formation called penance. He or she is incorporated into the body in a manner analogous to that which follows on the rite of becoming catechumen. The goal of the process will be full reconciliation, an event similar in significant ways to baptism. It will be a statement and accomplishment of a new apostolic identity for one who is already a member of another order.

2. Responding to the gospel announcement: penance. There is a striking similarity in formational purpose between penance as process and catechesis as process. Both are means of satisfaction in the root sense of the word. When understood in a broad sense satisfaction can signal an intimate human and divine interchange. Léonce Hamelin describes it well: "There is nothing against conceiving satisfaction as being the process of the free person's maturation, whereby all the energies of the human reality are gradually integrated into the free person's basic option. Satisfaction is not a kind of fine whereby we pray for God's forgiveness. . . . No, satisfaction is a talent given us that we are to make bear a hundredfold fruit; concretely, it is our recommitment to the Christian life" (Léonce Hamelin, *Reconciliation in the Church* [Collegeville: The Liturgical Press, 1980] 62).

Just as the Lenten journey of illumination and purification befits this mystical attentiveness to the rhythms of transformation for the initiate, so Lent has the same special meaning for the penitent. He/she undergoes the passionate process of illumination and purification specifically as a prayerful event of a threefold nature. In the Lenten sacramentary and in the rite of penance, it includes: 1. cleansing/forgiveness of sin or defilement; 2. strengthening/healing of sickness, debilitation, or weakness; 3. rescue/liberation from blindness, captivity, compulsion. The penitential process, further-

James Lopresti

more, is holistic. It is not merely a matter of the struggle against personal sin. It includes the more demanding and pervasive matter of the rescue from the power of evil in its systemic manifestations. True reform of penance requires a full, pastorally astute attention to each of these parts of the penitential journey. Hence the amount of time and care given to the process of illumination and purification.

3. *Acquiring a new set of relationships: the reconciliation.* As that penitential catechesis and mystical process of illumination and purification surges to a climax, it too comes to expression in a transformation event. A new relationship is realized in the ritual event of reconciliation, the laying on of hands. This ritual action, however, marks more than a return to an active status in the church. It inaugurates a new kind of apostolic life and witness. The reconciled member becomes an apostle and witness, on the other side of the breach. It is very important to understand that. The newly reconciled member is a living reminder of what the sacrament of penance is expected, above all, to manifest to the world, namely, the victory of Christ over sin (RP, no. 1). The reconciled member knows full well the meaning of the *felix culpa* and of amazing grace. Second reconciliation (penance) like the first (baptism) is not a return but an advance to a new identity, and it is an advance on behalf of the world. It announces the kingdom arriving in compassion, rescue, and forgiveness to transform the world. It is a showing of the victory in the wounds of the resurrected body as evidenced in the life of the newly returned member of the body.

4. *Celebration.* Rightfully, the eucharistic liturgy becomes the great event of celebration of the new life achieved in this grace-filled sacramental process. The reason is exactly the same as appears in the process of initiation (RCIA, nos. 37–40, RP, no. 6d). The unity and peace of the assembly become the living embodiment of the kingdom. The eucharistic summit of the process becomes the source for the further living of the Christian life of apostles and witnesses.

THE PROPHETICALLY ALIENATED

The journey of reconciliation between the church and the one who claims the role of prophet is akin to an ecumenical movement. It begins with a mutual discovery of the sin of separation and the

Reconciling the Alienated

mutual desire for reunion. These inaugurate a process of dialogue, a catechesis in its own right, and a search for common illumination and purification. It climaxes in the *pax* which is not a mere return, but a peace founded in new relationships. As in all other cases, the process leads finally to the valid and authentic gathering of apostles and witnesses around the table.

PASTORAL IMPLEMENTATION

We have briefly examined three journeys to the table. Each is marked by four events or processes. It now remains only to note how some of this could be put into pastoral practice. In particular we might ask how the penitential journey would be charted in a faith community. I think the Rite of Penance itself gives us the schema in the following progression:

RP, no. 16: welcoming the penitent. "The priest briefly urges the penitent to have confidence in God." As this describes the rite of individual reconciliation, so it could be expanded to give meaning to the process we have been describing. Recall that the goal of such a reevangelization is sorrow and the intent to lead a new life. As many of the fourth-century desert mystics testify, the best way for ministers in the church to call others to awareness of God's mercy is to attend to their own experience of that mercy. That shared humility and confidence is indispensable. There is no room for arrogance and righteous display on the part of the church's ministers. There is only room for rejoicing in God's mercy as it has met us all, each in his/her own circumstances of life. This level of self-revelation to the world in the life of a community is experienced by the seeker as an act of the truest hospitality. It is "Christ welcoming the sinner" (RP, no. 1), sacramentally manifested. It simply means living our reconciled life in full view and with compassion for the fallen and hurt. It is not a matter of paternal or condescending wisdom but of mutual and compassionate recognition of our common human struggle.

RP, no. 17: reading the word of God. "Through the word of God, the Christian receives light to recognize his [sic] sins and is called to conversion and to confidence in God's mercy." Undoubtedly the proclamation of the gospel is what leads to hearing, and hearing the gospel leads to confession of God's mercy. Gatherings of alienated Christians, like the gatherings of inquirers in the

James Lopresti

precatechumenate, should in some way lead to mutual acts of proclamation of, and attentiveness to, the Scriptures. Such experiences, when they eventually lead to the discovery and desire, that is, sorrow and the intent to lead a new life, prepare the hearts of the alienated for the celebration of the rite of confession. Certainly Ash Wednesday or the first Sunday of Lent would be appropriate times to celebrate that rite. Such a celebration would also inaugurate the Lenten season of purification and illumination for the newly enrolled penitents who would join with the elect and other members of the parish in prayer and practices of the season.

RP, no. 18. "This [act of penance] should serve not only to make up for the past, but also to help him [sic] with an antidote to weakness." We need merely ask what kind of antidote and satisfaction is needed. Prayer companions or sponsors? Spiritual directors? Prayer in common with one's fellow penitents? New experiences of the church at work in the world? What is needed should be done. Satisfaction is the goal. These choices would give shape to the Lenten retreat.

The ritual act of *imposition of hands* and the *prayer of absolution* complete the process. The *praenotanda* says this about the meaning of the prayer of absolution: "It underlies the ecclesial aspect of the sacrament because reconciliation with God is asked for and given through the ministry of the church" (RP, no. 19). Surely the climactic event of reconciliation celebrated at the end of the Lenten journey, perhaps on Wednesday of Holy Week, should be a corporate act of joy and consolation, the more so if some members of the community have joined the returning members as special participants in the Lenten journey. It may be a most appropriate gesture to manifest the community's deep love of the special witness performed by these apostles-beyond-the-breach by choosing them to be the ones whose feet are washed at the Holy Thursday *mandatum.*

The eucharistic table of the Easter Vigil is the goal of all processes of reconciliation. As the newly initiated take a special place around the table at this Eucharist, so too should the newly reconciled. Here apostles and witnesses of all kinds find the deepest experience of their new life. Validly and authentically gathered around the table, through the great fifty-day celebration of Easter, all can draw fruit from the experience of these journeys

Reconciling the Alienated

of reconciliation, whatever the distance or the estrangement overcome.

Clearly such a far-reaching reform of the rite of penance, like the RCIA itself, could not be accomplished without the active participation of many people in a life-giving community. Sponsors, or partners of some kind, spiritual directors, catechists, and people of hospitality arising from a community eager to embrace the world and its fellow poor are all needed. Such a reform is not only a matter of changing a rite, but also a matter of changing the heart and making life choices. Engaged in such deeply Christ-centered action, a community will discover for itself the struggles and joys of being ambassadors of reconciliation in a world divided against itself. It is only when living communities at the grassroots level decide for themselves that such a commitment to reconciliation is their primary call, that any reform of penance, indeed any implementation of the RCIA, will be more than changing furniture and rewriting texts. The process of reconciliation is the process of more deeply becoming the Body of Christ for the sake of the world. It is no more, and no less, than that.

James Lopresti

Joseph A. Hart

A Proposal for the Renewal of Penance in the Lenten Season

It is evident from the interventions of the 1983 Synod of Bishops that there are many in the Church who believe that with a little more tinkering with formulas, a few more heartfelt exhortations from pulpits, a bit more detailed explanations of the nature of sin and forgiveness, the line will form once again in front of our confessionals.[1] I think they are mistaken.

The sacrament is facing a crisis of meaning. The common experience of those who once frequented the confessional but now do so seldom or never is that sacramental penance does not seem to make much of a difference in their lives. In an earlier era all that was needed was an explanation that God works mysteriously and imperceptively and, although we do not see the results in our lives, nevertheless, God's grace is there *ex opere operato*. We automatically receive God's grace provided we place no block in its path. The educated laity of today seems less ready to accept that explanation.

Where God is present, they have been taught to believe, there is peace, joy, and love. But their lives still bear the scars of sin and disintegration in spite of frequent use of the confessional and the performance of the assigned penances. Simply to rehearse one's sins in the anonymous darkness and to hear in reply a juridical declaration of forgiveness leaves many still feeling empty and discouraged because this rite of reconciliation seems powerless to effect the real integration, wholeness and reconciliation that many so desperately seek.

This is not at all to call into question the power of God to transform us, or the reality of grace in our lives. It is rather to call into question some key assertions of the theological tradition that supported the practice of penance which we have inherited.

If grace is extrinsic to us, as the scholastic theologians all held, then in the ordinary course of things we cannot experience it. All that we can experience are the outward signs which point to the work of the unseen God. The fact that I feel nothing or have experienced no change in my life is insignificant in this theory of grace. But if Karl Rahner is correct, and grace is intrinsic to us,[2] then a person cannot be graced without the effects of the indwelling Trinity becoming accessible to experience. One cannot be graced without being transformed. One cannot be graced without the manifestation of faith, hope, and love. If Rahner's theory of grace is right then something is wrong with our theology and practice of the sacrament of penance.

Our present theology of the sacrament of penance is based not just on the theory that grace is extrinsic to us, but also on the thirteenth century Scotist and the later attritionist doctrines of penance. These theories tell us that, although we can be forgiven our sins because of an act of pure love, there is an easier way. We need muster only the most minimal sorrow and the sacrament does the rest. By an act of absolution which produces an infusion of unseen, unfelt grace, attrition becomes contrition, not through a subjective intensification of sorrow but as a type of objective completion of sorrow within.[3]

Such notions lend themselves to laxity in repentance and a too magical interpretation of the rite. With the use of the proper formula, God is forced into forgiving my sins, so to speak, whether or not there is true sorrow in me, whether or not there is true change in me.

But the twentieth century rejects the magical. It is suspicious of quick fixes and cheap grace. It judges the value of things by the results. It asserts that what costs nothing means nothing.

The early Church knew nothing of "magical" penance. Tertullian required the sinner to adopt a "mode of life which calls down mercy"[4] for satisfaction, propitiation, and reconciliation. Cyprian and Origen taught that baptism bestowed pardon by free grace while penance involved a painful process of purification.[5] Enrollment in the ancient order of penitents insured an intensive period of prayer, fasting, and almsgiving as well as the exclusion from the eucharist, the adoption of penitential dress, and the renunciation of sexual intercourse. Celtic penitential practice from the sixth century on produced a system of tariff penances which were based on a relentless notion of external atoning practices to bring about sincere internal contrition and conversion.

But the penitential practices of the ancient and early medieval Church, while not favoring magic, did tend toward an external

Joseph A. Hart

rigorism which, despite protests to the contrary, seemed to down-play the action of the grace of God in our healing. Repentance was something we achieve and offer to God rather than some-thing that God accomplishes in us. Although theologians like Augustine reminded those doing penance that it was not the difficulty nor the duration of the penitential act that was important but the depth of sorrow,[6] the act of penance often eclipsed the purpose of penance. And so by the eighth century the penitential order was bogged down in its own rigorism and Celtic penance was caught in a legalistic web of unrealistic penances and unhelp-ful substitutions or "redemptions." Hence, many maintain that these ancient and medieval practices can offer us little help in reviving the practice of penance in the twentieth century.

I believe they are wrong. As the Church in each age carries on a dialogue with its own times, forming and reforming its expres-sions of faith and practice, valuable insights are gained. Some in-sights are classic and some are period pieces, but all give us glimpses into the way we are made and how God deals with us. I wish to propose that, by drawing out the classic elements of the tradition of penance and rearranging them in a way that is con-sonant with an intrinsic notion of grace, the sacrament of penance may perhaps be given new life in our times.

THE CLASSIC TRADITION OF PENANCE

There are seven elements in the tradition of penance that I term classic:

1. The patristic era emphasized *exomologesis:* assuming a *peniten-tial attitude.* It recognized that genuine penance must have an in-terior and an exterior form. Merely verbal sorrow could be a delusion. Repentance was seen to be real only if it bore fruit inter-nally in a changed outlook and externally in a changed behavior.[7]

2. The third century understood that the immediate object of ec-clesiastical forgiveness was not God's forgiveness of sin but rather the *reconciliation of the sinner with the Church.* Not that this "peace of the Church" had no relationship to the forgiveness of God. On the contrary, the reconciled penitent was seen to receive, by the fact of reconciliation, the Spirit of the Father and the pledge of eternal life.[8]

3. The order of penitents from the fourth century on provided *community involvement* in the process of conversion and reconcilia-

Lenten Proposal

tion. The penitents looked to the prayer of the bishop and the intercession of the community of Christians to obtain the forgiveness of God and the return of the Holy Spirit to their lives. The community watched over the progress of conversion providing not just supervision but much needed encouragement and support.[9]

4. According to the testimony of the fifth-century popes, *Lent is the proper time for penance.* Leo the Great urged that this six-week period be used not just as a preparation period for those to be baptized at the Easter Vigil but also for those who looked forward to the forgiveness of sins through reconciliation to the Church on Holy Thursday.[10] Innocent I, in fact, expressly forbade reconciliation to take place at any other time during the year except in case of danger of death.[11]

5. Sixth century Celtic penance, through monastic influence, added *spiritual direction* to the practice of penance. It encouraged full openness with a spiritual father or mother in order to bring about complete healing and renewed spiritual growth. The spiritual director, manifesting his/her own sorrow for sin and a willingness to carry another's burdens, joined the penitent not just in prayer but in penitential activity.

6. During the Carolingian era *confession,* often a significant part of the penitential procedure, became one of the most important parts of that process. Carolingian theology, reinforced by popular piety, considered that a penitent received the grace of forgiveness more readily through the self-humiliation of confession. Although confession in the ancient Church was thought useful primarily in helping the confessor to assign a fitting penance, now the act of confessing came to be considered such an important penitential act that confession to one or more laypeople was encouraged to inculcate the virtue of penance.[12]

7. The Church of the tenth century began to break down the barrier between the ordinary Christian and those in the order of penitents. *All Christians were in need of repentance.* All were urged to confess their sins to a priest at the beginning of Lent, to receive voluntarily the imposition of ashes, to do penance side by side with those in public penance, and to be present on Holy Thursday for the reconciling prayer of the bishop.[13]

CONTEMPORARY CELEBRATION

These, then, are the classic elements from the first millennium. I

Joseph A. Hart

174

feel that they can be restructured into a thoroughly sensible celebration of penance as we begin the third millennium. They can be regrouped under five headings:

1. *Lent is the proper time for penance.* The evolution of the Church year adequately demonstrates that there is something deep within us which needs times of celebration and times of ordinariness, times of feast and times of fast. It seems psychologically and spiritually wise, then, to confine any intensive activity aimed at reforming our lives to a relatively brief period throughout the year. Someone who is always on a diet is never on a diet.

Although we are ever conscious of our sinfulness, we should heed the Council of Trent's admonition, based on the ancient Church's practice, that the eucharist is the chief antidote by which we are freed from our daily sins and kept free from more serious sin.[14] Likewise following ancient practice, during the ordinary time of the year, the sacrament of penance should not be celebrated, except in the case of emergency (for example, among the sick or for those especially burdened in conscience). Whenever such private reconciliation occurs, penitents would be reminded of their obligation to return to celebrate penance publicly with the community during the Lenten season. The Church cannot stress enough that there is but one extraordinary penitential time of year, a forty-day period of preparation prior to the celebration of the paschal mystery, when all Christians are reminded in a special way of their sin and need for repentance.

In order to make this penitential season really extraordinary, it would be ideal if the usual activities of the parish community were suspended: no committee or council meetings or parish social functions; no programs of sacramental preparation (with the exception of the RCIA), no scheduled baptism, no marriages. All these would be excluded for the time being in order that the community might focus completely on its most important task, conversion, as it prepares the catechumens for baptism and the community of penitents for reconciliation.

2. *Assuming a penitential attitude.* Unfortunately, the Lenten season in the past few years has become a season in search of a purpose. Since the drastic reduction in the laws of compulsory fast and abstinence, parish communities have sought clever but not wholly successful ways to give the forty days an expiatory mean-

ing. Although Christians are still encouraged to undertake acts of penance appropriate to their state in life, many are confused and disoriented for lack of community support and individual guidance. The only acts of penance with which most Catholics are familiar have been termed of late negative and inappropriate because their aim is viewed to be an appeasement of God's wrath or the subjugation of the "evil" body.

Twentieth-century psychology understands that exterior acts and interior attitudes are intimately interrelated. The modification of behavior can bring about a modification of attitude and vice versa. Likewise, our tradition of penance has always understood that true penance must have an interior and an exterior aspect and that these two are not really separable: change of life and change of heart are two sides of the coin of conversion. Therefore, to expect any significant change in life to happen during the penitential season, something more than an internal sentiment of sorrow is necessary. External concrete acts of penance are also needed. The Lenten season must be a time when Christians, by the help of God and with the prayers and support of the community, makes painful but positive changes in their manner of living. This has been traditionally done by prayer (a greater openness to God), fasting (denying oneself some good but unnecessary gratifications), and almsgiving (consciously giving more of oneself in loving service).

3. *The act of confessing and the involvement of the community.* If we have learned anything in this century, it is that in the long run rugged individualism accomplishes very little by way of changing hearts. The modern movements that have accomplished radical change in individuals have done so through some group support process. In a more secular context, the success of such movements as Alcoholics Anonymous and Gamblers Anonymous is well known. If the Church preaches a radical withdrawal of its very human members from the grip of sin, it can only expect this to be achieved with the prayerful support of a whole community of sinners.

The entire Lenten process should therefore stress the communal. According to custom, the community would first gather on Ash Wednesday. There, after the proclamation of the gospel of repentance, each member would come forward individually and, placing his or her hands in those of the confessor, relate the major sin or

Joseph A. Hart

sins of his or her current life. The priest, without comment, would then lay his hands for a moment on the penitent's head, pray for the grace of conversion and then impose ashes with the admonition "Turn away from sin and be faithful to the gospel." This face-to-face encounter is important not just because it has been commended since ancient times as an act of mortification but also because many twentieth-century psychologists have praised it as a mentally wholesome exercise. I must hear myself form the words of bitter honesty: I am a sinner.

Finally, the presider, reminding the community that the body is only as strong as its weakest member, would exhort all present to pray for one another, support one another, watch out for one another, and do penance for one another, especially for the weak, during the forty days of penance ahead.[15]

Then on each Sunday of Lent, when the community comes together once more, the presider would extend his hands over them and pray again for their conversion of heart. He would remind them that it is by God's power that all true change comes about and that their penance is only a sign of that change. In addition, he would insist that the penitents not practice their acts of penance on Lenten Sundays. This traditional Lenten break from penance on the Lord's Day keeps strong penitents from growing proud of their olympic activity and allows weaker penitents to break up Lent into six, more manageable blocks.

4. *Spiritual direction.* Spiritual direction is something that in the recent past has been a luxury for the few. Each parish should make it a priority that, during the Lenten season, it is available to many. On Ash Wednesday, everyone would be encouraged not just to confess their sins but to consult with a spiritual director at least once in Lent as the best means to break the habits of sin and to find appropriate penances for spiritual growth. By eliminating all meetings and functions from their calendar, every member of the parish staff would have sufficient time during the day and the evening to help people in their growth in the life of the Spirit. In addition, every parish has many good and holy people who, because of their practical experience of life, could also assist in this task of spiritual direction after proper education and training. Thus, the ancient and admirable practice of lay confessors and directors would be restored to the Church.

Lenten Proposal

During the Lenten season, parishes should also offer weekend retreats, bible study groups, faith-sharing groups, and other comparable spiritual programs to provide an environment conducive to the growth of the broadest possible spectrum of parishioners.[16] Although good leaders and much effort are required to conduct such programs, the more that people in the community are called upon to give to each other spiritually, the more they themselves will grow.

Moreover, during Lent, every parish should make available at parish expense professional marriage and family counselors. Through this counsel, those who have encountered blocks to their spiritual growth can gain insights into how to remove them. Whatever leads to wholeness leads also to holiness.

5. *Reconciliation with the Church.* Finally, on Tuesday or Wednesday of Holy Week (Thursday now presents practical difficulties), the community would assemble once again to celebrate the final part of the process of reconciliation. They have harmed each other by their sinfulness throughout the year, but now, in the Lenten season, they have built up each other in love. The presider recalls high points of the Lenten journey that is now ending. Perhaps singling out some particular acts of love that they have demonstrated, he will remind one and all of their need to continue this growth. After God's healing word has been proclaimed again, the presider prays over them one last time and begs the mercy of God for their sins. He then gives them sacramental absolution, forgiving them in the name of the Church for all the sins they had confessed on Ash Wednesday. All exchange the sign of peace. They are now ready to celebrate with joy the Easter mysteries.

CONCLUSION

In this new way of restoring the tradition, penance would not just have returned to Lent. It would have returned to its ancient order of celebration: confession, penance, reconciliation. It would have returned to its original communal context. The word "penance" would have been reinvested with its old meaning. By the time Holy Week dawns, the community has seen personal growth; it understands the purpose of Lent; it has experienced the action of grace in their lives; it has witnessed the growth of faith, hope, and love. The community truly celebrates the peace of the Church and the forgiveness of God.

Joseph A. Hart

Finally, and perhaps most importantly, though the sacrament has moved away from some venerable practices which no longer proved helpful in the ordinary life of the Christian community, it has regained its vitality by expressing to a new generation the loving forgiveness of God.

NOTES

1. Cf. *Origins* 13:18–22 (1983).

2. Karl Rahner, "Concerning the Relationship Between Nature and Grace," in *Theological Investigations,* vol. 1 (Baltimore: Helicon Press, 1961) 297–317.

3. John Duns Scotus, *Opus Oxoniense* IV d. 14, q. 2, n. 14.

4. Tertullian, *De Paenitentia* 9, 3.

5. Cyprian, *Ep.* 55, 22; Origen, *In Jer. hom.* 16, 15.

6. Augustine, *Enchiridion* 17, 65.

7. Tertullian, *De Paenitentia* 9, 1–2.

8. Cf. Cyprian, *Ep.* 57, 4; 55, 13.

9. Cf. Augustine, *Enchiridion in Ps.* 61, 23.

10. Leo I, *Serm.* 45; 49, 3.

11. Innocent I, *Ep.* 1, 7.

12. Confession to a lay physician of souls appears to have been of ancient origin. As early as the third century, Origen (*In Ps.* 37, hom. 2, 6) seems to have approved the practice which flourished among the Eastern desert fathers and mothers and eventually found its way into Western monasticism and later into common penitential practice. These confessors would listen and advise but not bestow ecclesiastical absolution. The suggested use of lay confessors continues even in the work of Thomas Aquinas (Cf. *Suppl.* a. 2) but dies out shortly after the Scotist emphasis on the power of absolution. Cf. Bernard Poschmann, *Penance and the Anointing of the Sick* (New York: Herder and Herder, 1964) 70, 176.

13. Beginning in the tenth century, faithful Christians who were not in the order of penitents and not excluded from the eucharist, gathered with the penitents on Holy Thursday to be included in the bishop's prayer of absolution. This seems to be the beginning of the practice of general absolution (see Poschmann, *Penance* 149). Although the recep-

Lenten Proposal

tion of ashes continued to be a sign of admission to the order of penitents, by the eleventh century the custom of having all the penitent faithful receive ashes was widespread and in some places even mandatory. See J. A. Jungmann, *Die lateinische Bussriten in ihrer geschichtlichen Entwicklung* (Innsbruck: Rauch, 1932) 59–60.

14. DS 1638.

15. It must be the entire community which celebrates penance. Cardinal Joseph Bernardin in an intervention at the 1983 Synod of Bishops (*Origins*, 13:324–386 [1983]) has suggested the re-establishment of an order of penitents modeled on the RCIA process. James Lopresti's "remembering" process (cf. his presentation elsewhere in this volume) seems to be the working out of this idea. Both of these plans suffer by repeating the mistakes of the past and failing to draw on its lessons. As long as some are singled out from the midst of the community as "the sinners," not only do few come forward but the fundamental truth of the gospel is missed: all are sinners in need of repentance.

16. In many parish communities inactive Catholics have asked to join the RCIA program in order to learn more about their faith as they return to active life in the Church. There seems to be a clear need for a special group process distinct from the RCIA to aid these people in rejoining the community. This can be accomplished during Lenten season by using a faith-sharing group with this particular focus. Thus these newly returned members can be bonded anew to the parish community without being isolated in the process from the larger parish community that is doing penance along with them.

Joseph A. Hart

Jon Nilson

"Opportunities Incalculable:" Reconciliation and the U.S. Economy

> Great questions of Faith, great questions of society are being
> worked out. The opportunities for God's Church are incalculable
> and Her obligations unmeasurable. She must take her part in the
> solution of these questions. . . . We, Her representatives and Her
> children, must take a part in their settlement.[1]

It is easy to imagine reading paragraphs like the following in a
future account of twentieth-century Catholicism:

> The revised Rite of Penance was finally promulgated in 1973. It did
> little, however, to restore the sacrament as a vital factor in Catholic
> life. Instead, it brought the contrast between the pre-conciliar and
> post-conciliar visions of sin and forgiveness into sharper focus. As
> the complexities and horrors of sin became more evident in an in-
> creasingly interdependent world, demands for a further revision
> could not be postponed.
>
> The latest rite of reconciliation, promulgated in 19??, offers many
> different ways to celebrate the sacrament. These ways reflect the
> reality of a multi-cultural Church as well as the analogous under-
> standings of sin and forgiveness that took root among Catholics af-
> ter Vatican II. As a consequence, the sacrament of reconciliation has
> been restored to its rightful place in the life of the Church.

Such a passage can hardly be considered a fantasy in light of
the widespread and well-founded criticisms of the 1973 Rite. This
revised ritual does not, for instance, adequately express a postconciliar awareness and theology of sin: indeed, the theology underlying the Rite seems identical with a post-Tridentine theology of
penance.[2] The new rite preserves a model of clerical domination,
whose theological and practical liabilities were obvious after Vatican II.[3] The new ways of celebrating the sacrament are also insufficiently grounded in human needs and rights.[4]

Informed, critical comment indicates that the appearance of
another "new" rite of reconciliation is only a matter of time—and
perhaps a short time at that. So it is providential that the U.S.
bishops' pastoral letter, *Economic Justice for All: Catholic Social
Teaching and the U.S. Economy*, is now completed and will enter

into the Church's bloodstream.[5] The letter offers an understanding of the reality and power of sin which urgently needs to be incorporated into a new Rite of Penance. Of course, *Economic Justice for All: Catholic Social Teaching and the U.S. Economy* can certainly be effective on its own terms. But it can and should play as well a major role in the Church's effort to restore the rites of reconciliation as signs and events of God's loving power over all the afflictions of sin in ourselves, our communities, our nations, and our world.

"SIN" IN THE LETTER ON THE ECONOMY

The pastoral letter begins as follows: "Every perspective on economic life that is human, moral and Christian must be shaped by three questions: What does the economy do *for* people? What does it do *to* people? And how do people *participate* in it?" (no. 1).[5] Why such questions? It is because the dignity of the human person, realized in community with others, is the criterion against which all aspects of economic life must be measured (no. 28). This conviction is the theoretical axis of the letter. Its main root is the biblical vision of creation in which woman and man are made in the very image and likeness of God. "As such every human being possesses an inalienable dignity which stamps human existence prior to any division into races or nations and prior to human labor and human achievement" (n. 32). Guided by this vision which is concretized and amplified in Catholic social teaching, the letter argues that human dignity so understood entails the recognition of certain basic human rights, without which "human dignity" becomes an empty rhetorical flourish.

> A number of human rights also concern human welfare and are of a specifically economic nature. First among these are the rights to life, food, clothing, shelter, rest, medical care and basic education. These are indispensable to the protection of human dignity. In order to ensure these necessities, all persons have a right to earn a living, which for most people in our economy is through remunerative employment. All persons also have a right to security in the event of sickness, unemployment and old age. Participation in the life of the community calls for the protection of this same right to employment, as well as the right to healthful working conditions. . . .
> These fundamental personal rights—civil and political as well as social and economic—state the minimum conditions for social institutions that respect human dignity, social solidarity and justice. . . .

Jon Nilson

Any denial of these rights harms persons and wounds the human community (no. 80).

The letter provides evidence, however, that these human/economic rights are being massively and systematically violated. For instance, unemployment afflicts about 7% of the labor force, about eight million people, who are disproportionately black, Hispanic, young adults and female heads of households. Among the devastating consequences of joblessness are child abuse, excessive drinking, divorce, and even suicide (nos. 15, 138–142).

Over thirty-three million of our fellow citizens fall into the category of poverty, as it is officially defined. They live "on the streets" and sleep in parks, subways, and flophouses. They find their food in garbage cans or soup kitchens. The children of poverty (estimated to be upwards of 25% of the children in the U.S.) are malnourished so that their physical and mental development are retarded, if not permanently impaired (nos. 16–17, 178–182).

Half the world's population live in countries where the annual per-capita income is $400 or less. Of every 100 children there, fifteen die before the age of five and many of the survivors are physically or mentally underdeveloped. Ample world food resources do not help the world's half-million people who are always hungry (no. 254).

These facts are essential to an adequate understanding of the contemporary reality of sin. Obviously, "sin" in this context does not mean the single act of a single individual. Rather, it refers to specific conditions of social existence which are contrary to the will of God.[6] It is closer to what we used to call a "state of sin," i.e., a condition of the person resulting from an unrepented, seriously evil act. But the act in question here is not that of one person but of many persons in concert. The denial of human rights which leads to unemployment, poverty, massive inequalities in the distribution of the world's goods and even death (no. 5) is structural, systematic, and political in nature. It is "social sin."

Gregory Baum discusses the depth and complexity of social sin by articulating four levels of it. "The first level of social sin is made up of the injustices and dehumanizing trends built into the various institutions—social, political, economic, religious, and others—which embody people's collective life."[7] This level of social sin is manifested, for instance, in laws which allow wealthy persons and major corporations to pay no taxes whatsoever and thus evade their fair share of the costs of public services.

"A second level . . . is made up of the cultural and religious symbols, operative in the imagination and fostered by society, that legitimate and reinforce the unjust institutions and thus intensify the harm done to a growing number of people."[8] The pastoral letter itself points to negative stereotypes of the unemployed and the poor (nos. 193–194). These often serve to justify government inaction and to paralyze individual efforts at remediation. As a symbol, the right to private property has been taken as a license to exploit natural resources without concern for the common good or the needs of future generations (no. 12).

"On a third level, social sin refers to the false consciousness created by these institutions and ideologies through which people involve themselves collectively in destructive action as if they were doing the right thing. This false consciousness persuades us that the evil we do is in fact a good thing in keeping with the aim and purpose of our collective well-being."[9] For example, the values of patriotism and loyalty are twisted to prevent criticism and alteration of the established order. Proposals for radical social change are called "communistic" and thus excluded before they are fully heard and evaluated. Executives speak of their responsibility to the corporation's stockholders and overlook their responsibilities to its employees, customers, and neighbors.

"Finally, . . . a fourth level of social sin which is made up of the collective decisions, generated by the distorted consciousness, which increase the injustices in society and intensify the power of the dehumanizing trends."[10] Social sin, therefore, is sin for which no single individual is fully responsible. It structures and scars the world into which each person is born. As we enter that world, however, we become deeply entangled in social sin. Inadvertently we ratify it and intensify its power. We buy the products of companies who, unknown to us, exploit their workers, deplete natural resources, and stimulate unhealthy cravings by their advertising. Our pension funds are invested in firms that manufacture and sell weaponry to countries whose people are chronically hungry. Our taxes support the "contras" in Nicaragua and pay for the nuclear missiles that may yet create a global holocaust.[11]

But we also become *victims* of social sin. Ideologies and stereotypes blind us to the plight of our sisters and brothers. Our vision

Jon Nilson

184

of them and of ourselves becomes distorted. The ways and means of a "consumer culture" infect our perspectives and sensibilities constantly and subtly (no. 334).[12] We pay in time, effort, and money for the injustices which produce shoddy goods, inflated prices, dangerous toys and drugs. We are deprived of the talents of the poor, the hungry, and the jobless.

RECONCILIATION IN LIGHT OF SOCIAL SIN
The Church's experience in dealing with individual sin is age-old and extensive. Its understanding of social sin is relatively new. In what ways should the Church carry out its mission of reconciliation vis-a-vis social sin? This question will be with us for a long time, but the Church's work of reconciliation is already well-begun.

The schools and social agencies sponsored by the Church have been the most pervasive and enduring of its institutional efforts to respond to social sin. The tradition of papal social thought (which actually predates *Rerum Novarum* in 1891)[13] has proven to be a powerful theoretical and practical resource. The U.S. bishops' 1983 letter, *The Challenge of Peace*, seeks to reconcile nations and heal the suicidal divisions between us. There are clear signs that the authors of *Economic Justice for All: Catholic Social Teaching and the U.S. Economy* also see their work as reconciling (nos. 5, 27). And they point out that laypeople must play the major role in that reconciliation which is the effect of justice in economic life (no. 332).

Still, an indispensable part of the contemporary task of reconciliation must be the incorporation of the pastoral letter's more adequate understanding of sin into a new rite of reconciliation. That sacrament is the "moment" when the Church attends most directly to the causes, power, and consequences of sin, only to realize and experience again God's power over it. As I have demonstrated, sin is not only the attitudes and actions of individuals. It is also "the injustices and dehumanizing trends built into the various institutions . . ., the cultural and religious symbols, operative in the imagination and fostered by society, that legitimate and reinforce the unjust institutions . . ., the false consciousness created by these institutions and ideologies . . ., (and) the collective decisions, generated by the distorted consciousness," as Baum points out. Thus, the rite for celebrating the sacra-

Reconciliation and the Economy

ment must come to grips with social sin. As long as it does not, it fails to express the full scope and power of Jesus' salvation. It misses the evil which pervades and infects contemporary social life and thus reinforces the current "crisis" in the celebration of the sacrament.

Some Church people assert that secularism and consumerism have robbed people of their sense of sin. They see our culture as the culprit responsible for the disuse of the sacrament today.[14] This explanation is surely too simple. Last year eight million people were looking for work but could not find it (no. 15). Today thirty-three million people are poor; another twenty to thirty million are needy (no. 16). Every day they suffer the contradiction between their God-given dignity and their deprivation. They know sin intimately, even though they may not use that word to name the cause of their suffering.

The public responses to starvation in Africa ("We Are the World"), to the plight of American farmers (Farm Aid), and to hunger and homelessness (Hands Across America) may be accompanied by hoopla and gimmickry that offend the purist in us. Nonetheless, events like these indicate that peoples' sense of sin is vivid and their desire to eradicate it is genuine. They do not avoid the sacrament of reconciliation because they are indifferent to the reality of sin. They ignore it because the rite does not come to grips with sin as they know it. Charlie Cappa, the "hero" of Martin Scorsese's film, *Mean Streets,* speaks for them all when he says, "You don't make up for your sins in a church. You do it in the streets, you do it at home. The rest is b_____s_____ and you know it."

THE TWO TASKS

As long as the 1973 Rite of Penance encompasses only personal sin, we have no corporate way to remember and to celebrate God's reconciling power over social sin. Thus, the sacrament's potential to transform us and the world in which we are both participants and victims is drastically truncated. The "continuing agenda" of reconciliation, then, must include at least two tasks, one interim and one long-range.

The first task is to develop ways to use the 1973 Rite to deal with the full reality of sin. The Rite needs to be creatively employed so that we can recognize social sin in our lives and find God's for-

Jon Nilson

186

giveness and healing for it. This means that the veins of sin running through our humanly constructed world must be exposed for what they are: homicidal and contrary to God's desire for God's people. My grasp of sin is inadequate, for example, until I begin to see how my tax dollars are spent, how my retirement funds are invested, and what kinds of companies my disposable income supports. My experience of sin is too pale and thin until I see how I supported policies and programs that deny people their dignity; how I often "blamed the victims" of poverty, hunger, and joblessness for their plight;[15] how I tolerated too readily what erodes the bonds of trust and understanding in the human community.

Can we celebrate the rites of reconciliation in a way that it empowers us to live in this world in the light and strength of the good news? Can the sacrament, for instance, help Christians so often faced with the difficult decisions in the economic order (no. 336)? If the laity are to play the main role in transforming the world (no. 332), they must be part of it. But we live "between the times." One cannot insist on perfect justice as a characteristic of every enterprise in which one engages. Consider the manager who is suddenly ordered to oversee the relocation of a factory. S/he may be anguished over those who will be put out of work. S/he may strongly disagree with the "profits over people" approach that can base a decision like this. S/he may be powerless to change it and deeply troubled at having to carry it out. Is there a way of celebrating the sacrament that brings this manager what s/he needs?

As we better grasp the centrality of justice in the gospel and see action for justice as an ingredient of our discipleship, our need for such a celebration will become more and more urgent. The justice agenda is massive, complex, and long-term. Its sheer intractability can overwhelm or depress people. Just as we learn not to rely upon our own efforts for our personal salvation, we must learn not to rely on our combined human effort to effect the social dimension of salvation. There, too, salvation is first, last, and always God's work. Only God's word will convince us that we can face the worst effects of social sin without despair. Only God's love can teach us to struggle without rancor. Only God's power can strengthen us for the long haul. Only God's patience can

Reconciliation and the Economy

enable us to be patient over our failures to cooperate in the work of the kingdom.[16]

The second task is to develop new rites for the sacrament which will effect and signify the reconciliation necessitated by social sin. True, individuals do not commit social sin. Social sin is not conscious or deliberate or willful. Yet it still devastates peoples' lives and alienates them from one another. Reconciliation is needed even for indeliberate acts. One may be alert while driving well below the speed limit, yet hit and injure a small child who runs into the street from behind a parked car. The injury is not your fault. But you will still seek pardon and not rest till you receive it.

We need new rites, therefore, which will bring divine forgiveness, healing, and power to use as victims and participants in social sin. We need rites that will restore the bonds between us and those whom we have harmed by our unconscious ratification and intensification of injustice. We need a way to celebrate the sacrament as a community of mutually dependent brothers and sisters. We need rites to seek and bestow the forgiveness that corresponds to our wrong. Until then we endure the diminished power of the sacrament to make this world ever more truly the kingdom of God and us ever more truly people of that kingdom.

NOTES

1. Words of James E. Quigley, Archbishop of Chicago, July 16, 1915, cited in Charles Shanabruch, *Chicago's Catholics: The Evolution of an American Identity* (Notre Dame: University of Notre Dame Press, 1981) 128.

2. Ladislas Orsy, *The Evolving Church and the Sacrament of Penance* (Denville: Dimension, 1978) 141 and 153–154, respectively.

3. James Dallen, "Church Authority and the Sacrament of Penance: The Synod of Bishops," *Worship* 58 (1984) 194–214.

4. Cardinal Bernardin, Archbishops Roach and Flores, Bishop Vaughn, "Questions About General Absolution," in *Origins* 13 (Oct. 20, 1983) 328–330. They also point out that "The clear intent of the Rite of Penance is to commend individual confession and absolution . . . to limit the types of circumstances in which recourse may be had legitimately to general absolution without previous individual confession of mortal

Jon Nilson

sins'' (329). Bernardin had actually proposed the sketch of a fourth rite to the Synod (ibid., 324–326).

5. This and the following numbers in parentheses refer to paragraph numbers in the text of the pastoral letter.

6. Paragraphs 35–55 paint a compelling and biblically-grounded portrait of social life according to the will of God.

7. Gregory Baum, *Religion and Alienation* (New York: Paulist Press, 1975) 201.

8. Ibid.

9. Ibid.

10. Ibid. 202.

11. If it is not already obvious, I speak as one white, middle-class male. Other standpoints—black, Hispanic, female, poor, unemployed, etc.— would engender different accounts of the impact of social sin.

12. See also John F. Kavanaugh, *Following Christ in a Consumer Society* (Maryknoll: Orbis Books, 1981).

13. My colleague Michael Schuck's work *The Question of the Coherence and Relevance of Papal Social Thought* will be completed soon. It provides important and illuminating evidence on this point.

14. From 1964 to 1974, the percentage of Catholics in the United States who confessed monthly dropped from 38% to 17%. See Dallen, ''Church Authority.''

15. For a persuasive account of this form of social sin, see William Ryan, *Blaming the Victim* (New York: Vintage, 1976).

16. I am grateful to my colleague, T. Jerome Overbeck, s.j., for this insight.

William Cieslak, O.F.M. CAP.

Reconciliation and Conversion in Pastoral Ministry: Problems and Possibilities

What are the signs that reconciliation is happening in the local parish? How can one tell whether conversion is taking place in people who call themselves Catholics? Monika Hellwig suggests that reconciliation is characterized by a genuine, practical, far-reaching sharing of life and resources and ideals, by an atmosphere of sincere welcome, mutual respect and support.[1] Gabriel Marcel, a Christian existentialist concerned with the quality of human living, would have added the term *disponibilité,* a word that defies exact translation but suggests availability, being open to the other, having sympathy with the other.[2] Walter Burghardt describes reconciliation in terms of communion: between God and ourselves, between ourselves and others, between ourselves and nature.[3]

Conversion, on the other hand, is characterized in terms of crisis resolution as a coming to one's senses, a turning from something to something else. Mark Searle describes the loss of tranquility, the feeling of dissatisfaction and disillusionment that is apparent at the outset of the conversion process.[4] That journey toward true conversion is marked by more than mere movement; it involves real struggle and searching, honest evaluation, recognition, and acceptance. Conversion demands change, a turning away from the way I now live to another way of living.

The two notions seem contradictory: reconciliation with its atmosphere of peace, communion, patience, sympathy, and open welcome; conversion with its atmosphere of disillusionment, dissatisfaction, painful recognition, humble admission, struggling return. Yet these two elements, reconciliation and conversion, are the very stuff of Christian living, the very fabric of the Church seeking to manifest threads of the kingdom. Reconciliation and conversion are the very way of life of the Church in the world as it waits in joyful hope for the coming of the Lord again.

The noun "conversion" as well as the corresponding verb is more frequent in Luke's gospel than it is in Matthew and Mark together.[5] This is because of the role that conversion plays in salvation. For Luke salvation is universal and conversion is its necessary condition.[6] The parable of the prodigal son (Luke 15:11–32) is but one example of Luke's understanding of reconciliation and conversion.

The parable begins in painful freedom. The younger son makes a bold request and the father obliges. He allows his son the freedom to act, the freedom to choose. The son chooses in favor of sin; the father waits in hope. Reconciliation and conversion both demand freedom as their base. Without human freedom reconciliation is forced, and forced reconciliation is no reconciliation at all. People then act *as if* reconciled, but in the depths of the human heart there is neither generous welcome nor heartfelt return. Without freedom, converting gestures are forced or conforming. Conversion has never taken place because there is no change of heart, nor even recognition of need.

Recognition of sinfulness. It is only in crisis that the son begins to realize his condition. The parable tells us just how estranged the son needed to be before crisis: he, a Jew, taking care of the pigs, even yearning to eat what they eat. The association is one of defilement and the story to the Jewish ear is disgusting. Only then does the son "come to his senses." Conversion by its nature demands some sort of unrest in the person, something that shakes the person out of a certain way of living, a certain way of viewing life. Without unrest there is no need to change. Discomfort, in this case radical need, is what initiates change. Discomfort, in this story, is good!

Naming the sin in the light of remembering. Coming to his senses the son remembers (Luke 15:18). The son begins to see his situation in the light of his former life. In this contrast of present and past he can begin to assess future direction. What is necessary first is acknowledgment of the crisis situation. What must follow is understanding of the cause of the crisis. The resistance that prevents one from coming to one's senses can be a combination of many factors: one's own trust in oneself, one's comfort in one's

Pastoral Ministry

lifestyle, denial of the seriousness of the situation, group or peer pressure, cultural pressure, and so on. Mark Searle, in relating the process of conversion to Elizabeth Kübler-Ross' stages of dying, notes the anger and refusal to see, the bargaining that is present in the conversion process.[7] We find in ourselves the ability to lie to ourselves in the most creative and imaginative way. Coming to one's senses is to name the sin, to identify oneself with the sin and to call oneself a sinner.

At the same time, coming to one's senses is an act of breaking away from the resistance of sin. Naming the sin gives one a certain power over the sin because it brings the sin to light as it really is and distinguishes the sin from the sinner. Naming the sin remembers who I am and who God is and acknowledges dependence upon God who alone can save.

Ultimately, coming to one's senses and naming the sin is an act of personal freedom. Jacques Pasquier writes, "Conversion is not only surrender: it is a choice for life."[8] Naming the sin unbinds the sinner and lets the sinner go free. It is an act of independence from the past and an act of dependence upon the hope or promise of something greater. One comes to see that one's vision has changed; that a new vision has been given, a revelation has been presented, the grace of self-transcendence, of a new life, of joy![9]

Memory also plays a significant role in this parable. The son remembers the security of his father's household. He remembers his immediate past: his dissolute living, his choice to move away, his "loyal friends." At the same time, with a longer memory, he remembers the love of his father, the care his father offers the hired hands. This longer memory is what allows him to break away from the present situation and hope for a better future. It gives him a new horizon for acting. The freedom experienced in conversion exists in the context of both kinds of remembering: of who I am and what I am and of what I've done; and in the context of a longer or larger memory: who God is and what God has done for me and for us.

Doing penance. The son realizes what he must do: return to his father's house. He rehearses in the parable what he must say. Conversion demands that one come to an understanding of that from which one is converting. One may need time to give this a name and identify the root problem. At the same time one must begin to understand what one must do to change the present

William Cieslak

situation: to see what moves one must make, what changes must occur. Penance means teaching ourselves how to change, uprooting old habits by establishing new ones. Penance means working at treating others differently, working at creating a different environment in which to live and work. Penance takes time and effort, and doing penance gives a person time to mature in a new way of being. This time is essential to true conversion.

Accepting reconciliation. The son thus begins his journey home (Luke 15:21). But the audience is immediately reminded that the younger son is not doing this on his own. While he is still a long way off the father catches sight of him and runs out to meet him. Thus, *in the same verse* we see the son setting out, doing penance, and the father running out to meet him. The converting attitude of the son is nourished in the embrace of the father. In fact, it is in the embrace of the father that the son confesses his sin, and it is in that same embrace that the father reconciles. In the parable the father is not exacting confession nor even demanding it. Instead he is surrounding his son with love and affection. The grace of conversion is met by the grace of reconciliation. The return made in freedom is supported by the free giftedness of the father. What is more, the father's tender excess is seen in the heartfelt embrace, the clothing from head to foot, and the festive celebration with choice food.

Conversion, no matter how much we might want to situate it in the power of the individual, is ultimately God's gift. Conversion from sin depends upon God's grace as does the reconciliation freely given. One does nothing of oneself, except sin. God's grace supports all movements of conversion. God's grace is manifest in reconciliation.

To accept reconciliation is to open oneself to God's healing love and forgiveness. Is this easy? Only for one who allows conversion to penetrate, only for one who truly stands powerless before God. Some people cannot love because they refuse to let the other truly love them. The same is true with reconciliation. The sinner must allow God to love freely and richly otherwise the reconciliation is rejected. But to be reconciled—that is to experience something of the kingdom of God. Then one sees God as God is and oneself as God sees.

The parable, of course, has a mixed ending. Another conversion story is in the making, this one of the older brother. This story, unfortunately, is left unresolved. We leave the brother angry, not converted. We see the father go out to him too, but there is no loving embrace—at least not yet. The brother has not yet undertaken the journey of conversion. The father waits in hope. Does the story repeat itself? Conversion needs human freedom—and time.

One sees in this parable the relation between reconciliation and conversion. Both elements are absolutely supported by God's grace. It is God's grace that provides the atmosphere of welcome for reconciliation, the reaching out in love to the sinner, the strong loving embrace, the *disponibilité*, the love. For conversion it is God's grace that provides the large memory, the sense of dissatisfaction, the power to step out and change, the ability to identify and name the evil, to see what must be done and the courage to move in the healing direction. Each depends upon the other for its completion. Together they manifest something of the kingdom of God alive in the world.

THE PARISH:
PLACE FOR RECONCILIATION AND CONVERSION

Richard McBrien argues that the parish is the local Church, the integral manifestation of the Body of Christ in a particular place.[10] In making his case he cites five criteria by which the local parish might be identified as ecclesial in nature:

1. It must confess Jesus of Nazareth as the Christ and Lord of history (Pastoral Constitution on the Church in the Modern World, no. 10).

2. It must be summoned together by the proclamation of, and in response to, the word of God embodied in Sacred Scripture (Constitution on the Church, nos. 25–26).

3. It must be moved to express its response sacramentally, especially in baptism and the eucharist (Decree on Ecumenism, no. 22).

4. It must have a sense of common purpose and common responsibility for the application of the gospel of Jesus Christ to the situation around it (Decree on Ecumenism, no. 23).

William Cieslak

5. It must designate some of its membership to fulfill specific services (ministry) for the sake of such a mission; these ministries are, in a Catholic local church, united by the pastoral ministry of the bishops and of the chief bishop (Constitution on the Church, no. 18).

What is not obvious from this list is the relation of these criteria to reconciliation and conversion. All of the criteria presume conversion. Without conversion one cannot confess Jesus as the Christ and Lord in any real way. Without conversion one cannot be summoned by the word or respond sacramentally. Without conversion there is no sense of common purpose in the Church and no sense of responsibility for spreading the gospel.

At the same time, the good news of the gospel is the good news of reconciliation. Eucharist and baptism, the sacramental and ecclesial foundations of the local Church, are both seen by the Church as sacraments of reconciliation.[11] Reconciliation is what the mission and ministry of the Church is all about.

To translate McBrien's position: the local parish as Church is called by its very nature to be an agent of reconciliation. The local Church is called to enflesh the good news of reconciliation in the way it exists in the world. It is also called to encourage conversion in its members so as to be a true sign of the kingdom of God.

The theological position suggested by McBrien is borne out in the experiences of the parishioners who belong to our local parishes. They find their Church identity fashioned and shaped by their Sunday experiences. They consider themselves Catholic because of their identity within the local Catholic parish and because of their baptism in the Church. They recognize their relationship between their parish priest, the bishop, and the pope. For many of them the local parish *is* the Catholic Church. What happens at Sunday worship, at the various other sacramental celebrations they attend, and in their personal dealings with the pastor and parish staff shapes and colors their understanding of Church.

These same parishioners have some very different understandings of what the Church is and of what it is to be about. Avery Dulles' *Models of the Church* continues to illustrate some of the different foci that are operative in people's understandings.[12] Any staff member will be quick to add that parishioners also view themselves quite differently with regard to their parish participation: some are more active than others, some more regular than others, some more contributing than others, some more accepting of responsibility for being Church than others.[13] Philip Murnion notes that in addition to all the above, today's parishioners view their membership in a local parish as voluntary.[14] Many of them "shop around" for the right parish and exercise great freedom in determining their membership.

The point that I wish to make is that this is the situation in which pastoral ministry is done. These are the people who constitute the converting, reconciling parish. The pastoral minister does not serve in some ideal parish or in some conceptual Church, but in a real Church, that is, in a real parish situation with real people who are there for different reasons, who have different expectations and different needs, who are from different demographic, economic, racial, and cultural settings. Pastoral ministry is service to this Church.

THE PASTORAL MINISTER

Who is the pastoral minister? In days gone by the term itself would have been foreign to most Catholic ears. Yet, since Vatican II the notion of ministry has burst into the local Church with a power! At first there were those who feared using the term "minister" in an inclusive way. These wanted to reserve the term to apply to the ordained alone. They were restrictive in their use of the term but to no avail. Some bishops were using the term "minister" inclusively, even if accidentally, while several theologians began using the term purposefully. People in the parishes picked up the term and used it even more indiscriminately: for some, everything one did was ministry and everyone in the Church was a minister.

Today there is still no clear understanding of the parameters of "ministry," even though much has been written on the subject.[15] Ministers are sometimes classified as either full- or part-time, ordained or non-ordained, temporary or permanent, skilled or formed or unskilled. Thomas O'Meara offers what I think to be a solid understanding of Christian ministry:

> Christian ministry is the public activity of a baptized follower of Jesus Christ flowing from the Spirit's charism and an individual personality on behalf of a Christian community to witness to, serve, and realize the kingdom of God.[16]

William Cieslak

196

The definition focuses on the public nature of ministry, the baptismal and Spirit-filled foundation for it, the role played by grace and human ability and willingness, and the kingdom mission which it serves.

Those who write about ministry focus on its servant nature. The model for ministry is Jesus Christ who came to serve and not to be served. The washing of the apostles' feet at the Last Supper is an image often called to mind in these writings as is the supreme self-emptying image of Christ on the cross. The minister is called to do what Jesus did and to live as he did. The minister is called to live a life for others, especially for the poor and the oppressed.

In terms of our topic, then, we must first of all see the ministry of Christ as one of reconciliation and calling to conversion. Mark's gospel lets us see how Jesus arouses faith in people and how he reveals little by little the kingdom present in his person.[17] We see how some come to believe in him. We also see how others harden their hearts. He reveals himself as Messiah and Suffering Servant (Mark 10:45) and asks those who would follow to take up their crosses and follow him (Mark 8:34). All the gospels reflect the ultimate unbounded love of Christ symbolized on the cross—all this so that sin would be forgiven and reconciliation established once and for all.

Second, we must see the Church as the continuing embodiment of God's forgiveness and reconciliation in Christ. On the local level, we must see the parish as a human body or assembly embodying forgiveness and reconciliation. It is only in the third place that we see the pastoral minister as agent of forgiveness and reconciliation—and that in the minister's role as *servant* of the local Church.

The pastoral minister, then, is called 1) to receive reconciliation through the assembly served; 2) to embody and proclaim the reconciling love and mercy of God to all those who will attempt it; 3) to support and join the community of believers in acknowledging its sinfulness so that all may be able to experience God's mercy; 4) to call the assembly to true and lasting conversion so that it might live life justly in the world.

The above points presume that the pastoral minister realizes that he or she is not the Christ but only a human Christian. Translated concretely, pastoral ministry must always be described in terms of the stage of conversion that the minister has reached in his or her own life and in terms of the needs of the real concrete community.[18] While Christ ministered perfectly, the Christian minister can do so only imperfectly. The minister lives and works with the sense of personal imperfection and sinfulness. Not to admit of pride or ambition or power, not to admit of the need for acceptance and approval in the midst of ministry is to presume a perfection which is not there. To deny feelings of anger or rejection or ingratitude is to deny the human quality of ministry. To base ministry on these feelings, however, is likewise a mistake. At best ministers are wounded healers, and their reactions in the concrete situation might be truly Christian, partly Christian, downright un-Christian, or some combination of the above.

TOWARD CONVERSION AND RECONCILIATION

If the parish is to proclaim the kingdom of God through its ministry and life, then the parish itself must be about the business of conversion and reconciliation. What might this mean in the concrete? Parishes may wish to review whether people and ministers, programs, structures, and processes support and encourage the conversion and reconciliation preached. What are some indications that conversion and reconciliation are happening?

1. *Recognition of sinfulness.* Conversion is present when a parish is able to recognize its own sinfulness. Since only Christ is truly perfect, a parish should not be surprised to find the presence of sin in its membership, its leadership, and even in its very structures. Anyone working on a parish staff can tell you about the sinfulness found in the membership of the parish. Pastoral ministers can point out, for example, the pettiness found in some members of the parish council or in those in charge of one of the sodalities or committees. They can also point to the back-stabbing, jealousy, envy, or gossip that plague too many of the people to whom they minister. They can see the self-serving and pride in these people; they can point out those compensating for poor self-images as well. Such people take their toll in the quality of meetings and in the general quality of parish life.

But the same can be said of pastoral ministers, ordained and lay, as well. Each of us struggles with sin in our lives, both those more social sins and those that hit home more personally. What we see in others is but a mirror of what lies hidden to ourselves.

William Cieslak

198

All sin takes its toll in human relationships as well as in professional ones. The quality of our attention to those in need, the quality of *disponibilité*, the ability for human communication—all are affected by the sinfulness that is part of who we are.

Then, of course, there are the structures that embody this sinfulness. The housekeeper refuses to acknowledge the associate and so fails to clean certain areas of the house (for example, his living area and office). The grade school principal locks horns with the director of religious education and thus locks office doors and drawers; both draw up job descriptions so narrowly that the two need never meet. The pastor sends memos to the head of the liturgy committee because he cannot stand being around the person. The same problems may be repeated with the janitor, the sacristan, the head of the evangelization committee, the permanent deacon, etc. When a pastoral minister's way of doing normal parish business allows for little or no human sharing about self, about the mission of the parish or the care of parishioners, or about some gospel concern, then one can say that something of sin is present in the very structures of the parish, either by commission or by omission.

Even the Sunday assembly bears the marks of sin, and is at times a battleground more than a sign of the kingdom. Priest and musicians lose patience with each other and lack appreciation for each other's roles; ushers treat people as if they had little brains, readers become condescending through their newfound knowledge of Scripture. Serious rifts appear in different parts of the country either when a sanctuary is filled with males or when females appear there, when a scripture text is changed to be more inclusive or when it is not changed. Some people are out to get poor preachers, but with a vengeance. Some preachers, in being prophetic, become condescending to their hearers; others never preach a prophetic word for fear that a reduced collection may result.

No one, in a moment of honesty, doubts that sin is part of our parishes, ourselves, and the people to whom we minister. But parishes and pastoral ministers must acknowledge the ways of sin found there if true conversion is to happen. Awareness and acknowledgment are the beginning of the process.

2. *Living a life of penance.* Conversion is present when a parish lives a life of true penance, that is, when the people and the

structures of the parish struggle to give way to the good news and strain to allow the gospel to shape both anew. Penance happens when the parish opens itself to honest criticism, when it is willing to hear the difficult and challenging word from the old timers, the adolescents wet behind the ears, the newly baptized adults—to name but a few. Penance happens when people who have been mistreated, or who feel they have, are free to speak out to pastoral ministers and be listened to. Penance happens when people who are imperfect reach out to other people who are imperfect and together support, sustain, and challenge each other.

Penance happens together, in a faith context, supported by other sinful people. Recovering alcoholics help each other to convert, day by day; overeaters do the same. Might the parishes not learn this one from the world? We are called to conversion and penance by the power of God manifest in the lives and struggles and woundedness of our fellow faith travelers. They are the ones who truly understand the cost; they are the ones who can give us the surest encouragement.

3. *Reconciling each other.* A reconciling parish accepts sin for what it is and accepts sinners for who they are. But all in the parish have sinned, all need healing: pastors, associates, sisters, school principals, members of parish councils, the wealthiest and the poorest, the healthiest and the seriously ill. This reconciliation comes from God, but always through other humans. Since the Church is called to reconcile through the power of God, the local parish, as Church, is called to reconcile. Since the parish is called to reconcile, those who constitute the parish are called to reconcile. Pastoral ministers must seek reconciliation from each other and from other members in the total parish; members in the total parish must seek reconciliation from each other and from their pastoral ministers. No one is exempt from the task of reconciling and seeking reconciliation. No one is "better off" than anyone else. What blocks reconciliation at this level more than anything else is personal self-righteousness. To be better because one is working and not laid off, because one is healthy, because one has economic security, because one has status, because one has not sinned publicly or caused scandal or not gotten caught, is to be no better.

Reconciliation *does* mean having to say "I'm sorry." Because true conversion takes time, however, reconciliation should not be

William Cieslak

200

ritualized too quickly. To ritualize reconciliation without true conversion happening isolates people from the very experience necessary for rich human growth.[19] It presents an empty sign without kingdom-content. Therefore, a reconciling parish can expect to be in relative disquiet most of the time, crying and rejoicing, in pain and in joy, dying and rising in its members again and again and again.

4. *Valuing people over programs.* A reconciling parish knows the value of people. People growing together in faith is what parish life is all about. Parish programs are meant to serve people, not vice versa. Since each person is somewhat different, since each is traveling in faith at a different speed and in a different place, all cannot be treated exactly alike. Therefore there must always be room for exceptions to parish policy. There will be converts who will not fit into the RCIA program (it's *supposed* to be a process, I know); there will be adults having their infant sons and daughters baptized without fulfilling all the parish requirements, without attending all the prebaptismal sessions; there will be young people who will celebrate marriage against policy and there will be people unlawfully returning to the sacraments of the Church. The gospels are filled with exceptions to rules and policies in favor of human kindness and reconciling love, and in most of the examples Christ is reconciling as well as healing physical diseases or teaching or sharing a meal.

The need for education of the masses and correct behavior are laudable parish goals; they give the appearance of order, concord, and good management. But they are not ultimate gospel goals. Forced learning and forced religious behavior give one the appearance of unity where there is none, but do not relate at all to the process of conversion that must go on. People need to be dealt with as rich human beings no matter how unacquainted they are with the latest theological and liturgical terms. They need to be listened to even when their faith language is disguised. They need to be welcomed as friends, as brothers or sisters, not as wayward children. When requirements for sacramental celebrations raise the status and power of some members of the parish over the status of others, there is need for reevaluation. The gospel is filled with paradox and struggle on this point.

5. *Doing it joyfully!* A reconciling parish does it with joy and humor! There are many ways to contend with the struggle and stress

of an atmosphere of conversion and reconciliation. One way is to become very serious about the process and about the people involved, careful to keep everyone on the straight and narrow. Another way is to relax in the presence of stress and disquiet and give people a chance to grow, to explore, to cry, and to laugh. Relaxation, play, and humor give people the distance they need to see themselves and their situations in context. A people who cannot relax cannot pray since prayer takes a certain amount of listening and recollection. A people who cannot stand back from the pains of life's situations and crises can only deal with them "from the inside," one-sidedly, without context. A people who cannot see the foolishness of some of our seriousness will never be able to appreciate the full mercy of God or, indeed, the deep revelation of God. Is it not the comedian who discovers the paradoxes in life and the incongruities of life? Is it not the clown who acts them out for the culture so that all may see? Is it not the jester who calls people to honesty through humor? Anxious tension, the opposite of joy and humor, has never begotten life or truth or freedom. It doesn't do much for reconciliation either.

CELEBRATING CONVERSION AND RECONCILIATION

Tears of sorrow and joy mark most of life's changes: from birth, to a child's first day at school, through an adolescent son's or daughter's moving away from parents to peer group, to moving out on their own, to marriage and new loyalties, to death and self-transcendence. A parish that celebrates conversion and reconciliation knows how to cry. Disquiet and new promise mark our moments of conversion and reconciliation in our own personal times and seasons as well as in our communal faith journey. We celebrate conversion and reconciliation in a variety of situations: among friends and family, and in professional and ministerial situations. There are embraces, hugs, kisses, tears spent, understanding looks, and so on. In the midst of these (and, to a certain extent founded on these) the Church's ways, the parish's ways, of celebrating conversion and reconciliation are built.

All sacramental moments celebrate God's tremendous love and healing, God's promise and kiss of reconciliation, in the midst of a community of the imperfect seeking to live in peace and justice.

Baptism, especially in its adult form, symbolizes and celebrates first conversion in the parish. Eucharist, not merely in its peniten-

William Cieslak

tial rite, but centrally in its eucharistic prayer proclaims the forgiveness of sin and effects that reconciliation in sacramental communion. Thus weekly the parish assembly celebrates in its midst God's tremendous love through Christ offered to itself; weekly the assembly acts out the reconciliation showered by a merciful and loving God. The sacrament of the sick embodies deep prayer for those in need of physical and spiritual healing and rubs that prayer and faith into the body of the ill person through the anointing with oil. Viaticum, the sacrament of the dying, accompanies the dying person in that final act of self-acceptance and self-transcendence.

Conversion is encouraged when Christians gather together for Scripture-sharing, when people break open the word and let it speak to them. Conversion is encouraged when friends disclose to each other their deepest yearnings and questions, when the frightened ill make known their needs to family, friends, and pastoral ministers alike, when the convert shares with his or her sponsor, when spiritual director and directee seek God's ways of conversion, when counselor and client discover sin and disease and work toward healing. Conversion is encouraged when people take on a life of penance together, struggling to reshape their lives in richer ways, making full use of retreats and days of prayer.

Conversion is celebrated when, in the quiet prayer of the reconciliation room, God is invoked and experienced as tremendously loving and merciful through the dialogued prayer of confessor and penitent. Here the weight of sin is lifted and new life springs forth. Conversion is celebrated when the Church, the parish, celebrates communal penance services, acknowledges social sin and the social dimensions of personal sin. Here in rhythmed fashion the parish acknowledges its need for constant renewal and conversion. Here the parish is seen in its primary role as sinful servant and reconciling minister in Lent, making its yearly penitential retreat, in Advent joyfully preparing itself for the full coming of the kingdom which it has already experienced. Here the Church becomes Church, not as in eucharist as the Body of Christ, but as a pilgrim people on journey, as a faith people in need for healing and direction, as a prophetic people, announcing the good news of peace, justice, and reconciliation.

As you can see, there are many rites of conversion and reconciliation in parish life. All demand a spirit of penitence and acknowledgment of sin. Yet each rite expresses the reality differently. All work together, for people, to proclaim the coming reign of God.

NOTES

1. Monika Hellwig, *Sign of Reconciliation and Conversion: The Sacrament of Penance for Our Times,* Message of the Sacraments 4 (Wilmington, Del.: Michael Glazier, Inc., 1984) 21–26.

2. Gabriel Marcel, *Le Mystere de l'etre, Vol.* 1 (Paris: Aubier, 1951) 178.

3. Walter Burghardt, *Towards Reconciliation* (Washington: United States Catholic Conference, 1974). These are the main divisions of this book.

4. Mark Searle, "The Journey of Conversion," *Worship* 54:1 (January 1980) 36–42.

5. Dom Marc-François Lacan, "Conversion and Kingdom in the Synoptic Gospels," in *Conversion: Perspectives on Personal and Social Transformation,* ed. Walter Conn (Staten Island, New York: Alba House, 1978) 97–118. See pages 112–117 for the section on conversion in Luke's gospel.

6. Ibid. 113.

7. Searle, "Journey" 40.

8. Jacques Pasquier, "Experience and Conversion," in Conn (ed.), *Conversion* 199.

9. Ibid. 198. Also Searle, "Journey" 39.

10. Richard P. McBrien, "The Parish We Are Shaping," in *Parish: A Place for Worship,* ed. Mark Searle (Collegeville: The Liturgical Press, 1981) 14–21.

11. *Ordo Paenitentiae* (Rome: Typis Polyglottis Vaticanis, 1974) no. 17; *Lineamenta* of the 1983 Synod of Bishops, "Reconciliation and Penance in the Mission of the Church," nos. 32, 36. See also Pope John Paul II, "Reconciliation and Penance: Post-Synodal Apostolic Exhortation" (Washington, D.C.: United States Catholic Conference, 1986) no. 2.

12. Avery Dulles, *Models of the Church* (Garden City, New York: Doubleday and Company, Inc., 1974).

13. Philip Murnion, *Forming the Parish Community* (Washington: United States Catholic Conference, 1978) 23.

14. Ibid.

William Cieslak

15. Among the many titles see William Bausch, *Ministry: Traditions, Tensions, Transitions* (Mystic, Conn.: Twenty-Third Publications, 1982); Bernard Cooke, *Ministry to Word and Sacrament* (Philadelphia: Fortress Press, 1976); David N. Power, *Gifts That Differ: Lay Ministries Established and Unestablished* (New York: Pueblo Publishing Company, 1981); Edward Schillebeeckx, *Ministry* (New York: Crossroad, 1981).

16. Thomas F. O'Meara, *Theology of Ministry* (New York: Paulist Press, 1983) 136.

17. Lacan, "Conversion and Kingdom" 99–108.

18. Regis Duffy, "New Forms for Parish Ministry," in Searle (ed.) *Parish: A Place for Worship* 99.

19. Searle, "Journey" 50.

Charles W. Gusmer

Penance and Anointing of the Sick

In this paper we want to review first of all the tradition of anointing of the sick. We shall then look at the theological issues, most especially the relationship between the sacrament of penance and anointing. Finally, we shall conclude with some pastoral applications.

THE TRADITION OF ANOINTING

In the year 416 Bishop Decentius of Gubbio sent his deacon Celestine to Pope Innocent I to inquire about some pressing liturgical matters. Letter 25 contains valuable data about the evolution of "confirmation," penance and the Roman Canon, and is especially helpful for our knowledge of anointing of the sick as practiced in fifth-century Rome. The letter had far-reaching importance, being cited 300 years later by Venerable Bede in England in 735, and would appear to reflect accurately the understanding and practice of anointing of the sick in the West for the first 800 years.

> Your next question concerns the text from the epistle of the blessed apostle James: "Is any among you sick? Let him call for elders of the Church, and let them pray over him, anointing him with oil in

the name of the Lord; and the prayer of faith will save the sick man, and the Lord will raise him up; and if he has committed sins, he will be forgiven." This must undoubtedly be accepted and understood as referring to the oil of Chrism, prepared by the bishop, which can be used for anointing not only by priests but also by all Christians whenever they themselves or their people are in need of it. The questions whether the bishop can do what undoubtedly can be done by priests seems superfluous, for priests are mentioned simply because bishops are prevented by other occupations and cannot visit the sick. But if a bishop is in a position to do so and thinks it proper, he, to whom it belongs to prepare the Chrism, can himself without hesitation visit the sick to bless them and anoint them with Chrism. But it may not be used on those undergoing penance for it is of the nature of a sacrament. How could one think that one kind of sacrament should be allowed to those to whom the rest is denied.[1]

Some comments are in order.

1. The practice is rooted in James 5:14–16, which Innocent quotes in full. There are some discrepancies however. James urges sick people to call upon the presbyters: if not priests as known today, at least office holders in the primitive Church. Furthermore, James attaches more importance to the prayer of faith than to the actual anointing itself; the blessing of the oil itself goes unmentioned.[2]

2. The blessing of the oil was reserved to the bishop. The application of the blessed oil could be performed by presbyters and laypeople—and for that matter, bishops. Liturgical formulas for blessing oil are very ancient in the Latin Church, but not its application; rituals for the latter begin to appear only at the middle of the eighth century. Antoine Chavasse has exhaustively studied the sources available for the first eight hundred years: liturgical prayers of blessing, hagiographical accounts, and patristic writings. The thirteen extant prayers of blessing pray for wholeness of body, mind, and spirit; nowhere is anointing foreseen as a ministration for the dying. The blessed oil could be applied externally to the body or imbibed internally.[3]

3. The phrase "the nature of a sacrament" (genus sacramenti) refers to the blessed oil: it does not refer to the technical sense of seven sacraments as evolved in the twelfth century and first articulated by Peter Lombard, but rather something "hallowed" or made "holy."

Charles W. Gusmer

4. Pope Innocent states explicitly that the anointing is not to be given to public penitents, but only to the faithful in good standing. The implication is that it would also not be given to catechumens who were not yet baptized.

Thus we begin *in medias res* with the Roman pontiff who describes the established custom in the fifth century, based on the letter of James, which was the practice for the first eight hundred years. During the Carolingian renaissance of the ninth century a change occurred in pastoral practice and liturgy which was to profoundly transform the meaning of anointing from a rite for the sick into a sacrament for the dying. Various local synods show that as a result of a reform movement seeking to renew the priestly ministry, lay anointing was abandoned and the anointing of the sick was henceforth reserved to priests. Rituals for applying the oil were now for the first time created; previously the only liturgical sources had to do with the episcopal blessing of oil. The rituals for anointing came to be associated with the rites of deathbed penance, which was the usual occasion for sacramental reconciliation at that time. According to the tradition going back to Pope Innocent I, a sick person had first to be reconciled and in the good graces of the Church before receiving the anointing. From this time onward two tendencies begin to mark the sacrament: a spiritualizing tendency associated with the penitential anointing of the five senses, and a growing perception of anointing as a rite for the dying. By the twelfth century the original order of penance, anointing, and viaticum had shifted to penance, viaticum, and anointing. Anointing had become quite literally extreme unction, the "last anointing."

This change in pastoral practice set the stage for the sacramental systematization of the Scholastic theologians. Anointing was numbered among the seven sacraments. Sacraments confer a spiritual grace *ex opere operato*. Although some early Scholastics still maintained anointing was a sacrament for the sick, the consensus grew that it was impossible for the recovery of health to be a promised benefit of the sacrament infallibly bestowed. From its close association with deathbed reconciliation, anointing was thought to forgive sin. Since baptism removes original sin and penance remits actual personal sins, the sacramental grace of anointing was thought to pertain to the removal of either venial sin (Franciscan school of Bonaventure and Scotus) or the remnants of sin (Dominican

Penance and Anointing

school of Albert the Great and Thomas Aquinas). The purpose of the sacrament was to prepare the dying Christian for the beatific vision, an anointing unto glory.

The Council of Trent (1551) in refuting the Protestant reformers affirmed that unction was a sacrament instituted by Christ, with an enduring salvific meaning which did not contradict the scriptural passage of James, for which the priest was the ordinary minister. But Trent declined to completely endorse the medieval approach to anointing as a sacrament for the dying. The original draft spoke of extreme unction as a sacrament to be administered "only (*dumtaxat*) to those in their final struggle and [who] have come to grips with death and are about to go forth to the Lord." The definitive text made a decisive alteration "This anointing is to be used for the sick, but especially (*praesertim*) for those who are dangerously ill as to seem near to death." Three times the recipients of anointing were described as sick (*infirmi*), not dying. The council taught that the specific effect of anointing was the grace of the Holy Spirit with spiritual, psychological, and physical ramifications.[4]

The post-Tridentine era, on the one hand, saw a progressive leniency concerning the interpretation of the danger of death required for unction and a gradual reassertion of anointing as a sacrament for the sick. Such teaching was reflected in the teaching of the Catechism of the Council of Trent and the encyclicals of Popes Benedict XV and Pius XI, who urged the administration of unction as the beginning of a "probable danger" of death. On the other hand, this century witnessed a resurgence of the Scholastic teaching regarding extreme unction as "anointing unto glory," preparing the soul of the dying Christian for the immediate beatific vision. This opinion, particularly popular in German dogmatic circles, held that granting the proper dispositions on the part of the recipient, the sacrament of unction has the power of canceling the total debt of punishment and thus preparing the soul for immediate entrance into heaven. One of the enthusiastic proponents in this country put it this way:

> Extreme Unction, if properly received, intends to eliminate purgatory for the recipient, intends to guarantee him the immediate beatific vision after death. . . . Nor is there any reason to suppose that such a disposition should be particularly difficult to obtain. In the sacrament of Penance, ordinarily not all punishments are remit-

Charles W. Gusmer

ted. The Council of Trent (XIV Sess.) tells us that Penance will cleanse us perfectly only if accompanied *magnis fletibus et laboribus* [by many tears and much work]. This sacrament is therefore not available for our purpose. One might say that we have the plenary indulgence and the apostolic benediction. I answer that these depend too much upon the disposition, the piety and exertion of the patient. A plenary indulgence presupposes remission of all sins, and in so trying a need it is altogether too uncertain a thing. We must have a sacrament; nothing else will do.[5]

This background is necessary in order to appreciate the theological issues at stake at the Second Vatican Council and the subsequent revision of the sacrament of anointing.

THEOLOGICAL ISSUES

There are at least three theological questions which have arisen regarding the sacrament of anointing since the Second Vatican Council.

First, is it a sacrament for the sick or for the dying? Here a remarkable evolution has taken place, greater than is generally observed. Paragraph 73 of the Constitution on the Sacred Liturgy represented a compromise. The name "extreme unction" was retained, but the Council fathers thought it would be better called "anointing of the sick." The condition of danger of death (*periculum mortis*) still prevailed, but the sacrament should be celebrated at the beginning of the danger of death from sickness or old age. The breakthrough is found in the 1972 Latin typical edition, the 1974 provisional ICEL green book (translation), and the 1983 ICEL white book (translation and adaptation). Anointing is clearly the sacrament for the sick; the sacrament for the dying is viaticum, and one half of the ritual is devoted to this important and much-neglected sacramental ministry to the dying. Nowhere are the misleading terms "extreme unction" or "last rites" used; the name of the sacrament is "anointing of the sick" (*unctio infirmorum*). Furthermore, the condition for reception in the 1983 Pastoral Care of the Sick reads: the "faithful whose health is seriously impaired by sickness or old age," a new rendering of the Latin *periculose aegrotans* previously translated as "dangerously ill."[6]

We mention in passing a second theological issue: what is the relationship of the sacrament of anointing to the charism of healing? If anointing is intended for sick people, what relationship

Penance and Anointing

does it have to the charism of healing expounded upon and practiced especially in Pentecostal-charismatic circles today? To address these issues one needs to admit the similarities of the two ministries based on the ecclesial community's full commitment to minister to the sick and its use of varieties of ritual prayer to further this ministry. But a clear distinction between the two ministries must also be made on the basis of different modalities of prayer rooted in scriptural origin, their respective places in the Church, and the expected results.[7]

The third theological issue with which we shall grapple is the subject of this paper: the relationship between penance and anointing. So much attention has been directed to the first two issues that this one still remains unfinished business. The brief survey of the tradition of anointing has surfaced the penitential aspects emanating from its association with deathbed penance which has profoundly shaped the history of the sacrament. A few examples will suffice. Until the revision in 1972 the essential sacramental sign consisted of the anointing of the five senses (matter) together with the words (form) first used in the tenth century: "May the Lord forgive you by this holy anointing and his most loving mercy whatever sins you have committed by the use of your [sight, etc.]." Another instance is the withholding of the sacrament of anointing from children. One popular moral manual explained the reason for this prohibition: "The subject must have attained the use of reason because Extreme Unction removes the consequences of sin, and one who has never had the use of reason has likewise never sinned."[8] Finally, the refusal to allow deacons to anoint the sick is in part due to the sacrament's longtime association with penance, although there are other issues, most notably canon 4 of Trent that the *sacerdos* (bishop or priest) is the proper minister. Behind all this lurks a mentality vaguely alluded to by Tecklenburg in the passage cited earlier that anointing is a safer way to forgiveness of sins for someone seriously ill, inasmuch as penance requires a conscious subject capable of making acts of contrition, confession, and satisfaction.

What are we to make of all this? It is true that the teaching of the Council of Trent on anointing included penitential effects. Chapter 2 of that teaching stated that one of the results was that "anointing takes away the sins if there are any still to be expiated." Canon 2 anathematizes anyone who would claim that

Charles W. Gusmer

anointing "neither confers grace, nor remits sins, nor comforts the sick." By way of assessment and interpretation let this be said: anointing is a sacrament of the living. Its lawful reception presumes the state of grace and proper disposition. Where there is no other recourse (as with all sacraments of the living), serious sins can be remitted, but there is no forgiveness of sins without *metanoia* or conversion of heart.

Put more positively, a relationship does exist between penance and anointing, but not in the way this is usually conceived, as a remnant of the unfortunate association with deathbed penance and the subsequent Scholastic speculation. The relationship between penance and anointing is grounded in a holistic anthropology which views sickness within the wider context of the mystery of suffering and evil. This means three things:

1. Some relationship exists between sin and sickness. The Greek verb used frequently in Jesus' healing miracles is *sōzein* (to save), which can mean both salvation from sin and salvation from sickness and disease: "Your faith has saved you." James 5:15b ("And if he has committed sins, he will be forgiven.") and the subsequent exhortation to mutual confession refers to a conditional effect of the rite. Herein is seen the close relationship between bodily and spiritual sickness and between physical healing and the forgiveness of sins. Many early Church writers and the Council of Trent felt this passage referred just as much to the penitential discipline of the Church as it did to the practice of anointing. It would also be an interesting project to reexamine the Scholastic teaching on original sin and the concomitant loss of the preternatural gifts of immortality, integrity, knowledge, and freedom from pain and suffering. In other words, sin—original and personal—has cosmic repercussions in terms of human solidarity and the ordering of the universe. This is not to say in a simplistic way that personal sin causes a given illness, an opinion reprobated by Jesus himself (Jn 9:3). Nor is this to state that sickness is a means of divine vindication, implying a "God of the ambush" waiting to get even! Rather, the whole human person in community suffers sickness as a consequence of evil in the world.

2. The good news is that the promised salvation in Jesus Christ encompasses the total person in community with the goal of the resurrection of all flesh. Within this holistic vision of human history Jesus comes to free us, to heal us from sin and evil and all its

manifestations, so that we can grow to full stature as children of God. In other words, God is on our side coming to save us.

3. Anointing of the sick is the complement or completion of Christian penance. This is not to be understood in the same sense that confirmation is the completion of baptism. Moreover, anointing is not given to persons because they are sinners or penitents but because they are sick. Anointing is the completion of penance not insofar as specified through sin but through sickness. Pain and suffering, accepted in faith and love, can purify a person more deeply from sin.

What is at stake here is a healthy concept of expiation. Suffering in and of itself has no value; suffering is ambivalent and can lead to either sin or to greater love. Moreover, God is not a sadist placated by the suffering of creatures. Recall also the opening paragraphs of the introduction to the anointing rite which refers to sickness as an evil to be resisted in the name of the kingdom of God.[9] Nonetheless, patient and courageous endurance of sickness can be a way of entering more deeply into the paschal mystery, experiencing poverty of spirit, dying to self-centeredness and allowing the risen Christ to penetrate our lives more completely. In his apostolic letter *Salvifici doloris*, Pope John Paul II puts it this way:

> Suffering is in itself an experience of evil. But Christ has made suffering the firmest basis of the definitive good, namely the good of eternal salvation. By his suffering on the cross, Christ reached the very roots of evil, of sin and death. He conquered the author of evil, Satan, and his permanent rebellion against the Creator. To the suffering brother or sister Christ discloses and gradually reveals the horizons of the kingdom of God: the horizons of a world converted to the Creator, of a world free from sin, a world being built on the saving power of love. And slowly but effectively, Christ leads into this world, into this kingdom of the Father, suffering man, in a certain sense through the very heart of his suffering. For suffering cannot be transformed and changed by a grace from outside, but from within. And Christ through his own salvific suffering is very much present in every human suffering and can act from within that suffering by the powers of his spirit of truth, his consoling Spirit.[10]

PASTORAL APPLICATION

The three questions most frequently asked about the sacrament of anointing are these: Who may be anointed? Who may anoint?

Charles W. Gusmer

What does the anointing do? We answer these with special application to the relationship between penance and anointing.

1. *Who may be anointed?* Some clarity may be gained from the new Code of Canon Law which appeared after Pastoral Care of the Sick and thus represents the Church's latest teaching on this matter.

> Canon 1004: The anointing of the sick can be administered to a member of the faithful who, after having reached the use of reason, begins to be in danger due to sickness or old age.
>
> Canon 1005: This sacrament is to be administered when there is doubt whether the sick person has attained the use of reason, whether the person is dangerously ill, or whether the person is dead.
>
> Canon 1007: The anointing of the sick is not to be conferred upon those who obstinately persist in manifest serious sin.[11]

All this would seem to imply the following conclusions regarding the recipient of anointing.

(a) *Catechumens* would not appear to be proper recipients of anointing. Although the Church already cherishes them as her own, they are not yet *fideles* (faithful) through the sacrament of baptism, the gate to the Church's sacramental life. In time of serious sickness, one might ponder if this is a moot question, since it might be more appropriate to celebrate first the initiation sacraments of baptism, confirmation, and first eucharist.

(b) *Penitents.* Recall the teaching of Innocent I and the above-cited canon 1007. Penitents should first have recourse to the sacrament of penance and be reconciled with the Church. No sins are forgiven without conversion of heart. The grace of anointing is not a blessing or a sacramental or the promise of a healing cure: the sacrament should not be received apart from a serious intention to live a Christian life. Anointing is not cheap grace, an easier way to have sins forgiven, or to save on medical bills!

(c) *Christians from other communions.* Here the same conditions apply as for eucharistic sharing as set forth in canon 844 of the new Code. There is a grave or pressing need, no access to one's own minister, the person spontaneously requests the sacrament, commensurate faith, and proper disposition. Note that the Eastern Orthodox and Episcopal (Anglican) Churches regularly anoint their sick members.

Penance and Anointing

(d) Children who are ill. As we have seen, the penitential understanding of anointing is why the sacrament was withheld from small children: they are not yet capable of serious sin. One detects an opening in pastoral practice here. For example, Pastoral Care of the Sick contains some newly created sections devoted to sick and dying children. The emendations in liturgical books flowing from the new Code now assert that children *are* to be anointed (earlier: may be anointed) if they have sufficient use of reason to be strengthened by the sacrament; in case of doubt whether the child has reached the use of reason, the sacrament is to be conferred.

2. *Who may anoint?* The penitential tradition of anointing is a partial reason why deacons are restricted from its administration. The question should ultimately be posed in the wider context of other pastoral ministers to the sick, both men and women. The current discipline is clear and is restated in canon 1003 of the new Code: "Every priest, and only a priest, validly administers the anointing of the sick." Other doctrinal issues to explore would be these. First, we are dealing with an evolving sacrament, as is most evident in the progress made from the Constitution on the Sacred Liturgy to the recent revisions: from a sacrament for the dying to a recovery of its original meaning as a sacrament for the sick. Second, how is the *presbyter* of James to be understood and how open is the teaching of the Council of Trent to this development? Third, there already exist precedents for the extension of the sacramental ministry, e.g., special occasions when priests may administer confirmation. Could this be applied to anointing when the Church now encourages an earlier time for anointing but is unable in many parts of the world to provide priests to administer it? Fourth, there is the situation of ecumenical convergence, although here the practice varies: the Eastern Orthodox reserve the *euchelaion* or "prayer oil" to presbyters, indeed seven of them when possible; the American Episcopal Church permits the anointing by a deacon or lay person in emergency situations using oil blessed by a bishop or priest. Fifth, and at the root of all this, is a conflict between two theological principles: a sacramental *tutiorist* position whereby the Church endorses the "safer" or surer theological opinion in matters pertaining to the salvation of its members (a particular concern here would be once again the penitential understanding of anointing restricting its administration to priests) and a

Charles W. Gusmer

pastoral principle that sacraments are for the people (*sacramenta propter homines*), and short of tampering with the substance of the sacrament every effort should be expended to make these means of grace available to people in need.

3. *What does anointing do?* A rich ambiguity of expectations is described in paragraph 6 of Pastoral Care of the Sick and is actually a paraphrase of the teaching of Trent:

> This sacrament gives the grace of the Holy Spirit to those who are sick: by this grace the whole person is helped and saved, sustained by trust in God, and strengthened against the temptations of the Evil One and against anxiety over death. Thus the sick person is able not only to bear suffering bravely, but also to fight against it. A return to physical health may follow reception of this sacrament if it will be beneficial to the sick person's salvation. If necessary, the sacrament also provides the sick person with the forgiveness of sins and the completion of Christian penance.

The Scholastic theologians spoke of the grace of unction as the forgiveness of venial sin/remnants of sin which prepared the dying Christian for the immediate vision of God. The grace was predicated on the assumption that the sacrament was intended for the dying and had the specific purpose of preparing them for heaven. This is indeed a beautiful and consoling teaching, but has to do with what we would now say is conveyed by the sacrament of penance and the apostolic blessing. If today we are returning to the earlier tradition that anointing is for the sick, the challenge presents itself: what, then, is the sacramental grace of anointing as the sacrament for the seriously ill? A more holistic anthropology is necessary and is captured in the revised liturgical action and liturgical word of the sacrament. The liturgical action (matter) consists of the anointing of the forehead and hands with the blessed oil, as well as additional parts of the body—the area of pain or injury. The liturgical word (form) during which the anointing takes place are these words incorporating the teaching of the Letter of James, the Council of Trent, and the earlier prayer of anointing:

> Through this holy anointing may the Lord in his love and mercy help you with the grace of the Holy Spirit. Amen.

> May the Lord who frees you from sin save you and raise you up. Amen.

We close with an excerpt from a graduate paper ''Penance and

Penance and Anointing

Anointing" written by a talented seminarian, Kevin Duggan, whom I was privileged to teach. He looks at the relationship between the two sacraments from the perspective of Karl Rahner's theology.

> In addition to viewing the human from the nature/grace perspective, we can also speak of the human in terms of the nature/person question. By this we mean to say that the human being is essentially project at birth. For the believer, one's life can be seen as a journey or pilgrimage; it is a project in which one builds one's person within certain parameters set by one's nature. The person grows as a person by disposing of oneself in free acts of knowing and willing always set within the horizon of God's call in grace. God is at one and the same time always the ground and horizon of human life, knowing and willing. This journey, one's life project, is one in which one faces obstacles; there is always the drag of one's nature which resists full disposition. Thus, the person under grace, can be said to grow according to the law of gradualness. Two realities which are inherent within this human condition, with its gradual growth, are sin in its personal sense of actual sin and sin in its objective sense of the sin of the world. This sin of the world is ratified in personal sin, it is present in sinful human structures and too it is present in the experiences of suffering, illness and death itself which are experienced as unnatural, resulting from the effects of original sin. Where there is a certain naturalness to the aging process and death, it is experienced as unnatural, threatening, dreadful. These can also be seen within the context of the mystery of evil; without attempting a full theodicy, one can say that a person's life journey toward wholeness and holiness, the call of grace, takes place within this situation marked by sin. The journey is involved with overcoming the effects of sin within our hearts subjectively, and within our world objectively. Given this, the sacraments of penance and anointing are inherently related and complementary as "healing sacraments." As a sacrament of the living, one needs to be reconciled in order to be anointed, but the two function together in the intended health of the whole person. Their efficacious grace overcomes, in the person rightly disposed, sin and the sins of which we speak, as all sacraments in their soteriological orientation are involved with this overcoming of sin and the victory of grace. They are encounters with the living Christ, in the Church through the action of the Holy Spirit and the encounter occurs in the situation of one's life—a situation marked by the "limit" experiences of one's personal sin on the one hand, and of the fact of the sin of the

Charles W. Gusmer

world on the other—with its resulting human experience of illness, suffering and death. Grace seeks always to move one beyond the "limit" experience through overcoming the resultant alienation and thereby leading to greater integral human wholeness.

Through penance, we overcome the "limit" experience of our sinfulness and the process of conversion is furthered. The alienation which is sin gives way to the reality of reconciliation and greater wholeness. Through anointing, we overcome the "limit" experience of human suffering, illness and the eventual spectre of death which is part of any experience of serious illness. While bodily health may be restored, it is only for a time for we all must die. However, the grace of anointing with or without a physical cure aims at the cure of the person as a whole allowing for new possibilities of being this being-in-the-world and we thereby grow to greater integral, human wholeness. In this too, our life's project of building our person and making this person an offering to God in love is furthered.

In these "healing sacraments," in a special way, we are embraced by Love, an all-consuming Love; one which we experience, only in part, in our human loving and being loved—but one which we hope for in full in the eschatological fullness of the Trinitarian Love's embrace. It is the experience of sin and sickness, of alienation and suffering being overcome through prayer, faith and the sacraments which draw us further into the Mystery. The limit experiences of human life and love, under grace, open out into the limitless eternal love of the God who creates, redeems and sustains in love. In this the cry from the cross of our life with its sin, suffering and death is transformed from that of: "My God, my God, why have you abandoned me;" to the prayer and self-offering: "Into your hands I commend my spirit."

NOTES

1. J. Neuner and J. Dupuis, *The Christian Faith in the Doctrinal Documents of the Catholic Church*, rev. ed., (New York: Alba House, 1982) 1603, p. 450.

2. While the Council of Trent taught that the anointing of the sick was instituted by Christ and "recommended to the faithful and promulgated by James" (Neuner/Dupuis 1636, p. 466), it was more nuanced in the third canon of 1551 suggesting that the rite and practice of extreme unction did not contradict the doctrine of James (Neuner/Dupuis 1658, p. 471).

Penance and Anointing

3. Antoine Chavasse, *Etude sur l'onction des infirmes dans l'église latine du IIIe au XIe siècle.* Vol. I: *Au IIIe siècle à la reforme carolingienne.* The insights of Chavasse's unpublished second volume are available to us through Placid Murray, "The Liturgical History of Extreme Unction," *The Furrow* 11 (1960).

4. For a more extensive treatment of the Council of Trent, as well as the tradition of anointing, see Charles W. Gusmer, *And You Visited Me: Sacramental Ministry to the Sick and the Dying* (New York: Pueblo, 1984) 3–47.

5. F. Tecklenburg, "The Primary Effect of Extreme Unction," *Ecclesiastical Review* 55 (1916) 291–99. Paul Palmer, "The Purpose of Anointing the Sick: A Reappraisal," *Theological Studies* 19 (1958) 309–44, was one of the first in this country to challenge this approach.

6. See *Pastoral Care of the Sick: Rites of Anointing and Viaticum* (Washington, D.C.: International Commission for English in the Liturgy, 1983).

7. See Charles W. Gusmer, "Healing: Charism and Sacrament." *Church* 2:2 (Summer, 1986) 16–22.

8. Heribert Jone & Urban Adelman, *Moral Theology* (Westminster, MD: Newman Press, 1962) para. 629, p. 445.

9. *Pastoral Care of the Sick* nos. 1–4.

10. John Paul II, "The Christian Meaning of Human Suffering" in *Origins* 13:37 (February 23, 1984) 621.

11. *Code of Canon Law.* Latin-English Edition (Washington, DC: Canon Law Society of America, 1983) 369. These canons have also necessitated some changes in the *Emendations in the Liturgical Books following upon New Code of Canon Law*. It is unfortunate that the Latin *periculum* was once again translated as "danger."

Charles W. Gusmer

Linda Gaupin, C.D.P.

"Let Those Who Have Faith Not Be Hasty:" Penance and Children

One of the more controversial issues which has emerged in the continuing agenda of reconciliation in the Church is that of penance and children. The issue impacts not only on our practices pertaining to the sacramental reception of penance, but also on our theological and catechetical understanding of the sacraments of initiation and on the entire shape of catechesis in the Church.

The issue of penance and children received great notoriety during the 1960's and 1970's because of the debate over first eucharist and first penance. While the issue was never satisfactorily resolved either on a theoretical or pastoral level, new developments have since emerged which raise the issue of penance and children to a new level of critical examination in the Church today. These events are vitally important because they form a backdrop for assessing the *status quo* of the present topic.

The promulgation and subsequent widespread implementation of the Rite of Christian Initiation of Adults (RCIA) has had a marked influence on the issue of penance and children for the 1980's. In restoring the integral unity and sequence of the initiation sacraments, the Rite forces us to reexamine the role and meaning of penance in early childhood.

Practically speaking, first penance interrupts this unity and thus alters the initiation sequence. In doing so, its position within the initiating sequence stands in contradiction to the underlying significance of these rites, i.e., to realize an initial union with Christ.[1] Thus the RCIA confronts us with the dilemma of our catechetical practices wherein we *reactualize* a union with Christ for small children who have yet to realize the *fullness* of their initial union received in baptism and completed in the eucharist.

The issue of penance and children also surfaced at the recent Synod of Bishops in Rome in October 1983. The issue was raised by Cardinal Silvio Oddi, Prefect for the Congregation of the Clergy, when he addressed the Synod on the topic of improved penance catechesis.[2] Noting that the area of catechetics had often been a source of concern and anxiety for his Congregation, Oddi cited the practice of admitting children to first communion without previous confession as one of the more *abusive* areas of practice. Oddi asserted further that the practice of admitting children to first eucharist without first penance was explicitly forbidden by the joint Declaration of the Sacred Congregations for the Discipline of the Sacraments and the Clergy issued May 24, 1973.[3] In terms of our current practices regarding penance and children, Oddi's assertion appears to be in conflict with the increasing practice of providing catechesis for penance with optional private confession available for those who want it.

The issue of penance and children is also considered in the new Code of Canon Law, and the controversial nature of the topic is evident in the somewhat contradictory statements that are made there regarding this practice.[4] Like the Code of 1917, the revised Code preserves the traditional initiatory sequence of baptism, confirmation, and eucharist. Furthermore, canon 913.1 which deals with first eucharistic reception, makes no mention of penance for children as one of the necessary requirements for eucharistic reception. Yet canon 914 asserts that sacramental confession precedes first eucharist for those children who have reached the use of reason. This regulation, however, appears to be in contradiction to canons 916 and 989 which require confession before communion only in cases of grave or serious sin.

The topic has surfaced also on a national level at the 1986 meeting of the USCC Committee on Education. In a communication to diocesan catechetical directors, Reverend Thomas P. Ivory indicates that the dialog regarding penance and children is continuing in terms of two different schools of thought on the issue of the celebration of first reconciliation and first eucharist.[5]

Considering all of the above, it would be naive to assume that the issue of penance and children will remain unnoticed in the continuing agenda on reconciliation in the Church for the future. The profound impact of this issue on our theological, catechetical, and pastoral understandings of reconciliation necessitates a systematic analysis of the problem.

The systematic analysis proposed in this paper is divided into three parts. The first examines the historical framework in order to determine the nature and scope of those factors which first provided a structure for linking penance to the years of childhood.

Linda Gaupin

The second examines the contemporary situation pertaining to penance and children as it has emerged in terms of the first penance/first eucharist debate. The third analyzes the state of questions and suggests a future direction for a catechesis for penance and children.

Attempts to systematically link penance with the years of childhood within a structured catechetical framework can be located in the seventeenth-century France.[6] The causes for this are germane to our discussion because they provide a historical rationale for understanding many of the difficulties and complications that face us today.

The need for a total reform of the entire catechetical structure arose in the wake of two critical events: (1) the virtual breakdown in the integral unity of the initiation sacraments, and (2) the general decline in the faith-life of the people following the deleterious effects of the Reformation. The first event left each of the initiation sacraments isolated from each other and bereft of any catechetical and pastoral practices.[7] This particularly affected those catechetical and pastoral practices surrounding first eucharist, which began to develop as a separate and distinct rite in the Church during this period. The second event was evidenced primarily in terms of ignorance of the most basic truths of the faith by a large majority of the faithful. This was acerbated by the high rate of success of the catechetical endeavors among Protestant reformers.[8]

Thus the reform of Christian life in seventeenth-century France provided the impetus for a complete catechetical reorganization. This reorganization took on three specific characteristics. The school became the shape of catechesis, new manuals or catechisms the major instrument, and catechized children its principle product.[9] The school constituted the ideal means for Christian reform and became the focal point for the Church's hopes for revival of faith among the people. It emphasized Christian formation as a necessary means to insure the complete Christian initiation of children into the faith. Thus, with the demise of the catechumenate, the parish school of the seventeenth century became the locus for the Christian initiation of children.[10]

Penance and Children

The structure of initiation was composed of four major stages which allowed for the gradual formation in faith of the child from infancy to young adulthood.[11] More importantly, however, it provided for the first systematic structuring of penance before first eucharist within a catechetical framework. The first stage or period addressed the catechetical formation of the child from the baptismal moment to the years of discretion. Centered in the home it acknowledged parents as the primary catechists of their children. During this time, the child was taught some of the basic prayers of the faith and a few rudimentary teachings of the Christian religion.

The second stage began with the child's entry into school and was designed for those having the use of reason. At the beginning of this stage, young children around the ages of five or six were introduced to the sacrament of penance. It also included preparation for the reception of the sacrament of confirmation. In fact, the primary purpose of this period was to lead the child to the reception of confirmation as a sacrament of initiation.

The third stage was directed towards the catechetical preparation and reception for first eucharist which was celebrated around the ages of twelve to fourteen years. The reception of the sacrament generally marked the close of one's formal education but did not, however, signal the end of one's religious formation. As such, first eucharist as a sacrament of initiation was seen as the crowning point of catechesis but not its conclusion.[12]

This third stage led directly into the fourth and final stage of catechesis which was ordered towards the ongoing religious formation for those who had been fully initiated in the Church. Centered around the "Catechism of Perseverance," its object was to secure perseverance in the study of religion and the practice of religious duties until marriage.

What is specifically significant for our discussion is the nature of the catechesis of penance for children. Initiated around the tender years of five or six, the catechesis respected the moral development of the young child and was developed in terms of a protracted catechesis for penance. At the outset of the second stage, young children were introduced to the sacrament of penance, but confessors were cautioned, however, not to give sacramental absolution to those who did not know the matter of the sacrament or who were judged incapable of receiving it.

Linda Gaupin

The intrinsic value of this system was that it allowed a long period of time for learning about penance.[13] From the young age of five or six, until the immediate preparation for first eucharist, the child had a five or six year period in which she or he was gradually introduced to and formed in the moral life. This protracted period also gave the child time to learn all those things required for a "good" confession.

What is underscored in the extended catechesis is the recognition of the difference in the catechetical requirements of penance from those of first eucharist. Catechesis for a "good" confession exacted a more demanding formation. Felix Dupanloup aptly described this recognition during the nineteenth century:

> A confession to be well made demands many things; a person must examine his conscience, must excite in himself contrition; when he presents himself at the confessional, there is a certain attitude to adopt, a certain language to use, certain forms to repeat; there is an order and a method even when accusing oneself of faults. No doubt all these points should be dwelt upon, and are very much dwelt upon, in the catechisms of the first communion; but is there time enough to do this, is there time, with so many children, to enter into the innumerable but necessary details? Above all, is there time to make oneself certain, by questions and individual answers, frequently repeated, that all the children have understood and learnt?[14]

Review of this period highlights several points germane to the questions of penance and children. First, it provides us with a historical framework for locating the first attempts to link penance and children within a systematic catechetical structure. One of the primary purposes of this structure was to provide some continuity for the sacraments of initiation. The retrieval of the integral unity of the initiating sequence was accomplished by means of a complete reorganization of the catechetical structure which focused on the Christian formation and initiation of youth.

Second, the inclusion of penance into the midst of the initiating sequence was not a deliberate action based on the theological premise that penance should precede first eucharist. Rather penance preceded first eucharist at a time when the preparation and celebration of that sacrament was delayed until the later years of childhood.

Third, the catechesis for penance was not confused with the catechetical preparation for any of the initiation sacraments. The

Penance and Children

unique feature of the catechesis for penance was that it respected the moral demands it required of the child, allowing for a five- or six-year period for introducing them to and forming them in the moral life. This was feasible within a catechetical structure which delayed first eucharist to the later years of childhood.

This catechetical structure was maintained until the twentieth century with one very important modification. A resurgence of rigoristic piety among the faithful, due to the influence of Jansenism, resulted in greater stress being placed on the intellectual and moral preparation of the child for first eucharist.[15] As a result, certain abuses crept into the catechetical system that remained unresolved until the promulgation of *Quam singulari* in 1910.[16]

The shape of catechesis was turned around when Pius X promulgated this decree.[17] The original intent of the decree was to correct those abuses associated with the practices surrounding the reception of first eucharist. What actually occurred, however, was a complete reorganization and renewal of the catechetical structure.

The abuses that Pius X sought to correct through the decree were essentially twofold: the advanced age required for the reception of first eucharist, and the exaggerated moral and intellectual demands placed on the child for its reception. In lowering the age for first eucharist, the decree made a major impact on the catechetical structure in two ways. First, it changed the focus of sacramental catechesis from adolescence to the early years of childhood. Second, it upset the catechetical structure by placing first eucharist in close proximity with the catechetical preparation and reception of confirmation and penance.

Catechists were suddenly confronted with the task of sacramental preparation for three sacraments in the early years of childhood. This challenge forced catechists to reexamine sacramental catechesis for first eucharist in light of a new realization: what was difficult at best for twelve- to fourteen-year olds was virtually impossible for a child of seven. In other words, catechists soon discovered that it was impossible to implement the decree within a system that did not recognize the realities of childhood. Complaints were voiced against the use of texts and methods that exceeded the comprehension and ability of the young child. Furthermore, catechetical methods which committed the child to memorize lengthy and abstract questions and answers were seen as unrealistic for a child of seven.

Linda Gaupin

As catechists struggled to inaugurate reforms for the sacramental catechesis for first eucharist, they soon became aware that these reforms pertained as well to all levels of catechesis. This insight confronted catechesis with a monumental task and consumed their creative efforts until the late 1950's. Thus, for the forty- to fifty-year period following *Quam singulari,* the catechetical reforms initiated in the wake of the decree centered around methodology, texts, and content for all catechetical levels.[18]

It was only after these issues were addressed that catechists began to explore the implications of *Quam singulari* in terms of sacramental sequence. When the decree was first promulgated in the United States, it created a considerable amount of havoc in terms of sacramental order. Concerned primarily with correcting abuses associated with first eucharist, the decree contained no directives whatsoever with regards to how catechists were to prepare children for confirmation, penance, and eucharist all of which were now placed in proximity with one another.

William Costello, leading catechist of this period, noted that following the promulgation of the decree, confirmation was being received at the same time as first communion in some cases and not until later in others. In some places, children received first penance before first eucharist while other children did not receive penance until afterwards.[19]

The situation regarding sacramental order was never resolved. In most cases, the pattern set out by the seventeenth-century catechetical reform, whereby penance preceded first eucharist, was maintained as the given order without any critical examination of the ramifications of this for the catechesis of young children. As a result, the protracted catechesis for penance disappeared since the catechetical preparation for first eucharist occurred around the same time in accord with the teachings of *Quam singulari.*

Thus, the catechesis for penance, which had formerly taken four to five years to complete, was now condensed into a process of several months. The catechesis for penance eventually took on the attitude of "learn it now and do it now even if you do not desire it," with the accompanying belief that in teaching everything we risk nothing. Furthermore, the catechesis for each of the sacraments became confused, with the catechesis for penance oftentimes dominating that for first eucharist.

This remained the situation until the early 1960's when catechists

Penance and Children

began to question the current catechetical practices surrounding penance and children. They were inspired by a number of factors: the fruition of the liturgical movement in the United States, advances made in eucharistic and sacramental theology which would ultimately be formative of the documents at Vatican Council II, the developments taking place in child psychology and moral theology, and the writings of Josef Jungmann.[20]

Based on these sources, catechists began to call for a separate and distinct catechesis for both penance and eucharist and for a delay in the reception of first penance until after first eucharist. The rise in the number of articles in many of the religious education journals attests to the widespread demand for this change during this time.[21] By 1970, fifty-one percent of the dioceses in the United States had implemented policies which called for the distinct and separate catechesis of penance and eucharist as well as a delay in the reception of penance until after first eucharist.

These changes marked the first substantial attempts to deal with the issue of penance and children since the time of *Quam singulari*. Much like the catechesis for penance from the seventeenth century until 1910, the changes restored the distinct and separate nature of the catechesis for penance from that of first eucharist and allowed for the development of a protracted period of catechesis for penance. Unfortunately, these changes received a major setback during the 1970's with the publication of the Addendum to the *General Catechetical Directory* (GCD) and the promulgation of the declaration *Sanctus pontifex* in 1973.

FIRST PENANCE/FIRST EUCHARIST DEBATE

The issue of penance and children surfaced in terms of the first penance/first eucharist debate during the 1970's. Since it is in this debate that the issue of penance and children will most likely surface in the future, it is important that we examine some of the more critical elements of this controversy.

As is well-known, the Addendum of the GCD created a pastoral crisis in the United States. It specifically addressed two experiments: the practice of permitting children to receive first communion without first confession and allowing some years to elapse between first communion and first confession.

When questioned regarding the status of the Addendum, John Cardinal Wright, Prefect for the Congregation of the Clergy, as-

Linda Gaupin

sured catechists that the Addendum did not have the force of legislation and was appended to the GCD to stimulate further research and inquiry into the situation. Wright deemed this necessary since the recent experiments with regards to first penance and first eucharist seemed to violate Church tradition and contradict the teachings of *Quam singulari*.[22]

Wright's repeated assurances that the Addendum was not a piece of legislation did nothing to clarify matters on a pastoral level. At their April 1972 meeting, the bishops of the United States voted to conduct a nationwide evaluation of the practice. A questionnaire was developed by the NCCB Committee on Pastoral Research and Practices and submitted to the Congregation for the Clergy for its approval.[23]

The results of the evaluation showed that eighty-five percent of the ordinaries agreed that the new practices made for a better reception of first communion especially since the reception of the eucharist did not make the higher intellectual, moral, and psychological demands that were required by penance. They also affirmed three other major points:

1. That the delay of first penance until the ages of eight or ten years of age had shown positive effects;

2. That the right to receive first penance before first communion be maintained;

3. That it was desirable to continue the practice in the United States after first communicating with the Holy See.[24]

After these results were presented at the November 1972 NCCB meeting, John Cardinal Krol, president of the NCCB, submitted a letter to Cardinal Wright pointing out that, as a result of the evaluation, the bishops of the United States were petitioning to continue the experimentation in this country for two more years. While the bishops waited for a response to their communication, the declaration *Sanctus pontifex* was issued on May 24, 1973.

Issued jointly by the Congregation for the Clergy and the Congregation for the Discipline of the Sacraments, the declaration called for the termination of all experimentation with regards to the delay of first confession by the close of the 1972/73 school year. The declaration, however, created just as much ambiguity as the Addendum and, like the Addendum, was based on an interpretation of *Quam singulari*.

Penance and Children

It should be noted that the declaration raised the binding force of the Addendum to a new legislative status. What was originally considered to be a document which merely raised the issue within the Church was now considered as adding strength to the custom of administering the sacrament of penance before first communion. Also, the legislative status and intent of the declaration itself was open to interpretation. When the representative committee of the Canadian Catholic Conference (CCC) met with both Cardinals Wright and Samore in Rome, they were told:

1. That the declaration did not impose the obligation of confession before first communion;

2. That the document was a declaration and not a decree;

3. That the intent of the declaration was to correct abuses regarding the reception of first confession; and

4. That this decision was based on an interpretation of *Quam singulari*.[25]

In the United States a twofold concern emerged regarding the declaration. First was a general dismay among catechists because the declaration lacked any explanation for the specific reasons for the termination; further, many leading catechists found the document theologically, legally, and pastorally unsound. Second, many catechists felt that the declaration would cause a credibility crisis on a diocesan level, since the document could also be used by more conservative groups to undermine other catechetical advances.

Considering the controversial nature of the declaration, many felt that it was important that diocesan directors of religious education and their bishops be made clearly aware of the teachings and legislative status of the declaration. Consequently, the bishops discussed the declaration and its impact on sacramental catechesis at their November 1973 meeting.[26] The bishops decided upon a broad pastoral interpretation of the declaration so that the impression of obligation to confess before first communion would not be insisted upon.

Rather than solving anything, the Addendum and declaration raised more questions than they resolved. Because of them, two schools of thought clearly emerged: one advocated the first penance of children before first eucharist, and another maintained

Linda Gaupin

228

a delay of first penance until after first eucharist. Religious educators were left to deal with the dilemma as best they could.

Thus, despite the attempts of Rome to resolve the issue, it remained in a state of ambiguity and confusion. This was made clearly apparent throughout the process of the formation of the National Catechetical Directory, *Sharing the Light of Faith* (SLF). The issue of first penance/first eucharist emerged repeatedly throughout each of the three consultative processes that were part of the formulation of this national document.[27] It was further complicated by a letter from John Cardinal Wright and James Cardinal Knox dated March 21, 1977. The cause of the letter stemmed from the fact that "in some parts of the Church and in some catechetical centers, dissention and doubts still remain about the ecclesiastical discipline which regards children's receiving the sacrament of penance before they receive communion."[28]

The letter clearly provided a negative response to the questions of whether the practice of first eucharist/first penance be allowed to continue after the declaration, but the letter appeared to be contradictory in two aspects. First, it reaffirmed the positions of the Addendum and declaration, yet in each of these cases catechists were assured that there was no intention of imposing the obligation of penance before first communion. Secondly, the letter treated both the Addendum and the declaration as having legislative status when in effect catechists had been told that the first was issued merely to surface the question and that the second, by its nature as declaration, did not have the force of a decree.

Ultimately, the letter of 1977, as well as the Addendum and declaration, led to the carefully worded distinction found in the SLF regarding the practice of first penance/first eucharist. After some revisions were made by the bishops at their November 1977 meeting, the statement regarding the practice of first penance/first eucharist read:

> Catechesis for the sacrament of reconciliation is to precede first communion and must be kept distinct by a clear and unhurried separation. This is to be done so that the specific identity of each sacrament is apparent and so that, before receiving first communion, the child will be familiar with the Revised Rite of Reconciliation and will be at ease with the reception of the sacrament, in accordance with the norms of the decree *Quam singulari* and in the communication from the Congregation for the Discipline of the Sacraments and the Congregation for the Clergy of March 31, 1977.[29]

Penance and Children

The entire draft of the SLF was submitted to the Congregation for the Clergy for approval in early 1978. On October 31, 1978, the Congregation for the Clergy, after consultation with the Congregation for Doctrine of the Faith and other experts, approved the Directory pending clarification in four areas. One of these dealt with paragraph 126 on the practices pertaining to first penance/first eucharist. Not satisfied with the wording, Rome recommended the text be changed to read "the reception of the sacrament of reconciliation should normally precede communion."

The bishops' committee did not accept exactly the recommendation of Rome. In their carefully crafted statement, they made a slight but significant change. Paragraph 126 now read: "The Sacrament of Reconciliation normally should be celebrated prior to the reception of first communion."[30] Omitted was any mention of the *obligation* to receive penance before communion.

STATE OF QUESTION

The importance of the first penance/first eucharist controversy is rooted in the bearing it has on the larger issue of penance and children in the Church. The material presented here confronts catechists with three fundamental questions which pertain to the continuing agenda of penance and children. They are the questions of 1) sacramental order, 2) the nature of the catechesis for penance, and 3) the meaning of penance in light of the initiation sacraments.

The historical evidence enables us to arrive at some clarifications regarding the question of sacramental order. First we are able to pinpoint the source of our present difficulties with *Quam singulari*. With the promulgation of the decree, the focus of sacramental catechesis was changed from adolescence to the early years of childhood. The pattern of first penance/first eucharist was maintained uncritically due to the overwhelming preoccupation with the many catechetical changes by the decree.

The critical question for the Church today is whether the decree *Quam singulari* ever called for the maintenance of this sacramental order. Herein lies the heart of the matter, since the Addendum of the GCD, the 1973 Declaration, and the other related documents rely on the decree as their fundamental source.

John Cardinal Wright believed that *Quam singulari* "clearly called for a simultaneity in the preparation for and the admission of

Linda Gaupin

these two sacraments."[31] Since the decree had not been abrogated, he felt that recent experiments violated Church teaching. He also maintained that the sacramental order of first penance/first eucharist represented the pristine practice of the Church.

Whether *Quam singulari* actually required this sacramental order, however, is open to discussion. It is important to keep in mind that the primary purpose of the decree was concerned with correcting abuses which essentially attempted to postpone or delay first communion. Within this context *Quam singulari* did not condemn delaying confession until after first communion and made no statement that the age of seven was "suitable" for first confession. Rather the decree says that children are to have access to confession from that approximate age. Thus *Quam singulari* only ensures the possibility of confession at the age of seven, but says nothing about the suitability, value, or propriety of this action.

Wright's statement that the first penance/first eucharist order has been the pristine practice of the Church also appears contrary to the historical tradition set out in the first part of the decree. Historical evidence is fairly clear that for twelve hundred years the normal practice in the Church was baptismal eucharist.[32] More importantly this study has shown that when first penance does precede first eucharist within the sacramental order, it does so within a context of special circumstances arising when first eucharist is received at a much later age in childhood. Even then the catechesis for penance was not considered as an integral part of the catechesis for first eucharist.

Further, it is important to note that *Quam singulari* did not intend to settle the question of the age at which a child can sin seriously. It did, however, reflect a sensitivity to the teachings of the Council of Trent which maintained that confession was obligatory only in the case of mortal sin.

In light of all this, it would seem to be imprudent to impose the sacramental order of first penance/first eucharist. The pastoral success of delaying first penance, substantiated by the U.S. bishops' evaluation in 1972, lends further support to this argument.

The historical evidence presented here also confronts us with a very important fact regarding our second fundamental question, namely, the integral nature of the catechesis for penance of children. Inherent in its nature is the need for a protracted catechesis which allows for the gradual introduction to and formation in the

Penance and Children

moral life. Even without the aid of the insights of developmental and child psychology, the seventeenth-century Church was aware of the importance of this fact.

One of the most important contributions of that era to our contemporary discussion is the recognition that there is a difference in the requirements for the catechesis for penance and for first eucharist. This was rooted in the premise that the catechesis for penance was more exacting on the child. Thus, it was not only crucial to keep this catechesis separate and distinct, it was also necessary to prolong its length.

It is interesting that this same perception was evidenced by the bishops in the results of their evaluation in 1972. In particular, they noted that the reception of the eucharist did not make the higher intellectual, moral, and psychological demands that were required by penance and that the catechesis was better when focused on only one sacrament.

The recent advances in child psychology and in the area of faith-development provide a further impetus for catechists to begin to examine the wisdom of restoring a protracted catechesis for penance. Critical attention must be given to our disjointed practices of a catechetical preparation for penance around the age of seven followed by another catechesis for penance some time later on in a catechetical program (if indeed this does occur). The lack of continuity in our programs for the sacramental catechesis for penance often risk overcatechizing for penance—and at too young an age.

One Dutch catechist admirably summarized our catechesis for penance in the following words:

> Let those who have faith not be hasty lest the spiritual impulses of the child be satiated before they are unlocked. Our education suffers from "too early and too much." We anticipate constantly. We drag the children towards God instead of letting them come . . . and not hindering them, as the Gospel teaches us. We say "learn it now and do it now even if you do not desire it." Meanwhile we think that we risk nothing because we have done everything.[33]

The challenge this presents for the future is the development of a sacramental catechesis for penance that is protracted and continuous. It points to the need for catechesis that respects the principles of faith and moral development by emphasizing the special nature of a catechesis for penance, i.e., the gradual introduction

Linda Gaupin

and formation into the moral life. This would have the added advantage of being adaptable to whatever sacramental order is maintained (first penance/first eucharist or first eucharist/first penance); of overcoming the dilemma of children who have never made first penance because they have missed the initial catechesis for one reason or another; and of helping to minimize the attitude of occasional catechetical participation only at sacramental moments.

Such an extended and continuous catechesis for penance would respect the ultimate goal of the penitential experience: interior conversion. It would also allow the child to be gradually catechized into the different ritual expressions contained in the rite.

Finally, serious consideration must be given to a third fundamental question, the meaning of penance for children in light of the initiation sacraments. The problem was stated in the beginning of this paper: what is the meaning of reactualizing a union with Christ for small children who have yet to realize the fullness of this initial union received in baptism and completed in the eucharist.

The insertion of penance into the initiation sequence impacts dramatically on our understanding of baptism and eucharist. The time of catechetical preparation for penance is often treated as a sort of mini-catechumenal period before first eucharist. Thus, there is a real tendency to look on baptism as a sort of entrance into the catechumenate and the moment of first eucharist as the time of initial initiation into the Church.

This notion is not so farfetched as it seems. During the controversy on first penance/first eucharist, John Cardinal Wright supported this sequence because he saw it as assuming "the role that baptism had for the Christian living in the ancient pagan context: they can become the sacraments of Christian Initiation." Wright further pointed out that since baptism is received in infancy "penance and eucharist mark for most Christians the *first* salvific encounters with Christ."[34]

Wright's remarks were published in December 1971. The following month the Rite of Christian Initiation of Adults was promulgated. Since this time, we have grown in our awareness of the meaning of sacramental initiation. As the Church has rediscovered the integrity of the initiation sacraments, the focus has returned to the total initiation action which incorporates the person into

Penance and Children

Christ. Within this context, baptism and eucharist are inextricably related as the supreme expressions of what it means to be Church. "In baptism, the eucharist begins, and in eucharist, baptism is sustained. From this premier, sacramental union flows all the Church's life."[35]

It is out of this understanding of the total act of initiation that we must consider the meaning of penance for children who have yet to receive eucharist. Peter Fink aptly states that "it is impossible to make reconciliation sense out of penance for children before their first communion."[36] He attributes this to the fact that over the centuries penance has taken on characteristics more akin to initiation than reconciliation.

Herein lies the crux of the problem. Francis Mannion comes close to resolving the issue in the careful distinction he makes between penance and reconciliation in a postbaptismal context. He refers to penance as the "comprehensive dynamic that involves the whole church, as well as the individual believer, in building up and ennobling corporate existence in Christ."[37] On the other hand, reconciliation is the "overcoming of the radical break with the community of believers, and with God, that takes place through a falling away from baptismal grace. It is the return to the communion of the church after the virtual withdrawal from it by what is traditionally and still properly called mortal sin."[38]

The distinction is useful for determining the proper meaning of penance with the initiation sequence. The need at this time is not so much that of reconciliation, but rather of fostering the sense of corporate existence in Christ and nourishing the process of conversion begun in baptism. Mannion suggests using this penitential conception of first penance before first communion. I would venture one step further and suggest that we begin to expand and enrich our catechesis for first eucharist to include these concepts.

This approach would respect the ecclesial reality of the moment: preparation for the celebration and reception of first eucharist as a sacrament which completes the union with Christ initiated at baptism. It would enrich our catechesis for first eucharist by including the concept of eucharist as the fullness of reconciliation. At the same time, it would allow us to incorporate the concepts of corporate existence and conversion in terms of an initiating paradigm.

This approach would also enable us to overcome the present dilemma of having to provide catecheses for penance and for eu-

Linda Gaupin

charist at around the same time, while yet having to keep them separate and distinct. All this could be followed by the sacramental catechesis for penance to be conducted along the lines of a protracted catechesis stated above.

An approach of this nature would also provide a viable alternative for reconciling Rome's concern that children be instilled with the desire for the sacrament of penance early in life with the significance of sacramental initiation for all catechesis in the Church.

The purpose of this study has been to identify some of the systemic problems that surround the issue of penance and children. A resolution to any of these problems must be rooted in a historical consciousness and in a serious consideration of our initiatory policy. Further consideration must be given to the fact that the confusion of sacramental order and the subsequent catechesis for penance, which followed the aftermath of *Quam singulari*, have never been critically examined nor satisfactorily resolved. The promulgation of the Rite of Christian Initiation of Adults provides us with an opportune moment to clarify these issues in light of the continuing reconciliation agenda.

NOTES

1. Aidan Kavanagh, "The Nature of Christian Penance: Metanoia and Reconciliation," *Resonance* 2 (1966) 11–12.

2. Cardinal Oddi's address can be found in "Congregation Head Asks Improved Penance Catechesis," *Origins* 13 (November 10, 1983) 373–376.

3. See *Documents on the Liturgy, 1963–1979: Conciliar, Papal and Curial Texts* (Collegeville: The Liturgical Press, 1982) 986.

4. *Code of Canon Law: Latin–English Edition* (Washington, D.C.: Canon Law Society of America, 1983). Commentaries on these canons can be found in James H. Provost, J.C.D., "Advisory Opinions: First Eucharist and First Penance," *The Jurist* 43 (1983) 450–453; and *The Code of Canon Law: A Text and Commentary*, eds. James A. Coriden, Thomas J. Green, and Donald E. Heintschel (New York: Paulist Press, 1985) 652–653.

5. Thomas P. Ivory to diocesan catechetical directors concerning the USCC Committee on Education meeting, May 5–6, 1986, Washington, D.C., NCCB Archives.

6. To support the French hegemony see Erwin Iserloth, Joseph Glazik, and Hubert Jedin, *Reformation and Counter-Reformation*, vol. 5, *History of the Church*, ed. Hubert Jedin and John Dolan, trans. Anselm Biggs and Peter Becker (New York: Seabury Press, 1980) 107–110.

7. For a detailed description see E. Diebold, "Du Concile De Trente au Decret 'Quam Singulari,' " *Communion Solennelle et Profession de Foi, Lex Orandi*, vol. 14, (Paris: Les Editions du Cerf, 1952) 46–48; ibid., *Histoire des Catéchismes de Saint-Sulpice* (Paris: Gaume Freres, 1983) 1–20; and Michel Sauvage, *Catéchèse et Laïcat* (Paris: Ligel, 1962) 272–273.

8. Sauvage, p. 362.

9. Mary Charles Bryce, "Evolution of Catechesis from the Catholic Reformation to the Present," in *A Faithful Church*, ed. John H. Westerhoff III and O. C. Edwards, Jr. (Wilton, CT: Morehouse-Barlow Co., Inc., 1981), 205–213. See also Sauvage, *Catéchèse* 272.

10. Jean-Claude D'Hotel, *Les Origines du Catéchisme Moderne* (Paris: Editions Montaigne, 1967). For a detailed description of this see also Sauvage, *Catéchèse* 387–422.

11. Diebold, *Trente* 58–59. Diebold describes the four different stages of the catechetical structure as it emerged in seventeenth-century France. This same information can be found in D'Hotel, *Les Origines* 411–412.

12. For a detailed history of first eucharist as a separate and distinct rite see Linda Gaupin, "First Eucharist and the Shape of Catechesis Since 'Quam Singulari' " (Ann Arbor, Michigan: University Microfilms, 1985).

13. Diebold, *Trente* 66, and D'Hotel, *Les Origines* 412–413.

14. Felix Dupanloup, *The Ministry of Catechizing* (London: Griffith Farren and Company, 1890) 275.

15. Michel Lagree, "La confession dans les visites pastorales et les statuts synodaux Brentons aux xix et xx siecles," in *La Practique de la confession* (Paris: Les Editions du Cerf, 1983) 244. See also Catherine Dooley, "Development of the Practice of Devotional Confession," *Questions Liturgiques* 64:2/3 (April/September, 1983) 107.

16. For a history of this period see Louis Andrieux, *La Première Communion* (Paris: Gabriel Beauchesne et Cie., 1911) 212–283. See also Dupanloup, *Catechizing*.

17. *AAS*, 2 (1910) 577–583. For the English translation see Joseph Collins, *Catechetical Documents of Pope Pius X* (Paterson, N.J.: St. Anthony Guild Press, 1946) 54–63.

18. For a detailed history of this reorganization, see Gaupin, *First Eucharist*, chapter 4.

Linda Gaupin

19. William Costello, "Christian Doctrine for Public School Pupils," *The Ecclesiastical Review* 51 (December 1914) 655–667. See also "The Assistant Pastor and the Decree on the First Communion of Children," *American Ecclesiastical Review* 44 (January 1911) 80; "An Ecclesiastical Conference on 'Quam Singulari,'" *American Ecclesiastical Review* 44 (January 1911) 82; and J. T. McNicholas, "The First Communion Decree," *American Ecclesiastical Review* 44 (January 1911) 76–79.

20. Jungmann's work was particularly formative. In *Handing on the Faith* (New York: Herder and Herder, 1959), Jungmann acknowledged that one of the chief obstacles thwarting the idea of early first communion was the necessity of preparing children for the sacrament of penance. Instead, Jungmann preferred the idea of returning to a more protracted period of catechesis for penance that would in turn respect the difficult nature of this catechesis. See especially pp. 290–340.

21. Gaupin, *First Eucharist*, chapter 5.

22. John Cardinal Wright, "The New Catechetical Directory and Initiation to the Sacraments of Penance and Eucharist," *L'Osservatore Romano* (English edition), October 7, 1971.

23. Minutes of the Twelfth General Meeting, USCC, April 11–13, 1972, Atlanta, Georgia. Washington, D.C., NCCB Archives.

24. "Evaluation," NCCB Committee on Pastoral Research, June 1973, Washington, D.C., NCCB Archives.

25. "Vatican Not Trying to Force Confession Before First Communion," N.C. News Service Documentation from Canadian Catholic Conference, National Center of Religious Education-CCD, November 7, 1973, Washington, D.C., NCCB Archives.

26. Thomas J. Sullivan, "The Directory and First Confession," *The Living Light* 16 (Summer 1979) 402.

27. For a history of this process see Gaupin, *First Eucharist*, chapter 7.

28. *AAS*, 69 (1977) 427.

29. "Sharing the Light of Faith: Proposed Amendments," Supporting Documentation, General Meeting of Bishops, November 14–17, 1977 (Washington, D.C.: NCCB Archives), 47–48.

30. Sullivan, *First Confession* 401.

31. John Cardinal Wright to Most Rev. William E. Power, D.D., President of the C.C.C., on the Declaration of 1973, September 28, 1973, Washington, D.C., NCCB Archives.

32. Andrieux, *La Première Communion*. See also *Baptism: Ancient Liturgies and Patristic Texts*, ed. A. Hamman (Staten Island: Alba House, 1967); J.D.C. Fisher, *Christian Initiation: Baptism in the Medieval West* (London:

Penance and Children

SPCK, 1965); and David Holeton, "The Communion of Infants and Young Children," in *And Do Not Hinder Them*, ed. Geiko Müller-Fahrenholz, no. 109 (Geneva: World Council of Churches, 1982).

33. H. Fortmann, "Zijdiegeloven, hassten niet," in *De geestelojklygienische problematick van de middelbare schooljeugd* (Utrecht, 1957) 43.

34. Wright, "The New Catechetical Directory."

35. Aidan Kavanagh, *The Shape of Baptism: The Rite of Christian Initiation* (New York: Pueblo, 1978) 122.

36. Peter J. Fink, "Investigating the Sacrament of Penance: An Experiment in Sacramental Theology," *Worship* 54 (May 1980) 220.

37. M. Francis Mannion, "Penance and Reconciliation: A Systemic Analysis," *Worship* 60 (March 1986) 109.

38. Ibid.

Ellen O'Hara, C.S.J.

Penance and Canon Law

In order to cover adequately the simple but wide-ranging topic of this paper, I first want to lay out what the 1983 Code of Canon Law says about penance. Then I will demonstrate with three examples the present challenge canonists face in interpreting the law; and I will conclude with some general observations about the spirit with which one approaches Church law in general and the legal aspects of penance in particular.

THE 1983 CODE AND PENANCE

When investigating what the Code of Canon Law says about penance, we might consider three groups of canons: those which set a context for interpretation, those where the sacrament of penance is mentioned specifically, and those which mention other areas or processes of penance and reconciliation.

First, certain canons concerning the interpretation and application of Code law are important for our topic. Canon 2 reminds us that liturgical laws hitherto in force remain in force, unless they are contrary to the Code. Canon 14 indicates that laws do not bind when there is a doubt of law. Canons 17 and 19 are the canons which indicate how one interprets the law. Canon 17 is especially significant since it contains a change which now allows canonists to look to other sources in trying to determine the meaning and application of law.[1] Canon 21 states that later laws should be harmonized to the greatest extent possible with earlier laws, and the revocation of previous law is not to be presumed. Finally, canon 27 says that custom is the best way to interpret the law. These canons serve from within the Code itself as an interpretative context for specific individual laws or groups of laws.

Second, we turn to five canons or groups of canons which mention the practice of the sacrament of penance specifically. The first is the discussion of the sacrament of penance per se in thirty-nine canons (959–997), and I will discuss these in more detail in the next section of this paper. In another place, canon 844 presents penance as one of three sacraments (eucharist and anointing of the sick are the others) for which there is a possibility of ecumenical reception: that is, a baptized non-Catholic can receive the sacrament from a Catholic minister, or a Catholic can receive the sacrament from a non-Catholic minister in whose Church the sacrament is valid. The diocesan bishop or the conference of bishops is to consult with the authorities of the non-Catholic churches before issuing norms. How this can or will occur remains to be seen, especially in light of the principle that the sacraments are not to be used indiscriminately in restoring Christian unity.

Another group of canons deals with the sacrament of penance and children. Canon 777.2 mentions that part of the pastor's responsibility is to see that the children in his parish are properly prepared for first confession by means of catechetical formation over an appropriate period of time and according to norms laid down by the diocesan bishop. Canons 914 and 916 (in the section on the eucharist) connect the reception of eucharist with sacramental confession. Canon 914 further indicates that it is the duty of parents and pastors to see that children who have reached the use of reason are properly prepared and receive first communion as soon as possible, "having made their sacramental confession." (Canon 916, however, places the obligation of sacramental confession before communion only on those aware of grave sin.)

A fourth group of canons deals with the sacrament of penance

Penance and Canon Law

for clerics and members of institutes of consecrated life. Canon 673 indicates that the witness of the consecrated life is nourished through prayer and penance: the reference here is to the larger context of penance and the works of penance as ascetical practices, not simply to the reception of the sacrament. In canon 630, superiors of religious are forbidden to induce any manifestation of conscience on the part of their members, and they are not to hear the confessions of their members unless members spontaneously request it. Canon 664 (in the section on the obligations and rights of religious) exhorts religious to strive for conversion of soul. In order to do this, two practices are mentioned: daily examination of conscience and frequent reception of the sacrament of penance.[2] Related to this is a final group of canons on the sacrament of penance and clerics. Canon 246.4 recommends frequent reception of the sacrament for seminarians, and canon 276.2.5 exhorts all clerics to do the same. Canon 916 mentions that anyone conscious of grave sin may not celebrate mass or receive communion without previously having been to sacramental confession, unless there is a grave reason and no opportunity to confess.

Third, beyond specific mention of the sacrament of penance, there are canons which mention other areas or processes of penance and reconciliation. For example, in Book IV of the Code, on the sanctifying office of the Church, we find legislation on the days of penance (canons 1248–1253). The obligation for all to do penance is affirmed, and the common practices of penance (prayer, works of piety and charity, self-denial, and fasting and abstinence) are described. Also, within the canons on the other sacraments, theological and pastoral statements are made of the connection with penance and reconciliation: baptism frees people from sins (canon 849); anointing of the sick cannot be conferred on those who "obstinately persist in serious sin" (canon 1007); and potential spouses are encouraged to approach the sacrament of penance prior to marriage (canon 1065).

Further examples suggest processes of penance and reconciliation in the wider life of the Church. Book VI, on sanctions in the Church, says that the Church may make use of penances (in addition to penal sanctions and penal remedies) in order to substitute for or augment a penalty (canons 1312.3, 1339, 1340). A penance is defined as "the performance of some work of religion or piety or charity" (canon 1340.1). In the section on the obligations and rights

Ellen O'Hara

of all members of Christ's faithful, there is mention of the obligation of all to provide for the needs of the Church so that the Church may accomplish its mission, and to promote social justice and assist the poor from within their own resources (canon 222). The following canon (223) mentions that, in exercising rights, all the faithful must take into account the common good of the Church, as well as the rights of others and their duties toward others. In the section on trials, canon 1446 exhorts all the faithful to strive to avoid disputes and to settle promptly and peacefully those that do occur. The canon goes on to urge a judge to do everything possible to assist conflicting parties to settle the matter equitably, to indicate various means and persons that would help in this, and to utilize conciliation and arbitration if it would be useful for resolving the controversy. These references clearly establish that there are the beginnings of structures for reconciliation outlined within the Code itself.[3]

INTERPRETING THE CODE

Scholars in various fields have pointed out the need for a context in interpreting and applying canon law, a kind of "hermeneutics of canon law" like that already recognized in the study of theology and scripture.[4] Reflection on the particular theology upon which the law is based and an understanding of whether a particular law is to be considered doctrinal, theological, perceptive or exhortatory, are necessary preconditions to a proper understanding of the Code. Thus the canonist's first task is to draw upon the pertinent sources that feed this reflection and understanding: magisterial teaching, liturgical law, and theology. In the case of the sacrament of penance, the following are all sources for the canonist: the teaching and legislation of the Council of Trent; the legislation of the previous Code of Canon Law (1917–1918); the teachings of Vatican Council II; the norms for general absolution (25 March 1944 and 16 June 1972); the General Catechetical Directory (1971); the 1978 National Catechetical Directory for the United States, *Sharing the Light of Faith*; the apostolic constitution *Paenitemini*, and the revised ritual for the sacrament of penance (1973).[5] In addition, the developments of the behavioral sciences, which aid our understanding of the human person, and knowledge of Thomistic philosophy are both helpful, even if at times there is disagreement between them.

Penance and Canon Law

One of the difficulties with sacramental law in the 1983 Code is its underlying theology.[6] Much of the language still reflects a Scholastic understanding of the sacraments and their operation. Some years ago, Karl Rahner offered a number of cautions which are relevant today.

1. There is always more in the memory of the Church than is present at any particular moment of her awareness.
2. Sober exactness and lucid abstractness, although good in themselves, may also lead to spiritual impoverishment in theology.
3. Mortal and venial as categories for sin differ essentially and not just in the matter of degree.
4. The terms "binding" and "loosing" are not alternatives, but rather two steps in the same process of reconciliation.
5. We always need to keep in mind the distinction between the entire penitential process and the one phase of that process which we identify as the sacrament.[7]

These cautions are useful to the canonist in reflecting on the theological foundations of law and the ways law enfleshes theology. Brief consideration of these examples will illustrate the difficulties and challenges for the science and art of interpreting canon law.

First, in the introductory canons of the section on the sacraments (834–839), the 1983 Code makes it clear that sacraments are ecclesial actions and symbols of the Church's unity which continue to build ecclesial communion. In the canons on the sacrament of penance, however, that sacrament's social and ecclesial dimensions are neglected, as are the role of the penitent as co-celebrant and the presence and participation of the community in the reconciliation process. It is true that the theological statement on the sacrament of penance (canon 659) differs from the previous code (canon 870 in the 1917 Code); but one notes that in the present canon there is no reference to Jesus, the Holy Spirit, the mercy or love or care of God, the involvement of the community in the celebration of the sacrament, or the liturgical celebration of the sacrament.[8] The theological statement and the vocabulary used to describe the sacrament of penance in the Code do not reflect the richness and development of the theology of the sacrament that has occurred over the last twenty-five years. There is no wording or thought comparable to the beautiful description and

Ellen O'Hara

discussion of the sacrament found in the introduction to the revised Rite nor the larger framework for it put forth in *Paenitemini*.[9]

A second example are the canons which treat of general absolution. Two legal documents effecting this discussion are the norms issued in 1944 and in 1972. The current Code is more specific than the Rite of Penance because the former seems to refer more to the 1944 norms than to the Rite itself; the Rite relies more on the 1972 norms. For example, the Code differs from the Rite in the fact that the Code gives greater priority to the danger-of-death situation as the circumstance in which general absolution may be used (canon 961). Unlike the Rite of Penance (no. 31), there is no mention or reference to mission territories or to other places or other groups of people where the need for general absolution may exist. Further, the new Code restricts the necessary permission to the diocesan bishop and not just to any local ordinary; and it leaves no option for the priest to make a decision apart from the judgment of the diocesan bishop about whether the conditions are present or not. The Rite of Penance (no. 32) called upon the bishop to *consult* with other members of the episcopal conference before making a judgment about the presence of conditions for general absolution; the Code speaks of criteria "agreed with other members of the episcopal conference" (canon 961.2).[10]

The Code and the Rite are in essential agreement on the matter of confession and forgiveness of sins. Canon 963 states the obligation of annual confession for all those who have reached the age of discretion and have committed grave sin. A person whose grave sins are forgiven by general absolution must make individual confession before receiving another general absolution "unless a just reason intervenes." ("Just reason" is a mercifully ambiguous phrase which should be left with legally binding interpretation!) The Rite of Penance (no. 34) indicates that the precept obliging individual confession remains in force. However, theological concerns challenge this position, and this canonist would need the assistance of competent theologians to explain how sins forgiven by general absolution require repetition in individual confession.

Theological concerns flow into pastoral practice, which in turn is informed by and informs the legal situation. The much-publicized case of Carroll T. Dozier, Bishop of Memphis, is an example. Bishop Dozier conducted a reconciliation service in his diocese, a

Penance and Canon Law

part of which included the Rite of Reconciliation of Several Penitents with General Confession and Absolution. The Sacred Congregation for the Sacraments and Divine Worship, after learning of the service, addressed a letter on the subject to the National Conference of Catholic Bishops, who in turn circulated it to all the bishops. The decision of the Congregation, while applauding Dozier's intent to draw Catholics back to the practice of the Church, was that the pastoral norms for general absolution had not been observed. The necessary conditions had not been met, and the letter cautioned that no assumption should be made that Rome agreed with Dozier's actions. The Congregation stated that the "celebration of the sacrament of penance with general absolution as the focal point of a pastoral ministry of evangelization or reconciliation does not accord with the pastoral norms." The exchange of letters[11] and the basis for the actions of both Bishop Dozier and the Holy See represent in a fairly clear way the different motivations and interpretations of conditions when using general absolution.

When we return to the canons on general absolution, the canonist would observe that their negative wording indicates a rather clear preference that general absolution not be used. Thus, while the rite with general absolution is one of the options for celebrating the sacrament of penance, the number of restrictions placed on it and the additional narrowing of the Rite in the new Code indicate both the disciplinary and theological unease with this form of the sacrament.[12] However, for one who knows the history of the sacrament, this unease may be the creative tension that presages another major shift in the way the sacrament is celebrated.[13]

A third example in this section is the question of whether or not reception of the sacrament of penance is a requirement for the first reception of eucharist. Canon 914 indicates that the pastor and the parents are to ensure that children who have reached the use of reason are prepared for and receive the eucharist, "having made their sacramental confession." Use of reason and proper preparation are the principal criteria in this canon for the reception of the eucharist. The previous canon (913) indicates the requirements for first communion: children are required to have sufficient knowledge, accurate preparation according to their capacity, and the ability to receive communion with faith and reverence. This

Ellen O'Hara

canon does not require previous reception of the sacrament of penance. Further, canon 988, as already noted, requires integral confession only for serious sins committed after baptism of which the faithful are aware after careful examination of conscience; and the obligation of annual confession (canon 989) is based upon having "reached the age of discretion." Without getting into all of the discussions which have emerged regarding the use of reason, sufficient use of reason, and age of discretion, it is clear (even to a canonist) that the canons are speaking of two different faculties: the use of reason versus the age of discretion.

The matter in question is extremely serious, particularly since interpretations of canon 914 suggest that the reception of the sacrament of penance must always precede the reception of first holy communion. Linda Gaupin describes well the assumptions regarding catechetical preparation and age which were collapsed by the change in process when *Quam singulari* encouraged the giving of first communion to younger children.[14]

The question which remains for the canonist is whether or not one can require or coerce the reception of the sacrament of penance as a precondition for receiving first communion. It would seem that the only sacrament required for the reception of eucharist is baptism, which is correctly referred to as the "gate to the other sacraments" (canon 849). The reception of the sacrament of penance cannot be coerced, as the very lack of freedom on the part of the recipient would in itself affect the central meaning of sign and sacrament. The decision about both first eucharist and first penance belongs primarily to the parents and the pastor, based on the child's readiness, preparation, and abilities. It may well be that the child meets all of the criteria necessary for the reception of first communion, and has attained the use of reason, but may still be lacking that discretion of judgment which would allow the capacity for serious sin, the only level for which integral confession is required.

As early as 1920, the Commission for the Interpretation of the Code replied to the question of whether the use of reason for the reception of holy communion and for the obligation for annual confession was the level necessary to commit a mortal sin or a level sufficient for the commission of a venial sin. It stated (rather vaguely) that the use of reason for holy communion is what was indicated in canon 854.2 and 3 of the 1917 Code, and the use of reason for the obligation of annual confession is as indicated in canon 906 of the same Code.[15] When one refers to those canons, one sees that the former canon requires an ability to distinguish the holy eucharist from ordinary bread, the ability to adore it, a fuller knowledge and more careful preparation compatible with their capacity, and as much devotion as can be expected of a child of that age. The discretion required by the latter canon is even less clear, since the obligation to confess is placed on all Catholics who have reached the age of discretion. The commentators have always explained that the obligation to confess pertains to mortal sins, since canon 902 of the 1917 Code clearly states that venial sins are not necessary matter for the sacrament of penance. The new Code repeats the recommendation that venial sins be confessed, but places no obligation to confess them (canon 988.2). Thus, as early as 1920 some distinction in the requirement of discretion for communion and penance was observed.

Some of the confusion which has emerged is based on the concern for the growing non-use of the sacrament of penance, both by adults and children, and on a perceived difference in the understanding or acknowledgement of personal sinfulness. For these reasons, there has been some renewed emphasis on frequent reception of the sacrament of penance as a source of grace and a practice of devotion.[16] Since the Addendum to the General Catechetical Directory in 1971, several Congregations of the Roman Curia have continually emphasized that experiments regarding reception of first communion without prior reception of the sacrament of penance were to be terminated. The emphasis was that reception of first communion as a general rule before the reception of penance was not to be permitted. In March 1977, the Sacred Congregation for the Sacraments and Divine Worship issued a private reply regarding the order of first communion and first confession. Maintaining the emphasis that it is wrong "as a general rule" to receive first communion without previous confession, the Sacred Congregation felt a need to explain once again the Church's norm regarding these questions. The letter states that the obligation of receiving both sacraments in this specifically designated order of confession before communion begins with the reaching of the age of discretion on or about the seventh year. It further cautions that the obligation of confession should be understood "according to the traditional doctrine of the Church." Ex-

Ellen O'Hara

plaining the need for confession before communion, the Congregation states:

> Moreover, St. Paul's admonition (1 Cor 11:28) truly establishes a directing norm which regards even children. Therefore these also, before receiving the Holy Eucharist, should examine themselves. But often a child is not able to examine his conscience clearly and truly by himself. This will be done more easily and safely if he avails himself of the help of a priest confessor. In fact there are many children who feel troubled by small and unimportant things while there are others who ignore and pass over more serious faults.[17]

The reply also states that the priest could not make a sufficient judgment about the child's disposition for first communion unless the child had gone to confession first. Finally, the reply says that the child has a right to the sacraments and it would be discriminatory and a violation of the child's conscience not to allow preparation for the sacraments.[18]

While this reply was private and therefore does not have the force of law, the argumentation is interesting. The line of reasoning suggests that the child needs to go to confession because she or he may not be able to examine her or his conscience, and may be so scrupulous as to be troubled by small and unimportant matters (which may not be sinful) while ignoring others which an adult might objectively consider more serious. Given the traditional doctrine of the Church recommended by the reply, it seems to me that the child who is not able to examine conscience or to distinguish between trivial matters and gravely sinful matters is also not capable of committing serious sin. It needs to be repeated that, unless one is talking about serious or mortal sin, the obligation of the sacrament of penance prior to communion does not hold and therefore need not be discussed. Preparation for the sacrament should precede and be separated from preparation for first communion (as recommended by Sharing the Light of Faith[19]), but there is a difference between allowing for reception of the sacrament of penance and demanding it. I do not see how one can require reception of penance before first communion if one takes into account the studies of the behavioral sciences (which indicate that children under age twelve are generally unable to form abstract concepts or to perform the necessary mental and moral processes for the commission of serious sin), and if one strictly maintains the traditional teaching of the Church on the require-

Penance and Canon Law

ment for confession and the ability to commit serious sin.[20] The reasons given simply do not match the seriousness being attached to the issue, and seem to reflect either agendas of authority or different notions of how to revive the practice of frequent reception of penance.

If a ruling is made at some point that the reception of the sacrament of penance is a necessary precondition to the reception of the sacrament of the eucharist for the first time, two things would require serious attention. The first would be the custom in some countries of giving a child first communion at the time of baptism. No one is obliged to the impossible (as a rule of law) and therefore the law itself would require exceptions. Second, if the reception of the sacrament of penance is considered a requirement, and its rationale would be the need to inculcate the practice of receiving the sacrament, the rite with general absolution might appropriately be used here. The restriction, of course, remains that those guilty of serious sin must confess these sins in individual private confession as soon as possible. This would be made clear during the ceremony, but in general the liturgical celebration of the sacrament of penance according to the third rite (general absolution) might be more appropriate to the conditions and circumstances of the children. The opportunity for individual confessions could be provided for anyone who wished it, but the group celebration could provide an excellent formation for the children of communal dimensions of penance and reconciliation. As they grow, children could then be provided with necessary and ongoing catechesis for individual confession.

CONCLUDING OBSERVATIONS ON THE LAW

Sacrosanctum Concilium (no. 11) states that in the celebration of the liturgy more is required than the legal minimum. That always needs to be kept in mind as the "more" toward which we are called in our witness and celebration as Church. As we live the daily reality of the Church with all of its tensions, we are keenly aware that there are different opinions, understandings, and assumptions about the functions of law in the Christian community.

When considering the sacraments in particular, Joseph Martos makes some helpful distinctions between theology and law. While the interest of theology is understanding the sacraments and explaining the function of sacraments and their nature, the law looks

Ellen O'Hara

more toward the regulation of the sacraments and the requirements for validity of celebration. Theology is more comfortable with the sacraments as signs and symbols, both revealing and imaging the mystery they express, while law is more concerned with the rubrics for correct celebration and with sacramental cause and effect. The theologian looks more toward the symbolic grace-movement of the community, while the lawyer is more comfortable with the questions of matter and form and observable behavior.[21]

These various distinctions, however, are tempered both by cultural and historical factors since the sacraments are celebrated in specific times and places. These factors may take the form of positive development or negative reaction, the accumulation of secondary elements or the purification of rites; but they clearly influence both the symbolic and legal shape of the sacraments. Considering penance in particular, Ladislas Orsy describes various models that have evolved in Church use over the centuries: the evangelical simplicity of Jesus' reconciling ministry, the public satisfaction and reconciliation or absolution, the Celtic model of tariff penances, and the Tridentine emphasis on a more legal and precise manner of confession.[22] As questions persist about the relevance of penance today and as communal celebrations seem to be the preferred form, one can legitimately ask whether or not we are in the midst of yet another paradigm shift with regard to the sacrament of penance.

If such is the case, it is imperative that we do not forget the following:

1. Law unconnected to life becomes a tyrant, whereas law should be "a friendly servant in an orderly house."

2. Not even canon law can create holiness. Those who look to law to create holiness are pharisees, whereas we are the people of Jesus Christ.

3. Making something law says nothing about its truth value or its validity in practice.

4. Only the naive would presume that theology and experience in pastoral practice would be enough to resolve the current tensions. Only those with little faith would presume that they are right without the necessary humility or openness to other points of view. Only those of little

faith would look to law, especially canon law, to solve the problems of the Church today, and only those with little faith would do things solely because they are law.

I suggest that only those with little faith would presume to speak with maximum certainty and ask for maximum clarification and uniformity. It is only those who love the Church deeply and truly believe in the presence of the Spirit among God's people who will discern the will of God and celebrate God's presence among the people. Now is truly a time when reconciliation among us is a necessary part of our witness to one another and to the world. Perhaps the most challenging call and most corrective part of the new Code of Canon Law is embodied in canon 1752 as the very last words of the Code and the very highest motive for any canonist: "the salvation of souls, which is always the supreme law of the Church."

NOTES

1. "Ecclesiastical laws are to be understood in accord with the proper meaning of the words considered in their text and context. If the meaning remains doubtful and obscure, recourse is to be taken to parallel passages, if such exist, to the purpose and circumstances of the law, and to the mind of the legislator." Canon 17, *Code of Canon Law*, Latin-English Edition (Washington, D.C.: Canon Law Society of America, 1983). The previous Code restricted canonists to parallel passages of the Code itself.

2. Canon 739 binds members of societies of apostolic life not only to the obligations mentioned in their constitutions, but also to "the common obligations of clerics, unless something else is evident from the nature of the matter or from the context." Canon 276.2.5 mentions frequent reception of the sacrament of penance as an obligation of clerics. In saying that this canon applies to all societies of apostolic life, I disagree with the commentary on this canon provided by Sister Sharon Holland in *Code of Canon Law: Text and Commentary* [= *CLSA Commentary*] (New York: Paulist Press, 1985) 537. Holland mentions that "The canon clearly is addressed only to clerical societies." In a parallel situation, canon 672 in the section on the obligations for religious applies the obligations of clerics to religious. The intent is clearly to put this obligation on all religious, and not simply clerical religious. I believe the same situation holds here.

Ellen O'Hara

3. On the personal level, I have found that the process of declaration of nullity for marriage can also be part of a reconciling ministry on the part of the Church.

4. For a good understanding of both the old and new canons on interpretation, the essays by James Coriden and Ladislas Orsy in *The Art of Interpretation* (Washington, D.C.: Canon Law Society of America, 1982) are most helpful. Father Orsy has also published two other relevant articles: "The Canons on Ecclesiastical Law Revisited" *The Jurist* 37 (1967) 112–159, on the equivalent canons of the 1917 Code; with reference to an earlier draft of the same canons in the 1983 Code, "The Interpreter and His Art" *The Jurist* 40 (1980) 27–56.

5. For the teaching and legislation of the Council of Trent, cf. Joseph Martos, *Doors to the Sacred* (New York: Doubleday, 1981) 114–121 and 346–356, or the series of three articles on the sacrament of penance by Charles Curran, especially "The Sacrament of Penance Today, III" *Worship* 44 (1970) 22–79. The norms of 1944 may be found in the *Canon Law Digest* (hereafter CLD), ed. T. Lincoln Bouscaren and James O'Connor, vol. 3, 377–379. The norms of 1972 are in *CLD*, vol. 7, 667–673. The constitution *Paenitemini*, which revised the entire penitential life of the Church, was issued Feb. 17, 1966; the dispositive part of the document can be found in *CLD* vol. 6, 675–677. The new ritual as promulgated Dec. 2, 1973, can be found in *The Rites of the Catholic Church*, vol. 1 (New York: Pueblo Publishing Company, 1976) 335–446. The *Lineamenta*, the interventions, and the report of the 1983 synod on "Reconciliation and Penance in the Life of the Church" are valuable sources for ongoing study and discussion. A small and excellent reference for the history of penance, some thoughts on change, and a good analysis of the new rite can be found in Ladislas Orsy, *The Evolving Church and the Sacrament of Penance* (New York: Dimension Books, 1978).

6. For a discussion on this issue, cf. Orsy, *Evolving Church*, in his critique of the new Rite of Penance, pp. 131–160; another good reference is "Guidelines on Sacraments," *National Bulletin on Liturgy* 17 (1984) 32–35.

7. Karl Rahner, "Forgotten Truths Concerning the Sacrament of Penance," *Theological Investigations*, vol. 2. *Man in the Church* (Baltimore: Helicon Press, 1963) 135–174.

8. "Guidelines on the Sacraments," *National Bulletin on Liturgy* 32.

9. Reference to the corresponding articles of the Rite of Penance often provides a necessary context and elaboration of the canons on the celebration of Penance.

Penance and Canon Law

10. Frederick R. McManus, "Commentary on Canon 961," *CLSA Commentary* 678.

11. *CLD* vol. 8, 554–561.

12. What is important is that canon 961 provides for the celebration of the third rite, with general absolution, despite the negative language and the restrictions. A close examination of the canon provides nuancing for the restrictions: both John Huels *(Pastoral Companion* [Chicago: Franciscan Herald Press, 1986] 117) and McManus *(CLSA Commentary* 679) point out that the "long time" during which one is deprived of sacramental grace or Holy Communion is a relative term and could mean one day. For another viewpoint, cf. Richard Malone, "General Absolution and Pastoral Practice," *Chicago Studies* 24 (1985) 45–58. Malone indicates that "subjective reluctance" for private confession is not the object of the canon, but rather *"objective* impossibility." Malone interpreting the "long time" as "a month, or at least a couple of weeks. This always supposes a strong common desire for individual confession if it were available" (p. 52).

13. For two recent discussions of general absolution, cf. the article by Richard Malone mentioned above and Ladislas Orsy, "General Absolution: New Law, Old Traditions, Some Questions," *Theological Studies* 45 (1984) 676–689. Malone argues against widespread use of general absolution as sound pastoral practice; Orsy argues for more sensitive openness to the possibility and advantage of the use of general absolution.

In any discussion of general absolution, note should be taken of the following canonical points:

1. To administer the sacrament of penance requires the grant of a specific permission or "faculty" (canon 966), although the methods for obtaining this faculty and exercising it are different from the previous Code. The 1983 Code does repeat the requirement of the previous Code that suitability for administering the sacrament should be established before the faculty is granted (canon 970), although no specific methods are suggested.

2. The 1983 Code indicates that the ordinary place for the hearing of sacramental confession is a church oratory. The new Code makes no distinctions in terms of places for confession for men and women as the previous code had.

3. The 1983 Code repeats the previous Code in its requirement (from the legislation of the Council of Trent) that the faithful must confess "in kind and number" all grave sins committed after baptism in individual confession at least once a year.

Ellen O'Hara

14. See Linda Gaupin, " 'Let Those Who Have Faith Not Be Hasty:' Penance and Children" in this volume.

15. *CLD* vol. 4, 268.

16. A good example of this line of thought can be found in the theological reflection developed for the 1983 Synod on reconciliation by the International Theological Commission. This report was published in 1984 in *Origins*.

17. *CLD* vol. 8, 603–607.

18. Clearly it would be discriminatory to violate someone's right to receive the sacrament if she or he wanted to receive it. But other factors also deserve consideration: the right of the parents to make a determination that the child is not ready, and the right of the child not to be coerced into receiving the sacrament of penance in order to participate fully in the eucharist.

19. "Catechesis for the Sacrament of Reconciliation is to precede First Communion and must be kept distinct by a clear and unhurried separation. . . . the Sacrament of Reconciliation normally should be celebrated prior to the reception of First Communion." *Sharing the Light of Faith*, National Catechetical Directory for Catholics of the United States (Washington, D.C.: USCC, 1979) article 126, p. 73.

20. Much has been written on the topic since the *General Catechetical Directory* in 1971. I would suggest the following articles: Most Rev. William Borders, "A Report to the General Meeting of the Bishops," *Living Light* 10 (1973) 604–613; Francis J. Buckley, "First Confession Before or After Communion?" *Homiletic and Pastoral Review* 72 (1972) 49–56 (this article is a reply to the article by Cardinal Wright mentioned below); John Huels, section on the sacrament of Reconciliation in *Pastoral Companion*, p. 82 (Huels argues that the child cannot be denied the eucharist if she or he does not wish to receive penance first); Thomas Sullivan, "What Age for First Confession?" *America* 129 (1973) 110–113; John Cardinal Wright, "The New Catechetical Directory and Initiation to the Sacraments of Penance and Eucharist," *Homiletic and Pastoral Review* 72 (1971) 7–24.

21. See Martos, *Doors* 85–96.

22. Orsy, "General Absolution" 684.

John Allyn Melloh, S.M.

Preaching Repentance

Three brief preliminary remarks will set the context for our topic.
First, these remarks on preaching repentance apply not only to
penance services, sacramental reconciliation, or worship settings,
but also to other preaching ministries (for example, retreat preaching, adult education, etc.). Second, it is not assumed that the
preacher will necessarily be an ordained presbyter. What follows
applies to any minister of the preached word. Third, the Introduction to the Rite of Penance (no. 13) speaks of the times for
sacramental reconciliation. Concerning the times for reconciliation,
three matters should be noted. (1) The faithful should know the
times scheduled for the sacrament. (2) Although it states that
reconciliation may be celebrated "at any time on any day," that
provision is made to accommodate the individual penitent. The
Roman tradition knew the communal reconciliation of penitents,
i.e., the *ordo paenitentiae*, on Holy Thursday day, that is, during
the last hours of Lent before the three-day Easter festival. The
sense of the tradition is that all the community should be able to
participate fully in the Triduum; hence, reconciliation precedes festival. Calendar and missal norms imply that reconciliation does
not take place during the Triduum, but rather before the Triduum
begins. (3) Thus paragraph 13 speaks of the lenten season as especially appropriate for reconciliation. Pastoral practice in the United
States suggests that Advent has also become a time for communal
penitential celebrations, showing that the French are correct in
calling Advent and Lent the *"saisons forts."*

With these remarks in mind, I want to describe what the
preacher is, and then proceed to explore the dynamics of preaching repentance. I will then draw some brief conclusions.

THE PREACHER
Since Christian preaching derives from the preaching of Jesus, a
brief examination of how Jesus is the model for the preacher is
necessary.

The New Testament scriptures show the historical Jesus to be a
prophetic itinerant preacher (Matt 4:23) in continuity with the

prophetic preachers of Israel and the figure of John the Baptist.[1]
Jesus preached the reign of God, beginning his public ministry
with the proclamation: "The time is fulfilled, and the kingdom of
God is at hand; repent, and believe the gospel" (Mark 1:14). His
preaching stressed that eschatological salvation is already experien-
tially available. The reply to John's question ("Are you the one
who is to come . . . ?") underlines the experiential aspect of
God's reign:

> Go and tell John what you have seen and heard: the blind received
> their sight, the lame walk, the lepers are cleansed, and the deaf
> hear, the dead are raised up, the poor have good news preached to
> them (Luke 7:22).

Proclaiming good news was understood as a form of liberation.
Jesus' own preaching must be seen in this light.[2] Evangelizing the
poor is liberating them with the spoken word, the good news.[3]
Great hopes were thus awakened through the proclamation, "The
kingdom of God is in the midst of you" (Luke 17:21). Not only did
the preaching of Jesus announce a future for the oppressed, but
the future had already begun.

Jesus did not announce God's reign solely in words, but
proclaimed its reality in action, especially that of table fellowship.
Hospitality was extended to the sinner. Mixing socially in a
classed society was taboo, but Jesus broke the social code, thereby
inviting the wrath of the "respectable." "This man receives sinners and eats with them" (Luke 15:21), scoffed the scribes and
pharisees. He expressed his solidarity with the outcasts, identifying with them: "Behold, a glutton and drunkard, a friend of tax
collectors and sinners!" (Matt 11:19). The effect on the marginalized was miraculous. The scandalous practice of Jesus took away
their shame, humiliation, and guilt: he liberated them. Because
Jesus was seen as a prophet and holy one of God, the gesture
could only mean that God viewed them as acceptable.[4] Table-
fellowship was thus an implicit forgiveness of sin. The sharing of
food and drink was a healing sign that the debt to God was can-
celed. The past history of the "outcasts" no longer dominated:
they were freed.

In sending out the twelve, Jesus commissioned them to go to
the "lost sheep," i.e., the oppressed, with this announcement:
"The kingdom of heaven is at hand" (Matt 10:11). The "content"

Preaching Repentance

of the preaching of Jesus' followers is the same: God's beneficent reign. The mission of Jesus, "to gather into one the children of God who are scattered abroad" (John 11:52), is continued in disciples, members of his Body and Church, through the outpouring of the Spirit.

The following conclusions may be drawn here by way of summary.

(1) "Ernst Troeltsch's succinct observation may be one of the great insights modern theology has given us: 'Jesus did not bring the kingdom of God; the kingdom of God brought Jesus.' "[5] The central symbol of the message of Jesus is God's reign. It follows that that is central to disciples' message too.

(2) Jesus, in identifying with the oppressed, expressed solidarity with humanity. "For our sake he made him to be sin who knew no sin, so that in him we might become the righteousness of God" (2 Cor 5:21).

(3) The proclamation of Jesus was the announcement of the decisive time of God's reign, calling for a response in faith: "to be converted and live out the new life in Christ."[6] Jesus' preaching and table-fellowship was both a judgment and a promise: a judgment on life in darkness and sin, and a promise of transformation.

(4) Thus the words and actions of Jesus constitute the expansion of a "horizon." The horizon is the range of vision that allows things to be seen from a particular vantage point. But additionally, it means that one is not limited to what is nearest, but can see beyond it. Horizon is something into which we move and which moves with us. Horizons change for people on the move. The reign of God becomes the new horizon for people on the move, in process of conversion.

(5) The reign of God cannot remain merely conceptual. It is experiential. In word and action the reign of God must be proclaimed as existential. "Jesus' *praxis* and *vision* of the *basileia* [reign of God] is the mediation of God's future into the structures and experiences of his own time and people."[7] So too must it be for us.

Christian preaching takes place in context of the Church, the People of God. The *ecclesia* is the assembly of the called, summoned by God's Word and accepting that Word in faith. It is the Word that forms a community of believers; conversion follows

John Allyn Melloh

upon proclamation. The preacher is a member of the Christian community, of that community where the ministry of preaching occurs.[8] The judgment of the Word, proclaimed and preached, falls upon the entire community, including the preacher. "The preacher as announcer and proclaimer of conversion to the community must further see himself as involved in the community's process of conversion."[9]

How does the preacher announce the good news and proclaim God's reign, which calls for conversion, and at the same time offer hospitality to the sinner, recognizing that he or she stands in solidarity with a sinful people? Is there a contradiction between the challenge of conversion and the proclamation of mercy?

In Jesus there was no contradiction. The announcement of God's reign was revealed in actions of hospitality and mercy. These were experienced as invitations to conversion: the story of Zaccheus (Luke 19:1–10) is just one of many examples. At other times, Jesus' words, especially his preaching in parables, called for conversion. In Jesus' self there is the definitive manifestation of salvation for the world. God's agenda is revealed as the human agenda. And Jesus, the fullness of God's revelation, shows this in word and action in both a normative and exemplary sense. But can the preacher today do the same?

First of all, it must be borne in mind that the word of the preacher is above all else God's Word. The "stewardship of God's grace" (Eph 3:2) has been given to the disciples. The preacher hands on what has been given: "For I delivered to you as of first importance what I also received" (1 Cor 15:3). And again: "And we also thank God constantly for this, that when you received the word of God which you heard from us, you accepted it not as the word of men but as what it really is, the word of God, which is at work in you believers" (1 Thess 2:13).

Second, the preacher is a hearer of the Word: ". . . the preacher will have to be a listener before he is a speaker."[10] Listening is the fundamental activity of the preacher; it is a listening *to* and listening *for* God's Word. The preacher listens to God's Word in prayerful reading of the Scriptures, in hearing the Word proclaimed in the assembly, and in study of the Scriptures. The preacher listens for God's Word in the world: in one's own life, in the experiences of sisters and brothers, in the events of history. "Listening is not an isolated moment. It is a way of life."[11]

Preaching Repentance

Homily preparation is fundamentally a movement of listening. It is a listening for that moment of existential conversion and giving it expression. If one effectively preaches to others, it is because one has first of all preached to oneself.

Third, the preacher stands as an interpreter. The homily interprets God's Word, proclaiming the good news that leads to conversion.

> Even as he mediates and announces the faith of the tradition to which the community is to respond, he is articulating the faith of the community. He is not only speaking to, but also out of the community. His leadership is a leadership of the community as member of it.[12]

Lastly, the preacher is mystagogue, that is, one initiated in the ways of the Spirit. Couching it in somewhat Jungian terms, Urban Holmes describes the task of all preaching:

> The sermon or homily . . . has as its object the inscape of existence, not the landscape. Preaching is not teaching. As an act of evangelizing the deep memory, it needs to reveal to us the inner person, not describe the externals.[13]

The one who can describe the "inscape of existence" and assist in permitting the Christ to become the dominant symbol of the deep structures is a mystagogue, one living a converted life. "The preacher whose words do not express his conversion has nothing to share with his congregation. His moral right to articulate their faith and lead their conversion is undermined."[14]

The Church continues the mission of Jesus in proclaiming the good news and offering hospitality to the sinner. The preacher is called on to give expression to both these aspects. The preacher does so from within the community, offering God's Word, not merely the preacher's own word, and shares with the assembly the Word that has been heard and seen by the preacher, interpreted within the context of the community, and shared as an existentially lived Word. The Word is the proclamation of God's mercy and hospitality for the sinner and the call, based on the experience of the Word, to ongoing conversion.

DYNAMICS OF PREACHING REPENTANCE

How is the preacher to preach repentance? Hans van der Geest's recently translated work, *Presence in the Pulpit*, makes a valuable

John Allyn Melloh

contribution to the study of preaching today.[15] His work presents the results of "effect analysis of worship service and sermon," a detailed study of more than 200 analyses of both Catholic and Protestant services. While van der Geest does not treat preaching repentance specifically, I will use his three "dimensions" of preaching to treat this question.

Effective preaching, from the hearer's point of view, must include these dimensions: (1) establishing a sense of security, (2) awakening a sense of deliverance, and (3) offering insight or understanding. These three dimensions are interconnected and interact in both the worship service and homily; each must be present if the preaching is to be effective. These three categories are theoretical aids for comprehending a more complex reality: thus, they are serviceable only in subsequent reflection.

(1) *Establishing security.* In discussing what he terms "the dimension of security," van der Geest makes two important points. First of all, people come to worship hoping to be moved in their depths. Participants, however, will allow themselves to be touched deeply only when they feel "spoken to" or "engaged." Secondly, the more that participants experience engagement the more are security and trust established. Without the experience of security, there is no real entering in to the worship event or hearing of the preached word.

Two corollaries flow from this second basic insight. (a) The actual content of the homily is less important than most preaching manuals would suggest. The conceptual content of the preached word is not the most important aspect of the homily. The orientation of the preached word is not fundamentally toward informational content, but rather geared toward engagement leading to transformation. (b) In establishing security and trust, what is critical is the relationship between the preacher and the congregation. In fact, the content of the preached word takes on its significance within this framework. The effect on the listener of the text preached is "inseparably connected with the effect of the preacher."[16]

How can the preacher work toward establishing this necessary sense of security? Or as van der Geest would phrase it: what behaviors are appropriate on the part of the preacher which foster trust? The relationship of trust is fostered before, during and after the preaching event.[17] The effective preacher will be an individual committed to the congregation and its life in Christ. This commitment will be revealed in attitudes of sincere love and genuine dedication. With regard to preaching in particular, it will mean taking this responsibility seriously, i.e., adequate preparation, assiduous study, and ardent prayer. During the homily, the effective communicator will attend to body language (e.g., stance, gesturing, etc.), vocal authenticity, conversational language, reverence, an inviting presence and "genuineness demonstrated through clarity."[18] After the homily, the effective preacher is willing to stand under the judgment of the preaching event and live by the word preached in the community of believers.[19]

What are the implications for preaching repentance? First, the homilist needs to establish trust all the more. Two attitudes on the part of the preacher are essential: solidarity with the community and vulnerability. Solidarity with the community means that the preacher recognizes that he or she stands as servant of the Word within a community that is at once sinful and yet justified. Vulnerability means that the preacher is open to the deeper dimensions of conversion in his or her own life. Secondly, the basic proclamation is of good news. "The church-goers hope and expect to discover and experience in the worship service that they are safe and secure with God, that the deepest qualification of their lives is to be loved."[20] Thus, the message, the content, is the good news of welcome for the sinner. A call to ongoing conversion will be heard only if a proclamation of good news precedes the challenge.

(2) *Proclaiming Deliverance.* If the first dimension of security touches what is deep within, the second reaches out with broader scope, embracing life in the real world, its opportunities as well as its impossibilities.

> The people in a worship service want to have light offered to them in the darkness of their lives; they want to see the hopelessness of day to day life, of life in this world, surpassed by a perspective which can't be found in that day to day life itself.[21]

This is the dimension termed "deliverance." Van der Geest's analysis demonstrates that security is not sufficient. Participants want the dark side of life to be taken seriously and yet, at the same time, expect that life will somehow become "new, better, whole."

John Allyn Melloh

In preaching repentance, what the preacher offers is deliverance—recognition that in Christ Jesus there is hope amidst despair and light in the darkness. But the proclaimed Word needs to address both dimensions: light and darkness, grace and sin. Both polarities of judgment and grace, law and gospel, cross and resurrection need to be preached, just on the basis of satisfying listener expectations! If only "law" is preached, the congregation experiences no deliverance; if only "gospel" is preached, there may be liberation announced, but it will be an abstraction; the hearers will not be able to identify with it, since it appears unrelated to life as experienced.

In preaching the law as one of the poles of deliverance, two things need to be avoided. First, "moralizing" on the scriptures has no homiletic place. Conversion is a movement that reaches far beyond the "limited moralistic change to which it is sometimes reduced."[22] The legalistic sermon, replete with "shoulds," "oughts," and "musts," is not only demonstrably ineffective, but runs contrary to the worship event's purpose, i.e., encounter with the Lord. Legalistic preaching leaves the individual in isolation, alone with injunctions and separated from community. Second, the "critique of the age" sermon is also to be avoided. Here moral indignation is mixed with the word of law. Such preaching leaves listeners bored or stirs the urge either to contradict or agree quite smugly. In any case, there is no movement of deliverance or call to conversion.

Both "law" and "gospel" make claims upon the individual and the community, but in different ways. Morris Niedenthal states[23] that the grammar of law is most apparent in the conditional sentence: if this, then that. For example, If you have faith, then you will be saved. The effects and implications of the grammar of the law are three. First, the future is made to depend on the past. Second, the grammar of law is safe and simplistic. If the future promise does not materialize it is because the conditions were not met. Third, the grammar of law presupposes strength, but does nothing to create it. "If you repent" presupposes the strength to repent, but does nothing to create repentance. Niedenthal continues that the grammar of the gospel stresses the declarative clause and sentence: because A, therefore B. The second clause ("therefore B") makes a claim upon us. Romans 12 begins: "I appeal to you, therefore . . . to present your bodies as a living sacrifice . . . ." The first eleven chapters are a "because": *because* God has delivered people from sin, the bondage of law, and the body of death, *therefore:* present your bodies.

Notice the effects and implications of the grammar of gospel. First, the grammar of the gospel opens a new future by declaring an action of God which alters the meaning of the past. Constrictions of the past are eliminated. Second, the grammar of gospel does not presuppose strength, but seeks to create it by ministering to needs and weaknesses. The "sermon on law" and the "sermon on gospel" are the same insofar as they both are proclamation of God's deed on behalf of humanity. What the law contributes to deliverance is to indicate from what misery people are freed; "it peers into the chasm from which we are saved."[24] Effective proclamation of deliverance embraces both law and gospel.

How is the preacher to do this? Two things follow from van der Geest's study. First, the preacher needs to open up the dimensions of everyday living, to help the congregation see life through gospel-colored lenses. The "ordinary" in life, the pain and sorrow as well as the joy and vibrancy, becomes grist for the homiletic mill. Secondly, the attitude of amazement should come through the preached Word: the surprise of redemption, the wonder of grace. If the preacher discovers grace in his or her own life, then the preached word will have the authenticity of personal conviction.[25]

(3) *The Dimension of Understanding.* People in a worship service desire to be convinced, to be persuaded. They seek comprehension and insight. This is the dimension of understanding. *Presence in the Pulpit* offers three insightful comments with regard to this dimension. First, what worship participants are seeking is existential truth which "precipitates engagement and participation, not cool ascertainment."[26] The desired understanding is more than cognitive knowledge: it is evidential insight. When it is seen, the person "is struck at the very roots, and his or her whole life is affected: feeling, thinking, inner vision and will."[27] Rational, logical argumentation will not be persuasive in this sphere. Second, listeners' expectations of being convinced anew by the homily require that preachers develop a sense for the hearers' questions. The preacher should be the first one to question. However, the effective preacher will deal with questions that are rooted in the experience of life and provoked by the proclamation. It is generally

John Allyn Melloh

ineffective to preach on religiously generic questions, such as the meaning of suffering, the mystery of sin, etc. These questions are not so pressing as the encounter with the Christ through the proclaimed and preached Word. Further, they can seldom be dealt with satisfactorily in the homiletic context. Third, the use of narrative and image is strongly recommended. Christian proclamation is better served by story and image, than by conceptual speech alone. Story and image engage the imagination, while leaving the person free to enter into the preaching event. While this notion is not new or unique to van der Geest, what is important is his data showing that effective use of story and image engage the congregation and contribute to comprehension.[28] He also points out dangers which undermine hearing the Word: a) if the story is too detailed, too finely worked out, listeners' imaginative engagement is diminished; further, it may prevent the listeners' experience from being integrated into it; b) multiplicity of images works against insight.

A corollary follows upon this third point. The use of conceptual speech can be in tandem with graphic speech. No one will complain about conceptual speech, if the homily relates vividly graphic experiences. Van der Geest argues for a balance of graphic and conceptual speech.

> The vivid, graphic element makes it possible to carry through the experience; the conceptual element makes it possible to get into that experience. Pregnant formulation and unusual expressions have a strong effect.[29]

Such speech is often useful in a "summarizing concept."

What are the implications for preaching repentance? First of all, if the truth that is sought is existential, then preaching must touch more than the cognitive level. Nor will the style of the preaching by syllogistic in form. Second, the generic homily on "sin," "grace," "forgiveness," etc., will be ineffective. The homiletic word that is effective will deal with the question that is provoked by the proclamation itself. Third, while the use of story and image will not necessarily guarantee good preaching, its absence will insure failure.

CONCLUSIONS

The Christian preacher, in continuing the ministry of Jesus, proclaims the reign of God as existential good news which calls for conversion, a lifetime process. It is a ministry of word and deed which at once offers hospitality to the sinner, on the basis of God's creative Word, and moves the sinner to accept the call to repent. Standing in solidarity with the community and under the judgment of God's Word, the preacher proclaims the Word of God that he or she has first heard. As mystagogue, the preacher interprets God's proclamation event in the here and now.

Effective preaching of repentance calls for the recognition that the preaching event is basically dialogical communication. The preacher faces the task of establishing the trust of the community, proclaiming both the cross and resurrection in a dynamic tension, and offering a word of truth that goes beyond the conceptual.

By way of conclusion, a story.

> A mother was trying to get her three-year old to bed. Since the family had guests, the child thought of every possible excuse for not going. Patiently, but firmly, the mother took the child upstairs and tucked her in.
>
> "Stay with me," pleaded the child. "I don't want to be alone."
>
> The mother thought and then with the instinct for right answers that mothers always seem to have, she said: "You won't be alone, *God* will be with you."
>
> A long silence followed, and then the plaintive cry of the child pierced the night. "I don't want God. I want somebody with skin on!"[30]

In sum, the preacher offers "a God with skin on!"

NOTES

1. Enda McDonagh, "Preaching and Conversion," *Furrow* 30 (April, 1979) 239.

2. Albert Nolan, O.P., *Jesus Before Christianity* (Maryknoll: Orbis Books, 1978) 45. Cf. Edward Schillebeeckx *Jesus*, trans. Hubert Hoskins (New York: Seabury Press, 1979) 179ff.

3. For a discussion of "good news," *euaggelion*, cf. William Barclay, *New Testament Words* (London: SCM Press, 1964) 101–106. Barclay points out on page 103 among other things that the good news is not of human discovery, but is of revelation (Gal 1:11–12); hence, the importance of Jesus' preaching and its continuance in the Christian community.

John Allyn Melloh

4. Nolan, *Jesus Before Christianity* 39. Elisabeth Schüssler Fiorenza points out that the reign of God spells out wholeness, the restoration of full humanity and life, especially in social relations. See *In Memory of Her* (New York: Crossroad, 1983) 120, 123.

5. Quoted in Thomas Franklin O'Meara, O.P., *Theology of Ministry* (New York: Paulist Press, 1983) 27.

6. McDonagh, "Preaching and Conversion" 239–40.

7. Fiorenza, *In Memory of Her* 121.

8. It is important to note that the NCCB 1983 document on preaching, *Fulfilled in Your Hearing*, begins with the assembly, not with the preacher; the document adopts a "receiver-oriented" view of the process of communication, pp. 3–8.

9. McDonagh, "Preaching and Conversion" 241–2.

10. *Fulfilled in Your Hearing* 10.

11. Ibid.

12. McDonagh, "Preaching and Conversion" 242. See also *Fulfilled in your Hearing* 7–8. Cf. Hans van der Geest, *Presence in the Pulpit: The Impact of Personality in Preaching,* trans. Douglas W. Stott (Atlanta: John Knox Press, 1981), chapters 2 and 3.

13. Urban T. Holmes, III, *Turning to Christ: A Theology of Renewal and Evangelism* (New York: Seabury Press, 1981) 216. I am grateful to my colleague O. C. Edwards, Jr., for this reference.

14. McDonagh, "Preaching and Conversion" 243.

15. What follows relies heavily on van der Geest's work. I am grateful to my colleague, O. C. Edwards, Jr., for his insistence on the importance of this work.

16. van der Geest, *Presence* 61.

17. I am grateful to my colleague, Mark Searle, for suggesting this division.

18. van der Geest, *Presence* 40; cf. 38–59.

19. I am told that Rev. Eugene Maly used to advise preachers: "Don't practice what you preach; rather, preach what you practice: It's far more difficult."

20. van der Geest, *Presence* 39.

21. Ibid. 70–71.

22. McDonagh, "Preaching and Conversion" 240.

23. For what follows, see Morris J. Niedenthal, "The Irony and Grammar of the Gospel," in Edmund A. Steimie, Morris J. Niedenthal, and

Preaching Repentance

Charles L. Rice, *Preaching the Story* (Philadelphia: Fortress Press, 1980) 141–150.

24. van der Geest, *Presence* 111.

25. Ibid. 75–76.

26. Ibid. 117.

27. Ibid. 118.

28. Ibid. 127, 135. Cf. Thomas H. Troeger, *Creating Fresh Images for Preaching* (Valley Forge: Judson Press, 1982).

29. van der Geest, *Presence* 139.

30. Fred A. Baumer, "Toward the Development of Homiletic as Rhetorical Genre: A critical Study of Roman Catholic Preaching in the United States since Vatican Council II" (Ph.D. diss., Northwestern University, 1985) 245.

James Lopresti, S.J.

Homily: Closing Eucharist
(Readings: Ezekiel 36:24–32, John 4:5–42)

There is much talk among liturgists about table fellowship, that unrivaled key image of the kingdom. But there is little talk about cup camaraderie. Though it is far less substantial a human matter than a banquet or a holiday meal, many curious things happen in places where people assemble to drink, whether it be the morning visit for coffee; the pause at the soda machine; or that secular analog of the confessional, 3 A.M. at the cocktail lounge. These less noble, or at least less celebrated, watering holes are often the places where pilgrims chance to meet on their way to somewhere else: a mother on her way to pick up the kids, a company executive on her way home to her apartment after work, Jesus at a well on his way to death in Jerusalem. The watering hole is a wayside stop. It is often not only a place to slake your thirst, but also to change your mind, your heart, even your direction.

All that is true of the unnamed Samaritan woman. (Have you ever noticed that Samaritans have no names in the Gospel? They are more like stereotypes than real persons.) Somehow because of the encounter with that strange man at the water she is immersed in a new world and, no longer a fourfold outcast, has become witness to a new set of promises to the town people who have shunned her up to now. The story is especially intriguing in that her transformation follows on nothing more than being recognized by this man. No miracle. No dispossessed demons. No exalted teaching. Only being recognized and a strange request to be let into her life. Such newness once again at the water! She apparently isn't used to all of that, at least from the other five men in her life.

And what of this well at which we have chosen to gather this week? We certainly had no lack of water on this pause in our journey. But I wonder what kind of difference our drinking together of some measure of wisdom will make in us, our communities, our dreams, and our priorities? What difference will there be in us because we've recognized each other chatting, singing, praying, and wondering out loud at this oasis?

Perhaps we've all learned some new things, or had some suspicions confirmed, or some certainties shaken loose. That's not bad at all. Some will go home to a pastor who wouldn't have understood anyway. Be that as it may, I'd like to think that we'll all leave this rebaptismal place a little more aware of who we are as a people, a little more given to compassion for those who hurt, a little more peaceful about our diversity, and a little more sure about our credentials as ambassadors. I'd like to think that our days together taught us that nothing from our past need be consigned to unredeemed forgetfulness, nothing in our present need remain an obstacle to union of hearts, nothing in our future need ever make us afraid. God's forgiveness is not measured out on a small scale; neither should the Church's be.

It's time, fellow pilgrims, to put down our water jars, our coffee mugs, our cans of Diet Coke and move on. Like the Samaritan woman, let's go tell our own townsfolk that we've met the Anointed One in the most unlikely place, awaiting the acceptance of outcasts at wells, remembering who they are and choosing to stay with them anyway. Let's go tell the townsfolk that we've found out that no one is alien anymore and that we will no longer forget how to forgive and be re-membered with each other. There are lots of people to tell, and maybe a few of them will believe us and find it possible to forgive and be forgiven, to heal and be

Homily

healed, to liberate and be freed. And if we're really lucky they won't even notice the egg on our face.

Tessa Bielecki

Celebrating Fast and Feast:
The Ascetical-Mystical Life

The Book of Ecclesiastes truly understands the mysterious alternating rhythms of our human existence in which everything has its season:

a time to be born and a time to die;
a time to plant and a time to uproot;
a time to kill and a time to heal;
a time to pull down and a time to build up;
a time to weep and a time to laugh;
a time for mourning and a time for dancing;
a time to scatter stones and a time to gather them;
a time to embrace and a time to refrain from embracing;
a time to seek and a time to throw away;
a time to tear and a time to mend;
a time for silence and a time for speech;
a time to love and a time to hate;
a time for war and a time for peace (Eccl 3:1-8).

To the list of polarities from Ecclesiastes may be added sacrifice and celebration, fast and feast, yes and no, crucifixion and resurrection, asceticism and mysticism. As folksinger Judy Collins sang these words years ago: "To everything there is a season—turn, turn, turn—and a time for every purpose under heaven."

It is in this spirit of alternating human rhythms that we must understand the mystery of asceticism. And there is no way to appreciate the perennial value of asceticism without its intimate connection to mysticism. At its best, classical Christian spirituality has always emphasized the unity of the ascetical-mystical life. William McNamara outlines the delicate balance: "Obviously, these are positive and negative sides to the spiritual life, times to resist and times to yield, times to gain control and times to let go, a world to deny and a world to affirm. The man who pulls off the human adventure, who reconciles the yes and the no, the yin and the yang . . . is the disciplined wild man."[1] Since our subject is asceticism, we will focus more on resistance, discipline, and gaining control. But we must never isolate this dimension from the world of yes, yielding, and affirmation—all of which come round in their season.

ASCETICISM AND MYSTICISM

Exactly what do we mean by asceticism and mysticism?

First of all, the words mysticism and contemplation are essentially the same and may be used interchangeably. One whole series of definitions relates mysticism to life: living in the now, living in the present moment, living on the spot where you are.

Another series describes mystical experience in terms of vision or seeing: beholding the manifold in the one, seeing everything against the background of eternity, seeing things as they really are. This seeing begins with a long loving look at the *real* and ends in a long loving look at the *Real*. In other words, whenever we take a long loving look at the reality of a rock, a cricket, or a chrysanthemum, we eventually come to see the reality of God as God reveals himself in rockness, cricketness, and chrysanthemumness!

These first descriptions of mysticism are deliberately non-theistic because most often our initial mystical experience is not explicitly theistic but more inchoate or confused. As we grow, our experience becomes more overtly theistic. In this higher stage, it is more appropriate to describe mysticism as loving experiential awareness of God, a pure intuition of God born to love, or, as the classical literature states, transforming union with God.

Viewed in this manner, we come to see mysticism as the fulfillment of all human desire. Asceticism is a means towards this end, a passionate preparation for divine union: union with God, unity within ourselves, communion among all human persons, oneness with all that is: animal, vegetable, and mineral.

Asceticism is best understood when we look at its Greek root *askesis,* a strong masculine word which means "training." Through our asceticism we train ourselves the way a soldier trains for war or an athlete for the contest. Both military combat and the athletic contest are ancient biblical metaphors for the life of the Spirit. "Blessed be the Lord, my rock, who trains my hands for battle, my fingers for war," we pray in Psalm 143. St. Paul describes the Christian life both in terms of fighting and running a race (1 Cor 9:24–27; 1 Tim 1:19, 6:12; 2 Tim 4:6–8; cf. Acts 20:24).

PERSONAL AND PLANETARY IMPERATIVE

Some people consider the ascetical-mystical life an illusion, a luxury, or a pleasant pastime for those who are "into that sort of thing." Some critics go so far as to call it an escape or a cop-out, an irresponsible evasion of pressing world problems.

On the contrary, any authentic ascetical-mystical life is not isolated but the source of realistic and responsible contemplative action in society. In fact, the ascetical-mystical life may be the only hope for the future of our perilously endangered planet. Why is this so?

Consider our contemporary world situation. Society moves at a frenzied pace, faster and faster, resulting in severe fragmentation, alienation, and neurosis. Education has deteriorated into mere utilitarian training for "making a fast buck." We have lost our deepest archetypal symbols and our roots in nature, in community, and in the home. Where are the integrated personalities and the uproariously happy people? We degrade sex, woman, and matter, and become obsessed with violence, control, and domination. We rape our land, pollute our air and water, and neglect the needs of our neighbors near at hand and around the globe, using up over fifty percent of the world's resources when we are only ten percent of the world population. Above all, the threat of nuclear disaster hangs heavy in the air and in our hearts.

These characteristics of our contemporary way of life are far from being unrelated. On the contrary, they are all manifestations of one central fact: an impoverishment of the human spirit, a loss of vision, the lack of ascetical practice and mystical life—in short, a crisis in contemplation.

Only the true contemplative is capable of truly effective action— whether apostolic, political, social, educational, or economic— because action without contemplation is blind. Only the true mystic takes a long loving look at the Real and ends up seeing things as they *really* are. This means that genuine contemplative persons and radical contemplative centers and movements are crucial

Tessa Bielecki

270

agents of social change and cultural transformation on individual, national, and global levels. History is full of examples of effective contemplatives in action: Sir Thomas More, Mahatma Gandhi, Dag Hammarskjold, Dorothy Day, Mother Teresa. As in previous ages throughout history, the renewal—and even survival—of Western civilization today depends upon the vitality of our ascetical practice and our mystical experience. The ascetical-mystical life, then, is not only a personal necessity but a planetary imperative.

HEALTHY GUIDELINES

As we ask what it means to "do penance" today and consider the role asceticism plays in the spiritual life of the individual and community called to ongoing conversion of mind and heart, we need to outline five essential guidelines.

1. Our asceticism must be *positive and not punitive*. In other words, through ascetical practices, we are not out to punish our "bad" bodies but to purify our inherently good bodies.

For many centuries, Christians have not given the body the attention it deserves. Our traditional suspicion of the body, leading to its neglect, is one of the weakest and most defective aspects of Christianity. This is perplexing, since this defect is diametrically opposed to the original and essential Christian teaching and strikingly at odds with the spirit of Jesus, our earthy founder, and his robust and vigorous disciples.

In Hebrew, there are no separate words for "body" or "soul." The Hebrew phrases we often mistranslate dualistically as "body" and "soul" or as "flesh" and "spirit" really mean the whole *living* person or the whole person *deadened* or dispirited. So where is the spirit, the soul, the divine image in us? The soul is in our eyes and ears and mouth. The soul is in our hands and feet. The soul is between our legs and in our blood and bones and bowels. This is why the whole human body-person—and the body of the planet—is sacred and must be treated accordingly.

The good news of the gospels is precisely this wholeness, oneness, unity: "The Word was made flesh and dwelt among us" (John 1:14). This is the incarnation we celebrate at Christmas—and how I wish we would call the feast "Incarnation" instead of "Christmas" (which has so many secular overtones and obscures the deeper mystical significance)!

Ascetical-Mystical Life

Throughout our Christian history, various heretics have crudely separated matter from spirit, body from soul, earth from heaven, as though one were evil and the other good. It is important to remember that this tendency—whether we call it Manichean, Jansenist, or Docetist—is heretical, and as such has always been condemned as well as criticized by the Church. At its best, the Church has preserved the genuine spirit of Christ, expressed so beautifully by William McNamara in his first book *The Art of Being Human:* "Ever since the Incarnation, no one is permitted to scorn or disregard anything human or natural"[2]—including the human body and the body of the planet.

In his latest book *Earthy Mysticism,* in the opening chapter entitled "God in the Flesh," McNamara goes even further: "The spiritual is not necessarily superior to the material. The material *is* spiritual."[3] This follows from the profound mystical insight of the French Jesuit Pierre Teilhard de Chardin who emphasized "the spiritual power of matter."[4] If we had grasped the wisdom of this essentially incarnational insight sooner, we would not have punished our human bodies so badly or damaged the body of the earth as carelessly as we have.

2. It is important to focus on the positive role of the body, the earth, and the material in Christian spirituality to offset the traditional suspicion of them which has historically characterized our tradition. But we must also be *realistic and enlightened* in our approach to asceticism. We would be naive and seriously remiss if we did not also admit the negative dimension and confess that the body can be an obstacle to the spirit as well as a vehicle of the spirit. "The soul loves the body," said Meister Eckhart, and this is true. But it is equally true to say with St. Augustine: "The soul makes war with the body." Or as St. Paul understood so painfully: "I fail to carry out the things I want to do, and I find myself doing the very things I hate" (Rom 7:15-16).

Any healthy and whole spirituality must take into account our "original sin"—whatever we mean by that term. Whatever happened in the garden of Eden—that is, "in the beginning"— something has gone awry. Genesis tells us that Adam and Eve disobeyed God and ate the forbidden fruit (Gen 3:1-7). Jesus explains that weeds have been sown among the wheat (Matt 13:24-30). C. S. Lewis says that an evil witch has invaded the gar-

Tessa Bielecki

den.[5] Jacques Maritain calls this life a "crucified paradise." The Buddhists call it "the wheel of samsara." Each case acknowledges the "bentness" or brokenness of the human person and our need for redemption, salvation, or liberation. Asceticism is precisely part of our path towards this personal and global liberation.

3. Our asceticism must be *natural and organic, not arbitrary or artificial.* This means that it needs to grow out of our natural situation and relate specifically to the problem at hand. For example, if we are proud and ambitious and tend to belittle our neighbor in order to accentuate our self-importance, then it will do no good to wear a hairshirt. It is far more effective to remain quiet about our own accomplishments and instead praise those of others. If we are gluttonous and greedy at supper and grab for the food, neglecting to notice the beauty of the meal, ignoring conversation and fellowship around the table, then it will do little good to sing the *Miserere* in Latin and flagellate ourselves every Friday. Far better to serve ourselves last and wait some time before eating in order to thank those who prepared the meal and comment on its lovely appearance, making sincere and concerned conversation with the family and friends around us.

4. In our ascetical efforts, we should usually *avoid extreme measures.* Again William McNamara cautions us against "strongman acts" which Thomas Merton calls "spiritual gymnastics" which Gerald Vann calls "self-regarding stoicism." McNamara's description of asceticism is characterized by sanity, sensitivity, and common sense. He says that Christian asceticism requires "no strongman acts, no glittering achievements, no spectacular successes. What it requires is total love that lasts forever. Such a commitment to perfect love may not involve anything big or dramatic at all, but demand instead a passionate fidelity to hundred little things."[6]

5. A systematic ascetical "program" may be initially helpful but it is often eventually dangerous and defeating because it can lead to pride and self-righteousness and foster rigidity. It is far healthier to *let life itself become our asceticism.* In other words, the greatest and most beneficial asceticism is our willing response to whatever God requires of us: not what we *want*—or even think we *need*—but what God *requires* of us. In my own community we speak of sensitivity to "God's Holy Ought."

Ascetical-Mystical Life

St. Therese of Lisieux, following her "little way," is a good ascetical model. As Ida Görres wrote in *The Hidden Face:*[7] "Life itself was her cross, not one or another event in it . . . she suffered life as simple and childlike folk must, suffered the permanence and inescapability of its demands." Like Therese, instead of trying to get out of what life asks of us, we should embrace and willingly suffer whatever demands life makes on our time and energy.

Speaking more personally, what does this mean in my own life? It means sometimes suffering the loneliness of my hermitage when I'd rather be with my community or out "on the road." Or it may mean the opposite: suffering the crucible of community or a busy lecture schedule when I'd rather be in the solitude of my hermitage. It may mean eating the cabbage and pickled herring that were donated to us instead of going out and buying hamburger. It usually means getting up in the morning for six o'clock Lauds when I'd rather stay in bed. (After twenty years of ascetical monastic training, I still find it difficult to get out of bed in the morning!)

You can draw up a list for your own life, depending on your vocation. Perhaps the ascetical "Holy Ought" demands taking care of a crying baby with colic, being kind to an indifferent spouse or a cranky old nun in your community, coping with a job or co-worker or family member particularly difficult or unpleasant. Everyone's "life asceticism" is unique. But the response required is the same for each of us: patience, humility, and creative fidelity.

RECOMMENDED PRACTICES

We all need to cooperate with God's wisdom and the plan of Divine Providence, and respond to the natural, organic, and enlightened ascesis life offers us. But oftentimes we need to engage in a more active ascetical effort. It is difficult to suggest what that effort might entail. In order to be effective, asceticism must be geared uniquely to each individual; therefore it varies from person to person. However, some general practices may be outlined because they grow out of our universal human weakness and the world's need. In each instance, we need to recognize both the personal and planetary value of the practice. Most of these ten practices are traditionally "tried and true," but their interpretation is both timely and contemporary.

Tessa Bielecki

274

1. *Simplicity*. We clutter our lives with too many consumer goods: clothes, cars, and gadgets of every kind. We waste too much food and too much energy. Simplifying our lives on every level and developing the habit of frugality is not merely a once-in-a-lifetime challenge but an ongoing process because of our pack-rat tendency to accumulate "stuff." The beginning of Lent and the New Year are particularly powerful "kairotic" moments to reassess, slim down, and get rid of any excess baggage that bogs us down and holds us back. Simplicity of life helps us identify more existentially with the Third World and leaves us freer for reading and prayer, celebration and service.

2. *Leisure*. American life is characterized by speed. We are all racing. But where? And why? In our topsy-turvy value system, the faster it is, the better it is: fast cars, fast foods, fast friends. We need to slow down and nurture the spirit of leisure. Leisure is not the result of external factors: spare time, no work, a holiday— we all know the frenzy of an unleisurely vacation. We also know that even in the midst of busyness, laden with heavy responsibilities, we can still be leisurely because leisure is a mental and spiritual attitude, a state of soul, a receptive stillness. As David Steindl-Rast says: leisure is "not the privilege of those who have time but the virtue of those who take time." Only those who leisurely take the time can come to see things as they really are, and know how to act accordingly on a family, local, national, or planetary scale. As St. John of the Cross teaches, those who rush headlong into action without first having acquired through contemplative leisure the wisdom and power to act, will accomplish little more than nothing, sometimes nothing at all, and sometimes even harm, so that those who come after us often have to undo what we did and start all over again.

3. *Solitude*. Blaise Pascal, that seventeenth-century Frenchman who was a genius in both science and spirituality, said: "All our troubles in life come because we refuse to sit quietly for a while each day in our rooms." According to Edward Ford, husband and father of eight, who wrote a book entitled *Permanent Love* to help spouses be better friends to one another: "Of all the things you can do by yourself . . . getting a job, going to school, working for charity—creative solitude on a daily or semi-daily basis (in brief, endurable chunks) will be the most important."[8] Solitude is not

Ascetical-Mystical Life

only meant for monks and hermits but for everyone, married people with families included. Paradoxically, when we are solitary, we best express our solidarity with the entire universe. William McNamara says, "Discreet solitude is a creative protest against the euphoric or chaotic togetherness that stamps our way of life in the modern world. But it is also the highest and most apt expression of our solidarity with the whole human race, with the whole of creation. The more solitary we are, the more divinely endowed and psychologically equipped to enter into a significantly profound relationship with all levels of life—animal, vegetable and mineral as well as human."[9]

4. *Reading.* "Tell me what you read, and I will tell you what you are," runs an old saying. In America today there is an alarming decline in reading of all kinds. Our culture becomes progressively anti-intellectual. When we do not read we cannot think and so we make uninformed and bad decisions. When we do not read, we do not know enough about the ascetical-mystical life, about God and prayer, about ecology and the energy crisis, about the sufferings in the world around us, their sources and their solutions. Reading is a good ascetical practice, an excellent meditation and preparation for prayer, and a crucial responsibility for every planetary citizen. But we must discipline ourselves to read with discrimination. Just as it is physically unhealthy to feed the body with junk-food, it is mentally unhealthy to feed the mind with junk-reading. We cannot afford to read what is merely good but only the very best.[10]

5. *Prayer.* We need to set aside a special time and place to pray every day. If there are no special times and places marked sacred, then life deteriorates and nothing is sacred. When we pray, we take the whole world with us: we pray for those in need, we pray for those who cannot pray because of illness or anguish, we pray for those who don't even know they ought to pray. After we have been faithful for some time to the asceticism of regular prayer, prayer changes from a discipline to a delight, from an exercise to an ecstasy, from a practice to a passion. Most of us don't persevere long enough to experience this transition.

6. *Fasting.* We all eat too much in general and too much of the wrong kind of food. The amount of food we waste when so many people go hungry is sinful; but this statement has become a

Tessa Bielecki

276

cliché, since our sensitivities are so dulled precisely by our over-eating, our lack of reading, prayer, and contemplative stillness. We need to eat less, more simply, lower down on the food chain. But we need to fast from more than food. We need to fast from too much talk and foster the spirit of silence; we need to fast from too much work and cultivate the contemplative spirit of celebration and play; we need to fast from too much togetherness and enjoy more solitude.

7. *Confession.* Communal penance services can never take the place of individual confession—and I deliberately use the word "confession." With so much emphasis on the psychological scars which form the background of our human behavior, we have lost a healthy sense of sin and the need to assume responsibility for our actions. Individual confession is a good "sin bin" but an even better "grace place"—an opportunity to probe into the root causes of our inhuman behavior, to uncover subterranean layers of being that block us from that ongoing conversion of mind and heart that is essential not only to peace of soul but to peace in our families, our businesses, our churches, and our world governments. As we acknowledge our own personal sinfulness, we take responsibility for the part we play in hurting the Mystical Body of Christ—a good first step in the healing of that One Body.

8. *Spiritual Direction.* The Celtic tradition calls spiritual direction "soul-friending." Confession and soul-friending are most effective when they occur together. But unfortunately not all confessors are spiritual directors and not all spiritual directors are confessors. The search for a soul-friend is not always easy. We should look for five qualities: personal prayer and holiness, reverence for the mystery of every human person, prudence, experience, and learning. In the absence of regular direction, however, we should never underestimate the guidance we can receive from books, family and friends, or from our own prayer. Psychological counseling is also a good aid in the ascetical-mystical life but should never be mistaken or substituted for spiritual direction.

9. *Rule of Life.* We not only need to eliminate the clutter in our houses but the clutteredness of our hours. We all need to reorder our priorities. Many of us are caught up in too many details, monumental trivia, peripheral activities that have very little to do with what we consider most meaningful in life, what Jesus called

Ascetical-Mystical Life

"the one thing necessary" (see Luke 10:42). Ordering our priorities is crucial so that we give our time, talent, and energy to what is most valuable: the celebration of life—celebrating family and friends and community through leisure and play, celebrating God through prayer and liturgy, celebrating the earth through enjoyment of birds and trees and stars and flowers.

The monastic expression for ordering our priorities by ordering the hours of the day is "horarium" or "rule of life." All of us need a rule of life so that we don't get dragged into the day, controlled and governed by external, inconsequential circumstances. When Henry David Thoreau said that he would give first prize to anyone who could live one day deliberately, he was admitting the great difficulty of this asceticism.

10. *Play.* Jesus said that unless we become like little children, we cannot enter the kingdom of God (see Matt 19:14). Entering the kingdom is synonymous with living the mystical life. Becoming like children means playing like children! But very few of us are capable of genuine play because we are driven by a neurotic compulsion to work in a utilitarian society that makes everything useful. We need to take more time to close the door on our routine, workaday world, and enter into a playful atmosphere of food, fun, and fellowship, rediscovering one another in leisure, laughter, and love. We need a play of the body—aimlessly paddling a canoe around the lake, climbing a tree, walking along with no destination and no purpose in mind. We need a play of the mind that comes to us through poetry, myth, music, art. Lives that are so gruelingly mundane, pedestrian, and prosaic need surprises, serendipities and festivities: flowers, candles, incense, picnics, bubble baths, lace tablecloths, café au lait laced with cinnamon and nutmeg—or something with a bigger kick! As Zorba the Greek said, "Every man needs a little madness. Otherwise he'll never be able to cut the rope and be free!"

CONCLUSION

How can we possibly conclude a discussion of asceticism by recommending more play? It is because play is the perfect antidote to utilitarianism, and utilitarianism is killing our culture. The culture can only be kept alive by whole, human, integrated personalities—*mystical* personalities who know the supremely non-

Tessa Bielecki

utilitarian value of leisure, celebration, contemplation, prayer, and play. Going against the prevailing utilitarian mood of our culture not only requires an enormous ascetical effort but an act of creative subversion, an act of heroism, and an act of faith in the highest human-divine values. St. Irenaeus said, "The glory of God is man fully alive." That is precisely the deepest meaning of the ascetical-mystical life, in keeping with the promise of Jesus: "I have come that [you] may have life and have it to the full" (John 10:10).

NOTES

1. William McNamara, *The Human Adventure* (New York: Doubleday, 1974) 160.

2. William McNamara, *The Art of Being Human* (New York: Doubleday Echo, 1968) 11.

3. William McNamara, *Earthy Mysticism* (New York: Crossroad Publishing Co., 1983) 5.

4. Pierre Teilhard de Chardin, *The Divine Milieu* (New York: Harper and Row, 1960), 81–87.

5. Cf. C. S. Lewis, *Chronicles of Narnia*, Book 6: *The Magician's Nephew* (New York: Macmillan, 1970).

6. William McNamara, *Mystical Passion* (New York: Paulist, 1977) 56.

7. Ida Frederícke Görres, *The Hidden Face: A Study of St. Therese of Lisieux*, trans. Richard and Clara Wilson, (New York: Pantheon, 1959).

8. Edward Ford, *Permanent Love* (Minneapolis: Winston Press, 1979).

9. McNamara, *Earthy Mysticism*, p. 103.

10. For an annotated list of what we consider to be the very best books, send $3.00 to READING LIST, Spiritual Life Institute, P.O. Box 119, Crestone, CO 81131.

Doris Donnelly

Reconciliation: The Continuing Challenge

My assignment is a pleasure. It is to issue a "continuing challenge" for reconciliation by summing up the many challenges presented at this conference. I need to be brief, and I leave it to you to fill in the blanks where I may have missed a challenge or two that spoke particularly to you and your situation.

The challenges I heard and pass on to you come in the form of simple, direct questions.

1. *Is the church a forgiving community?* Is your parish? Is my family?

Father John Catoir, the current director of The Christophers, offers some sobering testimony:

> After nearly ten years as the chief judge of a diocesan marriage tribunal and five years as a clergy personnel director during a period when 10,000 priests throughout the world were leaving the active ministry and now nearly seven years as the director of The Christophers, after having traveled around this country giving talks and listening to people . . ., I have come to believe that vast numbers of Catholics have distanced themselves from the church for a shocking reason: they perceive the church to be unforgiving. It is the image they have received and apparently the one we unconsciously keep sending . . ., "Shape up or ship out."[1]

Suppose Father Catoir is right. Suppose that *is* the perception people have of the Church. Then our challenge is to do something about it. We need to undo the harm that has been done by one of us by others of us apologizing, by asking forgiveness of those who have been dismembered, marginalized, rebuffed, condemned. We need to be the Murrays from *A Thousand Clowns* and say to these people, over and over again, "I'm sorry." Liturgists out there, we need you to fashion rituals to help us to do what we need to do and what we need to do is to make restitution to the divorced, to gays and lesbians, to former priests and nuns, and to anyone else to whom we have ever sent a message that their lives and choices are unredeemable failures.

2. *Is the Church a courageous community?* Do we speak out against the sins that really matter: discrimination, violence, violation of human rights, sexism, racism—even when the cause is unpopular and our own self interest is at stake? Do we understand that the repertoire of sins needs to include the unscrupulous, selfish, greedy, jealous, spiteful, cruel, unjust, brutal, arrogant, violent choices that all of us make and are tempted to make? Does our leadership ask forgiveness when there is awareness of sin in its ranks?

In her novel *Final Payments*, Mary Gordon writes of an encounter in the sacrament of penance:

> "Can you tell me your mortal sins since your last confession?"
> "I have had sexual intercourse with three men. Two of whom are married."
> "Go on."
> "I think those are the only mortal sins I have committed." Except I thought, the one I cannot tell, the one you are not interested in: that I put myself at the center of the universe.[2]

Those are the sins I mean. Does the Church call us to conversion from sins of putting ourselves at the center of the universe?

Sometimes the answer is yes. Do you recall Cardinal Vachon's intervention at the 1983 Synod on reconciliation?[3] We as Church, he said, need to recognize "our own cultural deformation," particularly "the ravages of sexism and our own male appropriation of church institutions and numerous aspects of Christian life." We need "to allow ourselves . . . to be confronted by the Spirit of God" in identifying "those aspects of our institutions which are unjust and demeaning" to women.

Sometimes the answer is no. Edward Daly, a Northern Ireland bishop, passes on an observation that ought to cause us to feel shame:

> If the churches are to be the witness of Christ in the world, they must be prepared to speak out and live Christ's teaching fearlessly and unequivocally and they must be prepared to speak the truth what ever the consequences. To sit and do nothing, to say nothing until any particular situation has resolved itself, and then link up with the winning side, is the ultimate betrayal.[4]

3. *Are we sensitive and attentive to signs and symbols that divide?* Are we attentive to language at liturgical celebration when it virtually excludes half the human race? More subtly, do we notice lip ser-

vice paid to "adult faith development" while treating those same adults as children by reinforcing the superiority and dominance of ecclesiastical office in the form of "guidelines"—a euphemism for rules and regulations that better be obeyed, or else?

It is of utmost importance, if we as Church intend to be credible in this area of reconciliation, that we practice what we preach. The Gospel says we need to leave our gifts at the altar while we straighten out our commitments as a repentant, forgiving, and reconciling people in the pews. It might just as accurately call us to leave our symbols at the altar if these are not paralleled elsewhere: in parish councils, in parish families, in parish rectories, in all relationships.

4. *Does the Church seek the initiative at being peacemaker?* We have some excellent role modeling for this activity with the peaceful revolution in the Philippines this year. A fine pastoral statement by the bishops of the Philippines told us that peace was not one choice among many, but the only choice. And the unexpected leadership of a Catholic laywoman, the President of the Philippines, reinforced and continues to reinforce some basic truths about forgiveness: that it is compatible with confrontation; that it is linked with justice; that its goal is the conversion of the offender and not his or her humiliation; and that it is a strength (not a weakness) capable of transforming people, certainly, but even nations.

Quality leadership like this prompts us to look into our own backyards—and beyond our own backyards—to uncover places in which we can be ministers and agents of reconciliation and where we can take the first step to offer hope in situations of despair.

I am reminded in this connection of the original version of the Humpty Dumpty nursery rhyme that someone sent to me when my children were little. It goes like this:

> Humpty Dumpty sat on a wall.
> Humpty Dumpty had a great fall.
> All the king's horses and all the king's men
> Couldn't put Humpty together again.
> But maybe *you* can!

What a terrific message for children to hear, for any of us to hear: that brokenness can be mended, that the pieces of a life can be put together, that there is possibility of recovery from some

Doris Donnelly

282

tough breaks of life and that some people (you and I and the children listening to the nursery rhyme) are called to help in the process!

5. *Is the Church an encouraging community, supportive of people who forgive, or do we regard the forgiving and reconciling approach to conflict and hostility as a weakness?* On the day after our hostages were released from Iran (January 23, 1981), the New York Times reported a conversation with newly elected President Ronald Reagan. Mr. Reagan was asked what retaliatory counteroffensive would be put into operation against the Iranians. He replied: "Well, you know, we have to forgive. We can't only be thinking of revenge."

President Reagan said that, and we did not pursue revenge.

I wonder how many people—how many of *us*—wrote encouraging letters to the White House saying "Well done." As many, do you think, as those who wrote supporting the recent retaliatory bombing of Libya? The point is, how much encouragement did we give the new president for his decision to pursue a nonaggressive, peaceful, forgiving policy; enough, do you think, to make him say to himself "I'm sure I made the right choice and the next time a conflict erupts, I'll do things the same way."?

On a more immediate and closer-to-home level, we need to support each other when someone says,

"I forgave my father for the way he abused me as a child."

"I'm tired of holding a grudge against my sister-in-law."

"I want to forgive my wife for her unfaithfulness."

"I need to forgive my son for his ingratitude."

We need to buy these people a beer. We need to celebrate their steps in the reconciliation process that begins with human hurt, moves through forgiveness where the pain is relived until, eventually, a reconciliation occurs.

Celebrating stages of healing, or even the desire for healing, in the dailyness of human life will make more sense out of a sacramental process and sacramental signs that also heal. Celebrating steps in any and all human reconciliations where forgiveness is pretty iffy and provisional, and where the style of forgiveness is more like putting people on probation ("I forgive you, but don't you dare do it again"), paves the way for the massive, foolish, unconditional, no-strings-attached love of God where the proper response is celebration with all the stops pulled out.

The Continuing Challenge

283

6. Are we a community that listens and responds to the human story? I think we do a good deal of our sacramental theology from the wrong starting point. We tell God's story; sometimes we tell only God's story, and we fail to link it with the human story. So, we tell people God feeds them, heals them, forgives them, and people say in return, "But I'm not hungry, I'm not sick, and what's forgiveness got to do with anything?"

Sacraments are the places where God responds to the human story, they are the places where God's story and the human story connect. Not only do we need to tell the human story; we need to hear the human story *first*—a story of loneliness, rejection, betrayal, alienation, brokenness, guilt, remorse, tragedy, pain, and an overwhelming desire to start all over again, to wipe the slate clean, to eradicate mistakes, to be new. Elicit those stories, tell your own, tell some you have heard, and the gospel news—that the events of human life, even when they turn out badly, are not beyond repair—will make sense. God's story will then connect with human life.

Let's go home more firmly convinced that love is the most powerful force in the world, far mightier than revenge, far stronger than hate. Let's go home firmly convinced that all we need to do is be human, to be fully human and fully alive, which is another way of saying we are living in God's grace.

We are a chosen race, a royal priesthood. Let's get the word out that in Jesus Christ and our own forgiving fellowship with one another we never had it so good.

NOTES

1. John Catoir, "Is the Church Unforgiving?" *America* (January 19, 1985) 47.

2. Mary Gordon, *Final Payments* (New York: Ballantine Books, 1978; 11th printing, April 1986) 275.

3. Archbishop Louis-Albert Vachon, "The Reconciliation of Women and Men in the Church," *Origins* 13:19 (October 20, 1983) 334.

4. Bishop Edward Daly, "In Place of Terrorism," *The Furrow,* 26 (October, 1975) 596.

Doris Donnelly